STUDY GUIDE
CHAPTERS 1-13

ACCOUNTING

STUDY GUIDE
CHAPTERS 1-13

Ann DeCapite
Coastal Carolina Community College

ACCOUNTING
Sixth Edition

Charles T. Horngren
Walter T. Harrison
Linda S. Bamber

PEARSON

Prentice
Hall

Upper Saddle River, New Jersey 07458

VP/Editorial Director: Jeff Shelstad
Assistant Editor: Sam Goffinet
Manager, Print Production: Christy Mahon
Production Editor & Buyer: Wanda Rockwell
Printer/Binder: Courier, Bookmart Press

10 9 8 7 6 5 4 3 2 1
ISBN 0-13-144583-9

Contents

Chapter 1—Accounting and the Business Environment

CHAPTER OVERVIEW

Chapter One introduces you to accounting. Some of the topics covered in this chapter are the types of business organization, the basic accounting equation, analyzing business transactions, and preparing financial statements. Like many disciplines, accounting has its own vocabulary. An understanding of accounting terminology and the other topics covered in this chapter will give you a good foundation towards mastering the topics in upcoming chapters. The learning objectives for this chapter are to

1. Use an accounting vocabulary
2. Apply accounting concepts and principles
3. Use the accounting equation.
4. Analyze business transactions.
5. Prepare the financial statements.
6. Evaluate business performance.

CHAPTER REVIEW

Objective 1 - Use accounting vocabulary.

Accounting is the information system that measures business activities, processes that information into reports, and communicates the results to decision makers.

The users of accounting information are:

- **Individuals** use accounting information to make decisions about whether to purchase or rent (lease) a home or vehicle and to manage their bank accounts.
- **Business managers** use accounting information to set goals for their businesses and to evaluate progress toward achieving those goals.
- **Investors** use accounting information to evaluate the prospect of future returns on their investments.
- **Creditors** use accounting information to evaluate a borrower's ability to make the scheduled payments to repay the loan.
- **Government regulatory agencies, taxing authorities, and nonprofit organizations** also use accounting information.

The users of accounting information are further categorized into external users and internal users. This distinction relates to the two fields of accounting:

1.) **Financial accounting** focuses on providing financial information for individuals *outside* (external to) the business or organization.
2.) **Managerial accounting** focuses on providing financial and other business information for individuals *within* (internal to) a business or organization.

> Helpful hint: Review Exhibit 1-2 to review the relationship between financial and managerial accounting.

The Financial Accounting Standards Board (FASB), the Securities and Exchange Commission (SEC), the American Institute of Certified Public Accountants (AICPA) and the Institute of Management Accountants (IMA) are four groups that influence the practice of accounting in the United States. **Generally Accepted Accounting Principles** (GAAP) are the rules governing accounting. In addition, accountants are expected to maintain high ethical standards. Similarly, many corporations also have standards of ethical conduct to which they expect their employees to adhere.

> Helpful hint: Review Exhibit 1-3 in your text to review the key accounting organizations.

The three forms of business organization are:

1. **Proprietorship** - a business owned by one person who has *unlimited* liability for the debts of the business
2. **Partnership** - a business owned by two or more individuals who all share *unlimited* liability for the debts of the business
3. **Corporation** - a business owned by many owners called stockholders (or shareholders) whose liability for business debts is *limited* to the amount the stockholders invested in the corporation.

In the United States, proprietorships are the largest form of business numerically, whereas corporations are the dominant form in terms of total assets, income, and number of employees.

> Helpful hint: Review Exhibit 1-4 in your textbook for the comparison of the three forms of business organization.

Objective 2 - Apply accounting concepts and principles.

As previously mentioned, the rules governing accounting practice are called Generally Accepted Accounting Principles (GAAP). GAAP includes five important concepts and principles:

1.) **The entity concept:** The financial records of a business entity should be separate from the personal financial records of the owner. For example, if a business owner borrows money to remodel her home, the loan is a personal debt, not a debt of the business.

2.) **The reliability (or objectivity) principle:** Accountants should attempt to provide reliable, accurate records and financial statements. All data that the accountant uses should be verifiable by an independent observer. Ideally, accounting records should be determined by objective evidence. For example, the most objective and reliable measure of the value of supplies is the price paid for the supplies. The objective evidence documenting the price is the invoice from the supplier.

3.) **The cost principle:** Assets and services should be recorded at their actual (historical) cost. For example, if a business pays $25,000 for land, then $25,000 is the price actually paid for the land or the "cost" and the amount recorded in the accounting records, even if an independent appraiser estimates that the land is worth $34,000.

4.) **The going-concern concept:** Assumes that the entity is expected to remain in operation for the foreseeable future. This assumption provides accountants with the guidelines on how to record the value of the entity's assets in the accounting records. If an entity is assumed to be a going concern, then the relevant measure of the entity's assets is the historical cost, as established by the cost principle. However, if the entity were going out of business, meaning it is no longer expected to be a going concern, then, the relevant measure of its assets would be market value.

5.) **The stable-monetary-unit concept**: Assumes that the purchasing power of the dollar is relatively stable. Therefore, the effects of inflation are ignored in accounting, which allows accountants to add and subtract dollar amounts as though each dollar had the same purchasing power as any other dollar at any other time.

Objective 3 - Use the accounting equation.

The **accounting equation** is expressed as:

Economic resources = Creditor's claims to economic resources + Owner's claims to economic resources

Total claims to economic resources

Or,

ASSETS = LIABILITIES + OWNER'S EQUITY

Assets are a firm's resources that are expected to provide future benefits. You can also think of assets as the things that the business owns. **Liabilities** are claims by outsiders (creditors) to those resources. If a business purchases a piece of land and borrows money from the bank for the purchase, then the bank, the creditor, has claim to the land until the loan is repaid. The land would be an asset of the business because it is a resource of the business, and the amount of money borrowed to purchase the land would be a liability until the loan is repaid. Claims by insiders (owners) are called **owner's equity** or capital. If a creditor does not have claim to the assets of the business, then the owner does. The accounting equation must always reflect what the business has, assets, and who has claim to those assets, either creditors or the owner(s).

Some of the most common examples of assets are cash, accounts receivable, notes receivable, supplies, land, and buildings.

- A business acquires cash from capital investments made by the owner, from borrowing money, and when the business makes sales to customers and collects from those customers either at the time the sale occurs or sometime in the future.
- Accounts receivable and notes receivable both arise when a business makes sales to customers on credit, meaning the cash payment from the customer is expected sometime in the future. Accounts receivable result from general trade credit where the customer promises a future payment of all amounts owed to the business.
- Notes receivable are similar to accounts receivable in that they both represent a promise of future payment for sales; however, they are different in that notes receivable are evidenced by a written promissory note whereas accounts receivable are not.
- Supplies represent things that will be used up in the normal course of doing business, such as office supplies, restaurant supplies, and medical supplies to name a few.
- Land represents unimproved real property.
- Buildings are structures that may be located on the land.

Liabilities represent claims on assets by outsiders (creditors) or things that the business owes to others. A business can owe cash, inventory or services to other businesses or its customers. The most common examples of liabilities are accounts payable and notes payable, which arise when the business makes purchases on credit.

- An account payable results from general trade credit where the business promises to pay all amounts owed to its supplier.
- Notes payable are similar to accounts payable in that they both represent a promise of future payment for purchases; however, they are different in that notes payable are evidenced by a written promissory note whereas accounts payable are not.
- Other liabilities will be introduced and explained in future chapters.

Owner's equity represents claims on assets by insiders (owners). Owner's equity is also referred to as the net assets (or residual equity) of the business and reflects, in total, what is left of the assets after subtracting the liabilities. The accounting equation can be rewritten to reflect this relationship:

$$\text{ASSETS - LIABILITIES = OWNER'S EQUITY}$$

There are only four things that will affect a change in owner's equity:

- Owner's investments of assets into the business (increase owner's equity)
- Owner's withdrawal of assets from the business (decrease owner's equity)
- Revenues generated by delivering goods or providing services to customers (increase owner's equity). Revenues result when the business does what it is in the business of doing. For, example an attorney will generate service revenue from providing legal services because that is what an attorney is in the business of doing. Gay Gillen eTravel will generate service revenue when the business provides travel services to its customers because that is that is what a travel agent is in the business of doing. Amazon.com will generate sales revenue when it sells products to its customers because that is what Amazon.com is in the business of doing. As these examples indicate, the nature of revenue may differ according to each different type of business; however, revenue is always generated when a business does what it is in business to do.
- Expenses result from using assets or increasing liabilities to deliver goods or provide services to customers (decrease owner's equity). Expenses are those costs incurred to support the generation of revenues. Examples of expenses include rent, utilities, and employees' salaries.

> Helpful hint: Review Exhibit 1-6 in the textbook to review the transactions that increase or decrease owner's equity.

The owner's investment or withdrawal of assets represents transactions that occur between the business and insiders or the owners of the business. The generation of revenues and the incurrence of expenses represent transactions that occur between the business and outsiders or the business's customers, suppliers, or creditors. Profitability results from the transactions that occur between the business and those entities outside of the business. If the business is profitable, then owner's equity increases when the revenues are greater than the expenses of the business.

Objective 4 - Analyze business transactions.

Every transaction will have, at minimum, a dual effect on the accounting equation, meaning that each transaction has at least two parts. Recording the two (or more) components of each transaction maintains the equality of the accounting equation or we might say that the accounting equation always remains "in balance". Study carefully the eleven business transactions analyzed in the text, and reinforce your understanding by following the demonstration problem and explanations in this chapter of the Study Guide. Pay particular attention to how each transaction affects the accounting equation. Take notice of the duality of each of the transactions. You should also pay attention to how each time a transaction is determined to have an effect on owner's equity; the type of owner's equity transaction is noted. Next, study how the summary of the transactions is reflected on the Balance Sheet. The balance sheet reports the assets, liabilities, and owner's equity of the business at any given moment in time. You should observe that the balance sheet is very similar to the accounting equation, except that only the ending balances in each of the accounts are shown on the balance sheet. You must have a thorough knowledge of how transactions affect the accounting equation and how they are reflected on the balance sheet in order to proceed further in this course.

Objective 5 - Prepare the financial statements.

Accountants summarize the results of business activity in four primary financial statements:

1.) The **income statement** presents a summary of the firm's revenues and expenses for some period of time, such as a month, quarter or year, and reports **net income** if total revenues exceed total expenses. A **net loss** occurs if total expenses are greater than total revenues. The information used to prepare the income statement comes from the Owner's Equity column of the accounting equation. Notice that only those transactions that represent revenues and expenses should appear on the income statement. Remember that revenue and expense transactions result from transactions that occur between the business and its customers and vendors. Owner's investments and withdrawals are do not appear on the income statement because they represent transactions that occur between the business and the owner(s).

2.) The **statement of owner's equity** presents a summary of changes in owner's equity during the same period of time as the income statement. As we have mentioned before, owner's equity increases with owner's investments and net income, and decreases with owner's withdrawals and net losses. The net income or net loss information will carry forward from the income statement and the owner's investment and withdrawal information will come from the Owner's Equity column of the accounting equation.

3.) The **balance sheet** reports all assets, liabilities, and owner's equity, as of a specific date. The date shown on the balance sheet will be the same date as the last day of the period for which activities are summarized in the income statement and the statement of owner's equity. The information that appears on the balance sheet will come from the ending account balances for each asset and liability account off of the accounting equation, and the ending balance in owner's equity from the statement of owner's equity.

4.) The **statement of cash flows** shows the cash inflows and outflows, organized into three areas—operating activities, investing activities, and financing activities. The statement of cash flows is prepared from the "Cash" column of the accounting equation with each item of cash classified according to whether it resulted from an operating, investing or financing activity. This financial statement is covered in detail in Chapter 17.

> Helpful hint: See how the data provided in Exhibit 1-7 correlates with the financial statements in Exhibit 1-8.

Objective 6 - Evaluate business performance.

All financial statements begin with three line headings, as follows:

Name of Business
Name of Financial Statement
Date or time period covered

The income statement is prepared first, listing the revenues and expenses for the period. The result is either net income (when revenues are greater than expenses) or net loss (when revenues are less than expenses). This result is carried forward to the next statement, the statement of owner's equity.

The statement of owner's equity is prepared after the income statement. It details the amounts and sources of changes in capital during the period, as follows:

Beginning Capital Balance
+ Owner's Investment
+ Net Income (or − Net Loss)
<u>- Owner's Withdrawals</u>
<u>Ending Capital Balance</u>

Ending capital is carried forward to the next financial statement, the balance sheet.

The balance sheet is a formal listing of the accounting equation as of the last day in the financial period. The individual assets are added together to equal total assets. The liabilities are totaled and added to ending capital.

The statement of cash flows reports cash flows (receipts and payments) for the same period covered by the other financial statements, and groups these into three types of business activities—operating, investing, and financing. The amount of net cash increase (or decrease) will, when added to the beginning cash balance, agree with the ending cash balance reported on the balance sheet.

TEST YOURSELF

All the self-testing materials in this chapter focus on information and procedures that your instructor is likely to test in quizzes and examinations.

I. Matching *Match each numbered term with its lettered definition.*

_____	1.	AICPA	_____ 9.	IMA
_____	2.	Assets	_____ 10.	Partnership
_____	3.	Corporation	_____ 11.	Proprietorship
_____	4.	Expenses	_____ 12.	Revenues
_____	5.	FASB	_____ 13.	SEC
_____	6.	GAAP	_____ 14.	Statement of Cash Flows
_____	7.	Income Statement	_____ 15.	Statement of Owner's Equity
_____	8.	Liabilities	_____ 16.	Balance Sheet

A. A summary of revenues and expenses for a period.
B. A business owned by one person.
C. A professional organization of Certified Public Accountants.
D. A financial statement summarizing changes in capital.
E. A legal entity, owned by stockholders, which conducts its business in its own name.
F. The body that formulates GAAP.
G. Resources expected to provide future benefit.
H. The "rules" of accounting.
I. Claims on assets by outsiders.
J. Inflows of assets from the sale of a product or service.
K. A business co-owned by two or more individuals.
L. A federal agency with the legal power to set and enforce accounting and auditing standards.
M. Costs incurred to generate revenue.
N. A professional organization of management accountants.
O. Details the net change in cash from one period to the next.
P. Lists an entity's assets, liabilities, and owner's equity as of a specific date.

II. Multiple Choice   *Circle the best answer.*

1. An example of a liability is:

    A. Fees earned
    B. Supplies

    C. Note payable
    D. Investments by the owner

2. When cash is paid on an account payable:

    A. total assets increase.
    B. total assets decrease.

    C. total assets are unchanged.
    D. Cannot be determined

3. A receivable is recorded when a business makes:

    A. sales on account.
    B. purchases on account.

    C. sales for cash.
    D. purchases for cash.

4. When cash is received on an accounts receivable:

    A. total assets increase.
    B. total assets decrease.

    C. total assets are unchanged.
    D. Cannot be determined

5. An investment of equipment by the owner will result in:

    A. an increase in both assets and liabilities
    B. an increase in both liabilities and owner's equity

    C. an increase in both assets and owner's equity
    D. no change in assets or owner's equity

6. An investment of cash by the owner will result in:

    A. an increase in both assets and liabilities.
    B. an increase in both liabilities and owner's equity.

    C. an increase in both assets and owner's equity.
    D. no change in assets or owner's equity.

7. If the date on a financial statement is June 30, 20X5, then the financial statement must be:

    A. the income statement.
    B. the statement of owner's equity.

    C. the balance sheet.
    D. the statement of cash flows.

8. On March 17, 20X5, ShopJLo.com sold 700 swimsuits on account for $78 each. How would this transaction affect the accounting equation?

    A. An increase in both assets and liabilities, $54,600
    B. An increase in both assets and owner's equity, $54,600

    C. An increase in both assets and owner's equity, $70,000
    D. No change in assets or owner's equity

9. On April 10, 20X5, ShopJLo.com collected $30,000 on account from the previous sale on March 17. What is the effect on the accounting equation?

A. An increase in cash and a decrease in accounts receivable, $30,000

B. A decrease in cash and an increase in JLo, Capital, $30,000

C. An increase in both cash and JLo, Capital, $30,000

D. No change in assets or owner's equity

10. If the financial statement is dated For the Month Ended June 30, 20X5, then the financial statement must be:

A. the income statement.

B. the statement of owner's equity.

C. the statement of cash flows.

D. All of the above

11. Net income equals:

A. Assets - Liabilities

B. Liabilities + Owner's equity

C. Revenues + Expenses

D. Revenues – Expenses

12. If total assets equal three times the liabilities, and owner's equity is $90,000, what are total assets?

A. $45,000

B. $90,000

C. $135,000

D. $80,000

13. On January 1, 20X5, David Designs had assets of $265,000 and owner's equity of $130,000. During the year, assets decreased by $75,000 and owner's equity increased by $24,000. What were the liabilities on December 31, 20X5?

A. $36,000

B. $135,000

C. $99,000

D. $154,000

14. If the beginning balance in owner's equity was $300, the ending balance is $544, net income for the month was $325, and there were no investments by the owner, how much did the owner withdraw during the month?

A. $72

B. $119

C. $369

D. $81

15. For the month ended June 30, 20X5, if revenues were $57, 500, and the expenses for the period were $67,250, owner's investments were $10,000 and owner's withdrawals were $27,500, was the business profitable for the month of June?

A. Yes, it generated $9,750 in net income

B. No, it generated a $9,750 net loss

C. Yes, it generated $19,750 in net income

D. No, it generated a $27,250 net loss

III. Completion   *Complete each of the following statements.*

1. The four primary financial statements are: 1) _____
   2) _____ , 3) _____
   and 4) _____ .

2. Keeping accounting records for a business separate from the owner's personal accounting records follows the _____ concept.

3. Revenues are _____ .

4. _____ are the costs incurred in operating a business.

5. Outsider claims against assets are called _____ and insider claims are called _____ .

6. What is the accounting equation?
   _____ .

7. When a firm purchases assets, they are recorded at _____ .

8. _____ is the clerical recording of the data used in an accounting system.

9. What is the three-line heading with which all financial statements begin?
   _____
   _____
   _____

10. Assuming the purchasing power of the dollar remains relatively stable over time underlies the _____ concept.

IV. Daily Exercises

1. For each of the following questions, indicate the financial statement where the answer can be found:

Question	Financial Statement
a. Where did all the money go?	_____
b. How much is the business worth?	_____
c. How much does the business owe?	_____
d. Is the business profitable?	_____
e. Is my investment in the business more or less than last period?	_____

2. At the beginning of the year, a business purchased a building for $100,000, paying $35,000 cash and signing a promissory note for $65,000. By the end of the first year, the amount due on the note had been reduced to $60,000, and real estate values had increased by 20% in the area. At what amount should the building be listed on the balance sheet? Which decision guideline supports your answer?

3. At the end of its first month of operations, a business had total revenues of $7,300, cash receipts from customers of $6,500, total expenses of $5,500, and an owner's withdrawal of $1,800. Was the business profitable during its first month of operations?

4. Refer to question #3 above. Assuming the owner made no additional investments during the month, did the value of the business increase or decrease during the period? Explain your answer.

V. Exercises

1. Ashley Granger operates a small tax preparation business. During the first month of operations the following events occurred:

   A. Ashley invested $20,000 to start the business.
   B. She paid rent of $675.
   C. She purchased $5,000 of computer equipment on account.
   D. She purchased $475 of supplies for cash.
   E. She performed tax services on account, $2,750.
   F. She paid $1,000 on the computer equipment purchased in C.
   G. She received $425 from a customer on account.
   H. She sold supplies (which cost $40) to a friend for $40.

   Prepare an analysis of transactions showing the effects of each event on the accounting equation. (Helpful hint: You may want to refer to Exhibit 1-7 in your text.)

| | ASSETS | | | = LIABILITIES | + | OWNER'S EQUITY |
| | Accounts | | Computer | Accounts | | Granger, |
Cash +	Receivable +	Supplies +	Equipment	= Payable	+	Capital
A.						
B.						
C.						
D.						
E.						
F.						
G.						
H.						

2. Presented below are the balances in the assets, liabilities, revenues, and expenses for Clarence's Clunker Repair and Body Shop on June 30, 20X7.

Accounts Payable	$ 250
Accounts Receivable	200
Cash	120
Clarence, Capital	?
Equipment	160
Service Revenues	220
Supplies	70

Prepare a balance sheet for Clarence's Clunker Repair and Body Shop for June 30, 20X7.

Clarence's Clunker Repair and Body Shop
Balance Sheet
June 30, 20X7

Assets:		Liabilities:	
Cash	_____	Accounts Payable	
Accounts Receivable	_____	Total Liabilities	_____
Supplies	_____	Owner's Equity:	
Equipment	_____	Clarence, Capital	
	_____	Total Liabilities	_____
Total Assets	======	and Owner's Equity	======

3. The following are the balances in the accounts of Paul's Delivery Service on August 31, 20X6.

Accounts Receivable	$ 220
Accounts Payable	260
Equipment	2,980
Notes Receivable	130
Salaries Payable	240
Salaries Expense	500
Service Revenue	3,210
Supplies	180
Supplies Expense	280
Telephone Expense	270
Paul, Capital	1,160
Truck Rental Expense	500

Prepare an income statement for Paul's Delivery Service for the month of August, 20X6.

Paul's Delivery Service
Income Statement
For the Month Ended August 31, 20X6

Service revenue		$_____
Expenses:		
Salaries	$_____	
Truck Rental	_____	
Supplies	_____	
Telephone	_____	_____
Net income		$_____

VI. Beyond the Numbers

Can a profitable business (one where revenues consistently exceed expenses) become insolvent (unable to pay their bills)? Conversely, can an unprofitable business remain solvent?

_____
_____
_____
_____

VII. Demonstration Problems
Demonstration Problem #1

Nick Russell, CMA (Certified Management Accountant) opened a consulting practice in Midtown, USA. Solely, Russell owns the business, which is named Russell Consulting. During the month of May, 20X8 (the first month of operation), the following transactions occurred:

5/1	Russell invested $25,000 of personal funds to start the business and deposited the funds in a checking account in the name of the business.
5/1	An office was located and rent of $1,250 was paid for the first month.
5/3	Office equipment was purchased for cash at a cost of $2,100.
5/5	A computer and a laser printer to be used in the business were purchased on account for $3,200.
5/8	Office supplies costing $200 were purchased on account.
5/10	Services of $1,500 were provided on account to a client.
5/15	Russell provided consulting services, $2,300 during the first half of the month. The fees for these services were collected from clients at the time the service was provided. Russell made one deposit in the business checking account.
5/16	Cash of $1,300 was collected for the services rendered on 5/10.
5/18	Paid for the office supplies purchased on 5/8.
5/21	Russell withdrew $3,000 from the business for personal use.
5/31	Consulting services, $4,100, were performed during the second half of the month. The fees for these services were collected from clients at the time the service was performed. Russell made one deposit in the business checking account.

Required:

1. Prepare an analysis of transactions of Russell's Consulting. Use Exhibit 1-7 and the Summary Problem in Chapter 1 of the text as a guide and the format below for your answers.

2. Prepare the income statement, the statement of owner's equity, and balance sheet of the business after recording the May transactions. Include proper headings. Use Exhibit 1-8 as a guide for completing the financial statements.

Requirement 1 (Analysis of transactions)

		ASSETS			=	LIABILITIES	+	OWNER'S EQUITY
Cash +	Accounts Receivable +	Supplies +	Equipment	=	Accounts Payable		+	Capital

Requirement 2 (Income Statement, Statement of Owner's Equity, and Balance Sheet)

Income Statement

Statement of Owner's Equity

Balance Sheet

Demonstration Problem #2

Mildred Mann Amis is an artist living in the Outer Banks of North Carolina. Her business is called Mann Made Designs. From the following information, prepare an Income Statement, Statement of Owner's Equity, and Balance Sheet for Mann Made Designs for the month of May, 20X9.

Accounts Payable	$ 700
Accounts Receivable	1,800
Advertising Expense	500
Building	55,000
Cash	8,200
Commissions Earned	12,000
Equipment	6,600
Interest Expense	200
Interest Receivable	100
Mildred Amis, Capital 5/1/20X9	59,325
Mildred Amis, Withdrawals	2,000
Notes Payable	14,000
Notes Receivable	1,000
Salaries Expense	1,750
Salaries Payable	250
Supplies	2,325
Supplies Expense	2,900
Utilities Expense	100
Vehicle	3,800

Income Statement

Statement of Owner's Equity

Balance Sheet

SOLUTIONS

I. Matching

1. C	5. F	9. N	13. L
2. G	6. H	10. K	14. O
3. E	7. A	11. B	15. D
4. M	8. I	12. J	16. P

II. Multiple Choice

1. C   Of the choices given, only "Notes Payable" meets the definition of a liability. Fees Earned is revenue, supplies are assets, and investments by the owner are increases in equity.

2. B   When cash is paid an account payable: cash is decreased and accounts payable is decreased. This results in a decrease in total assets and a decrease in total liabilities

3. A   Only sales on account cause a receivable to be recorded. Purchases on account cause a payable to be recorded, sales for cash and purchases for cash do not affect receivables.

4. C   When cash is received on an account receivable, two assets are affected: cash is increased and accounts receivable is decreased. Since the increase in cash is equal to the decrease in accounts receivable, total assets are unchanged.

5. C   The owner's investment of equipment in the business causes an increase in the assets of the business. Since the owner has a claim to those assets he or she invested in the business, there is also an increase in owner's equity.

6. C   The owner's investment of cash in the business causes the same result as if he or she had invested any other asset into the business. Therefore, the investment of cash causes an increase in the assets of the business. Since the owner has a claim to those assets he or she invested in the business, there is also an increase in owner's equity.

7. C   The balance sheet lists all the assets, liabilities, and owner's equity as of a specific date. The income statement, statement of owner's equity, and statement of cash flows cover a specific time period.

8. B   The sale of swimsuits would result in an increase in assets, specifically the accounts receivable account, for $54,600 (700 swimsuits x $78 each) and an increase in owner's equity resulting from the generation of revenue.

9. A   The collection of $30,000 on the account affects two asset accounts: cash is increased and accounts receivable is decreased. Since the increase in cash is equal to the decrease in accounts receivable, total assets are unchanged. There is no effect on owner's equity because the sale (revenue) was recorded on March 17 at the time the sale was made.

10. D   The income statement, statement of owner's equity, and statement of cash flows all cover a specific period of time. The balance sheet lists all the assets, liabilities, and owner's equity as of a specific date.

11.   D   Revenues minus expenses equal net income. Assets minus liabilities equals owner's equity. Liabilities plus owner's equity equals assets. Revenues plus expenses has no meaning.

12.   C   Let "L" stand for liabilities. Given that total assets equals 3L and that owner's equity equals $90,000, then according to the accounting equation:

$$3L = L + \$90,000$$

Subtract L from both sides of the equation.

$$2L = \$90,000, \text{ therefore } L = \$45,000$$

Total Assets = 3L or 3 x $45,000 = $135,000

To double check your work, plug the amounts into the accounting equation:

Assets   = Liabilities + Owner's Equity
$135,000 = $45,000 + $90,000

> **Study Tip**: Memorizing and understanding the basic accounting equation is important and will be helpful in future chapters.

13.   A

Assets	=	Liabilities	+	Owner's Equity	
$265,000	=	$135,000	+	$130,000	Jan. 1
-75,000				+24,000	
$190,000	=	$36,000	+	$154,000	Dec. 31

14.   D

Beginning balance in owner's equity	$300
+ Net income	325
Subtotal	625
- Withdrawals	81
Ending balance in owner's equity	$544

> **Study Tip**: There is an important concept in this problem that you can use over and over throughout your accounting course. In general terms the concept can be stated:
> Beginning balance + Additions - Reductions = Ending balance.

15.   B   Profitability is determined by evaluating revenues and expenses.
Revenues – Expenses = Net Income (Loss)
$57,500 – $67,250 = (9,750). Therefore, the business was not profitable for the month of June.

III. Completion

1. Income Statement, Statement of Owner's Equity, Balance Sheet, and Statement of Cash Flows
2. entity (The most basic concept in accounting is that each entity has sharp boundaries between it and every other entity.)
3. amounts earned by delivering goods and providing services to customers
4. expenses
5. liabilities, owner's equity
6. Assets = Liabilities + Owner's equity
7. cost
8. Bookkeeping
9. Name of business, name of financial statement, date or time period covered
10. Stable Monetary Unit

IV. Daily Exercises

1.
   a. The statement of cash flows lists the cash inflows and outflows (i.e., receipts and payments) for the period and would, therefore, answer the question.
   b. The balance sheet indicates the financial position of the business on any particular date. The net worth of the business would be equal to the owner's equity.
   c. The balance sheet includes a list of all liabilities (amounts owed to creditors) on any particular date.
   d. Profitability is determined by comparing revenues with expenses and is reported on the income statement.
   e. The statement of owner's equity starts with beginning capital and calculates ending capital by adding net income and additional investment for the period then deducting any owner withdrawals.

2. The building should be listed on the balance sheet at $100,000. This amount is supported by the cost principle, which states that assets and services should be recorded in the accounting records (the books) at the actual price paid for the asset or service.

3. Yes. A business is profitable when revenues exceed expenses (net income) and is not profitable when expenses exceed revenues (net loss). Therefore, net income was $1,800 ($7,300-$5,500). Cash receipts from customers and owner's withdrawals are irrelevant with respect to determining profitability.

4. The value of the business to the owner did not change during the period. Net income of $1,800 was offset by the $1,800 the owner withdrew during the period. Therefore, beginning capital and ending capital were the same amount. The change in owner's equity shows the change in the value of the business. The value of the business is equal to owner's equity.

V. Exercises

1.

	Cash	+	Accounts Receivable	+	Supplies	+	Computer Equipment	=	Accounts Payable	+	Granger, Capital
A.	$20,000							=			$20,000
B.	(675)							=			(675)
	$ 19,325							=			$19,325
C.							$5,000	=	$5,000		
	$ 19,325					+	$5,000	=	$5,000	+	$19,325
D.	(475)			+	$ 475			=			
	$ 18,850			+	$ 475	+	$5,000	=	$5,000	+	$19,325
E.			$2,750					=			$ 2,750
	$ 18,850	+	$2,750	+	$ 475	+	$5,000	=	$5,000	+	$22,075
F.	(1,000)							=	(1,000)		
	$ 17,850	+	$2,750	+	$ 475	+	$5,000	=	$4,000	+	$22,075
G.	425		(425)					=			
	$ 18,275	+	$ 2,325	+	$ 475	+	$5,000	=	$4,000	+	$22,075
H.	40				(40)			=			
	$ 18,315	+	$ 2,325	+	$ 435	+	$5,000	=	$4,000	+	$22,075

2.

Clarence's' Clunker Repair and Body Shop
Balance Sheet
June 30, 20X7

Assets:			Liabilities:	
Cash	$ 120		Accounts Payable	$ 250
Accounts Receivable	200		Total Liabilities	250
Supplies	70		Owner's Equity:	
Equipment	160		Clarence, Capital	300
			Total Liabilities	
Total Assets	$ 550		and Stockholders' Equity	$ 550

3.

Paul's Delivery Service
Income Statement
For the Month Ended August 31, 20X6

Service revenue			$3,210
Expenses:			
Salaries	$	500	
Truck Rental		500	
Supplies		280	
Telephone		270	1,550
Net income			$1,660

VI. Beyond the Numbers

The answer to both questions is yes. How is this possible? Profitability is presented on the Income Statement and occurs when revenues exceed expenses. Solvency is analyzed by examining the Balance Sheet and comparing assets (specifically cash and receivables) with liabilities. A business is solvent when there are sufficient assets on hand to pay the debt as the debt becomes due. Remember, however, there is a third financial statement—the Statement of Owner's Equity—which links the Income Statement to the Balance Sheet. A profitable business will become insolvent if, over time, the owner withdraws cash in excess of net income. In addition, if the company invests heavily in long-term assets or inventory, solvency will decrease even if the company is profitable. Conversely, an unprofitable business can remain solvent over time if the owner is able to contribute personal assets in excess of the net losses.

VII. Demonstration Problems

Demonstration Problem #1 Solved and Explained

Requirement 1 (Analysis of transactions)

5/1   Russell's investment of $25,000 increased his equity in the business by the same amount. Thus:

Assets	=	Liabilities	+	Owner's Equity
Cash				Russell, Capital
+25,000		no change		+25,000

5/1   Monthly rent of $1,250 was paid, so Cash decreased by $1,250. In return for the rent payment, Russell's business received the right to use the office space. However, since Russell owns no part of the office, his right to use the office cannot be considered an asset. By a process of elimination you can evaluate that since Russell has paid $1,250 cash but has not received an asset in return, nor paid a liability, his equity in the business has decreased by $1,250 attributable to rent expense. Russell must have an office from which he can conduct his business, therefore, the payment of rent can be considered a cost incurred to generate revenue or an expense.

Assets	=	Liabilities	+	Owner's Equity
Cash				Russell, Capital
-1,250		no change		-1,250

5/3 $2,100 was paid for office equipment. In exchange for cash, Russell's business received ownership of the office equipment. When a business owns a resource to be used in the business, that resource is an asset. Since the $2,100 cash was exchanged for $2,100 worth of assets, owner's equity was not affected. Remember: When cash is exchanged for an asset, owner's equity is unaffected.

Assets		=	Liabilities	+	Owner's Equity
Cash	Office Equipment				
-2,100	+2,100		no change		no change

22

5/5   A computer and laser printer were purchased for $3,200 on account. Russell's business now owns some additional equipment, which we already established as an asset on 5/3. The words "on account" indicated that payment was not made at the time he purchased this equipment, but rather promised sometime in the future. The promise of payment represents money that is owed and is a debt or liability. By promising the computer sales company $3,200, Russell has added $3,200 to his company's liabilities. Up to this point Russell had no liabilities.

Assets	=	Liabilities	+	Owner's Equity
Computer +3,200		Accounts Payable +3,200		no change

5/8   Office supplies costing $200 were purchased on account. As indicated in the 5/5 transaction, when a business incurs a debt in exchange for an asset, the business has added the asset and it has also added a related liability.

Assets	=	Liabilities	+	Owner's Equity
Supplies +200		Accounts Payable +200		no change

5/10   Consulting services of $1,500 were provided on account to a client. The words "on account" indicate that the customer did not pay for the services at the time the services were rendered. Therefore, the client has promised to pay for the services rendered sometime in the future. This promise represents an asset to the business, or an account receivable. A business earns revenue when it performs a service, whether it receives cash immediately or expects to collect the cash later. Revenue transactions cause the business to grow, as shown by the increase in total assets and equities. Note that both the assets and the owner's equity in the business have increased.

Assets	=	Liabilities	+	Owner's Equity
Accounts Receivable +1,500				Russell, Capital +1,500

5/15   Fees totaling $2,300 were earned and collected. When services are rendered and cash is collected, the asset cash increases by the amount collected and the owner's equity also increases due to the earning of revenue. We determine that revenue has been earned because the services were rendered.

Assets	=	Liabilities	+	Owner's Equity
Cash +2,300		no change		Russell, Capital +2,300

5/16 Collected $1,300 cash on the account receivable created on 5/10. The asset Cash is increased and the asset Accounts Receivable is decreased by the same amount. Note that revenue is unaffected by the actual receipt of the cash since the firm already recorded the revenue when it was earned on 5/10.

Assets		=	Liabilities	+	Owner's Equity
Cash	Accounts Receivable				
+1,300	-1,300		no change		no change

5/18 Paid for the supplies purchased on 5/8. The payment of cash on account does not affect the asset Office Supplies because the payment does not increase or decrease the amount of supplies available to the business. The effect on the accounting equation is a decrease in the asset Cash and a decrease in the liability Accounts Payable. The business has simply paid for an amount that it owed to the business from which it purchased the office supplies.

Assets	=	Liabilities	+	Owner's Equity
Cash		Accounts Payable		
-200		-200		no change

5/21 The owner withdrew $3,000 for personal use. The withdrawal of cash decreases the asset Cash and reduces the owner's equity in the business. Note that the withdrawal does not represent a business expense.

Assets	=	Liabilities	+	Owner's Equity
Cash				Russell, Capital
-3,000		no change		-3,000

5/31 Fees totaling $4,100 were earned and collected. When services are rendered and immediately collected, the asset Cash increases by the amount received, and the owner's equity increases as well attributable to the earning of revenue.

Assets	=	Liabilities	+	Owner's Equity
Cash				Russell, Capital
+4,100				+4,100

RUSSELL CONSULTING

| | ASSETS | | | | = | LIABILITIES | + | OWNER'S EQUITY | |
	Cash +	Office Supplies +	Accounts Receivable +	Equipment	=	Accounts Payable	+	Russell, Capital	Type of owner's equity transaction
5/1	+25,000							+25,000	Owner investment
5/1	-1,250							-1,250	Rent expense
5/3	-2,100			+2,100					
5/5				+3,200		+3,200			
5/8		+200				+200			
5/10			+1,500					+1,500	Service revenue
5/15	+2,300							+2,300	Service revenue
5/16	+1,300		-1,300						
5/18	-200					-200			
5/21	-3,000							-3,000	Owner withdrawal
5/31	+4,100							+4,100	Service revenue
	$26,150	$200	$200	$5,300		$3,200		$28,650	

$31,850 $31,850

Requirement 2 (Income Statement, Statement of Owner's Equity, and Balance Sheet)

Russell Consulting
Income Statement
For the Month Ended May 31, 20X8

Service Income		$7,900
Less: Expenses		
Rent		1,250
Net Income		$6,650

Russell Consulting
Statement of Owner's Equity
For the Month Ended May 31, 20X8

Russell, Capital 5/1/X8		$0
Add: Capital Investment	$25,000	
Net Income	6,650	
Less: Withdrawals	(3,000)	28,650
Russell, Capital 5/31/X8		$28,650

Russell Consulting
Balance Sheet
May 31, 20X8

ASSETS		LIABILITIES	
Cash	$26,150	Accounts Payable	$ 3,200
Accounts Receivable	200		
Office Supplies	200		
Equipment	5,300	**OWNER'S EQUITY**	
		Russell, Capital 5/31/X8	28,650
Total Assets	$31,850	Total Liabilities & Owner's Equity	$31,850

Demonstration Problem #2 Solved

Mann Made Designs
Income Statement
For the Month Ended May 31, 20X9

Commissions Earned		$12,000
Less: Expenses		
Advertising	$500	
Interest	200	
Salaries	1750	
Supplies	2900	
Utilities	100	
Total Expenses		5,450
Net Income		$ 6,550

Mann Made Designs.
Statement of Owner's Equity
For the Month Ended May 31, 20X9

Mildred Amis, Capital 5/1/X9		$59,325
Add: Net Income	$6,550	
Less: Withdrawals	2,000	4,550
Mildred Amis, Capital 5/31/X9		$63,875

Mann Made Designs
Balance Sheet
May 31, 20X9

ASSETS		LIABILITIES	
Cash	$ 8,200	Accounts Payable	$ 700
Accounts Receivable	1,800	Notes Payable	14,000
Notes Receivable	1,000	Salaries Payable	250
Interest Receivable	100	Total Liabilities	$14,950
Supplies	2,325		
Equipment	6,600		
Vehicle	3,800	**OWNER'S EQUITY**	
Building	55,000	Mildred Amis, Capital 5/31/X9	63,875
Total Assets	$78,825	Total Liabilities and Owner's Equity	$78,825

Chapter 2—Recording Business Transactions

CHAPTER OVERVIEW

Chapter Two uses the foundation established in the previous chapter and expands the discussion of recording business transactions. A thorough understanding of this process is vital to your success in mastering topics in future chapters. The learning objectives for this chapter are to

1. Use accounting terms
2. Apply the rules of debit and credit.
3. Record transactions in the journal.
4. Post from the journal to the ledger.
5. Prepare and use a trial balance.
6. Analyze transactions without a journal.

CHAPTER REVIEW

Objective 1 - Use accounting terms

The terms used in accounting sometimes have meanings that differ from ordinary usage. You must learn the accounting meaning of terms now. Some key terms you must learn are:

- **Account:** The basic summary device used to record all the changes that occur in a particular asset, liability, or owner's equity during a period.

- **Ledger:** The record holding all of the individual accounts used by a business. The list of accounts that appear in the ledger are referred to as the **chart of accounts**. Each account is assigned a unique number (this account number is used as a reference in the posting process). The order of the accounts and the corresponding account numbers in this list parallels the accounting equation. In other words, assets are listed first, followed by liability accounts, and lastly, owner's equity. Owner's equity is subdivided into capital, withdrawals, revenue and expense accounts. The numbers are assigned in ascending order so assets are assigned the lowest numbers while expenses carry the highest numbers.

- **Journal:** The chronological record of an entity's business transactions. In practice, when a business transaction occurs, the transaction will first be recorded in the journal. So, you can think of the journal as the first place a business transaction will appear in the accounting records. Transactions are recorded in the journal chronologically, or in the order in which the transactions occurred.

- **Trial Balance:** A list of all the accounts with their balances. The trial balance is prepared from the ledger and the accounts are listed in the order in which the accounts appear in the ledger.

- **Assets:** Economic resources that will benefit the business in the future. When we talk about assets, we are referring to the category, or classification of accounts. Within each category or classification, there are specific account titles that are used that are representative of the nature of each type of asset. Examples of asset accounts are Cash, Notes Receivable, Accounts Receivable, Prepaid Expenses, Land, Buildings, Equipment, Furniture, and Fixtures.

- **Liabilities:** Obligations that the business owes to an entity in the future. Remember that liabilities represent creditor's claims to the assets of the business. The term "liabilities" represents the category of accounts that summarizes the total debt of the business. Within the liabilities category, there are specific liability accounts. Examples of liability accounts include Notes Payable, Accounts Payable, Taxes Payable, Interest Payable, and Salary Payable to name a few. Notice the word "payable" implies that cash will be paid in the future. So, whenever you see an account title that includes the word "payable" you will know that it is a liability account. A business can have obligations where it owes something other than cash. A business can owe a service or a product, too. We will address these other obligations in future chapters.

- **Owner's equity:** The claim that the owner has on the assets of the business. Owner's equity represents the value of the business and can also be referred to as the net worth of the business. Owner's equity is the category that houses the individual owner's equity accounts. The individual owner's equity accounts are:
    - **Capital:** The specific account that reflects the owner's claims to the business assets.
    - **Withdrawals:** The assets that the owner removes for personal use
    - **Revenues:** The account classification that represents the increases in owner's equity created by delivering goods or services to customers or clients. Examples of specific revenue accounts are Service Revenue, Sales Revenue, and Interest Revenue.
    - **Expenses:** The account classification that represents decreases in owner's equity resulting from the using up of assets or the creation of a liability in the normal course of doing business. Remember that expenses are created to support the generation of revenues. Examples of specific expense accounts are Rent Expense, Salary Expense, Utilities Expense and Interest Expense.

- **Double-entry accounting**: The accounting system that records the dual effects of every business transaction. Every transaction affects at least two accounts.
    - **T-accounts:** In accounting education, the T-account is an abbreviated version of the general ledger used as an illustrative tool used to show the dual effects of a transaction in specific accounts. In practice, you would ask to see the ledger. You would never ask to see the T-accounts.
    - **Debit (Dr)**: The left side of the T-account.
    - **Credit (Cr)**: The right side of the T-account.

Helpful Hint: Debit means left and credit means right. That's all! In order to learn the accounting use for the words debit and credit, you must depart from your personal knowledge of debits and credits as they relate to your bank account.

Objective 2 - Apply the rules of debit and credit.

To learn the rules of debit and credit, you need to start with the basic accounting equation. You know that the accounting equation must always be in balance. This rule will carry forward as you learn about the rules of debit and credit. The account category (assets, liabilities, or owner's equity) governs how increases and decreases are recorded in each individual account. The rules of debit and credit refer to the side of the T-account on which an increase or decrease is recorded. It is easiest to first focus on the side of the account on which increases are recorded. According to the rules of debit and credit, when a business transaction results in an increase in assets, the increase is recorded on the left side of the T-account or the debit side. In accounting language, we would simply say to "debit the account" when we mean to increase the account balance of an asset. When a business transaction results in an increase in liabilities or owner's equity the increase is recorded on the right side of the T-account or the credit side. In accounting language, we would say to "credit the account" when we mean to increase the balance of a liability account or to increase owner's equity.

Assets = Liabilities + Owner's Equity

Notice that when we say that assets equal liabilities plus owner's equity, we are really saying that the left side must always equal the right side of the equation. Or, using accounting language, we could simply say that the debits must equal the credits.

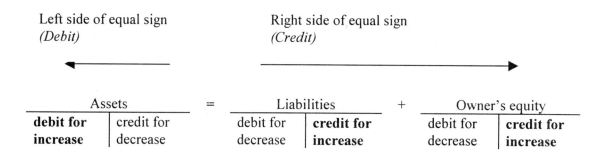

Once you understand which side of the T-accounts increases are recorded, it stands to reason that decreases would be recorded on the opposite side. Thus, to decrease an asset account, you would "credit" the account, and to decrease the liabilities and owner's equity, you would "debit" the account.

Study Tip: Refer to the basic accounting equation to understand the debit/credit rules. Increases in items on the *left side* of the equation are placed on the *left side* (debit) of the account. Increases in the items on the *right side* of the equation are placed on the *right side* (credit) of the account.

Take some time to make sure that you understand the basic rules of debit and credit as they apply to the accounting equation illustrated above. Once you are comfortable with the accounting equation, then we need to look a little more closely at Owner's Equity.

Remember that Owner's Equity has four components:

1. **Owner's investments** that increase overall owner's equity and are always recorded in the Capital account.
2. **Owner's withdrawals** that decrease overall owner's equity and are always recorded in the Withdrawals account.
3. **Revenues** that increase overall owner's equity and are always recorded in a specific revenue account such as Service Revenue.
4. **Expenses** that decrease overall owner's equity and are always recorded in the specific expense accounts such as Advertising Expense and Utilities Expense.

To apply the rules of debit and credit to owner's equity, you must first understand the difference between these four components and the effect of each (increase or decrease) on owner's equity. Now review the following illustration:

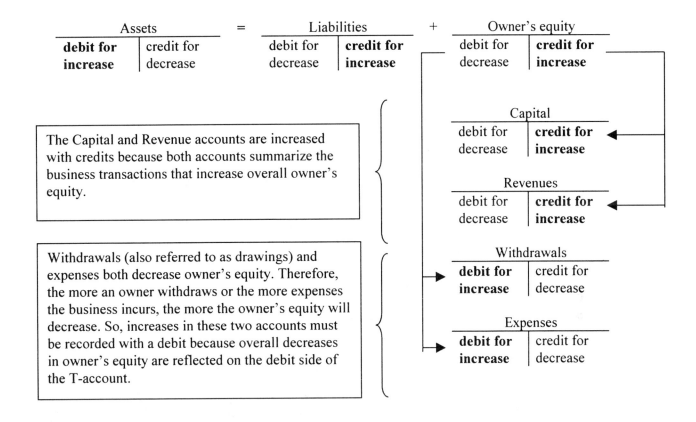

Helpful Hint: You can use a pneumonic to learn the rules of debit and credit: **DEAD CLRC** or

Debit to increase:	Credit to increase:
Expenses	**L**iabilities
Assets	**R**evenues
Drawings (withdrawals)	**C**apital

The term **normal balance** refers to the type of balance (debit or credit) the account usually carries. The normal balance for any account is always the side of the account where increases are recorded. Therefore, the normal balances are:

Account	Normal Balance
Assets	debit
Liabilities	credit
Capital	credit
Withdrawals	debit
Revenues	credit
Expenses	debit

> Helpful Hint: See Exhibit 2-13 for a summary of the rules of debit and credit and the normal balance of accounts.

Objective 3 - Record transactions in the journal.

Remember, the journal is a chronological record of a business's transactions. It is the first place where a transaction is recorded. To record a transaction in the journal, follow these three steps:

1. Specify each account affected and determine whether it is an asset, a liability, or an owner's equity account.
2. Determine whether each account balance is increased or decreased, and then use the rules of debit and credit to determine whether to "debit" or "credit" the account. (Note: The rules of double-entry accounting also require that every journal entry will consist of at least one debit and at least one credit. A journal entry that affects more than two accounts is referred to as a compound entry.)
3. Record the transaction in the journal:
   - Enter the date of the transaction
   - Record the debit first
   - Record the credit second
   - Last record a brief explanation of the transaction.

To illustrate, suppose that Bob Bush, borrows $10,000 from the bank to expand the business. What is the journal entry for this transaction?

1. The accounts affected are Cash (an Asset) and Notes Payable (a Liability).
2. Both accounts will increase by $10,000. Debit Cash for $10,000 to increase Cash, and Credit Notes Payable for $10,000 to increase Notes Payable.
3. Record the journal entry:

Date	Accounts	Debit	Credit
Jan. 10	Cash	10,000	
	Notes Payable		10,000
	Bank loan for business expansion.		

(Notice that the debit appears on the left and the credit is indented below the debit to the right, which is consistent with the definitions of debit and credit that you have learned.)

As you become more proficient with journal entries, you will be able to "read" the entries and work your way backwards to describe the transaction. For example, when you see the debit to cash, you will know that cash was increased meaning the business received some cash; and, the credit to notes payable indicates that an account titled note payable was increased meaning that the business now owes some money. If the business receives cash from increasing a liability, then you know the original transaction has to be that the business borrowed some money.

Study Tip: If you determine that one of the accounts affected is Cash, first determine whether Cash increases or decreases. This allows you to use a process of elimination to determine the debit or credit for the other account affected by the transaction. Using the example above, if you determine that the account Cash has increased, and you know that the increase has to be recorded with a debit, then you can conclude that the other account you have identified, Notes Payable, will have to be the credit, since every transaction must have at least one debit and at least one credit.

Examples of some typical journal entries are:

Accounts	Debit	Credit
Cash	25,000	
Smith, Capital		25,000
Owner invests money into the business.		
Prepaid Insurance	3,000	
Cash		3,000
Purchased a three-year insurance policy.		
Supplies	1,500	
Accounts Payable		1,500
Purchased supplies on account.		
Accounts Payable	1,500	
Cash		1,500
Paid amount owed for supplies.		
Accounts Receivable	2,200	
Service Revenue		2,200
Billed clients for services rendered.		
Cash	1,400	
Accounts Receivable		1,400
Received payments from clients previously billed.		
Salary Expense	2,800	
Cash		2,800
Paid salaries.		
Withdrawals	2,000	
Cash		2,000
Owner withdraws cash for personal use.		

Objective 4 - Post from the journal to the ledger.

Posting means to copy the amounts from the journal to the appropriate accounts in the ledger. The journal entry for the bank loan in the previous example would be posted this way:

Cash		Notes Payable
10,000		10,000

Posting updates the ledger by transferring all of the transactions that affect a specific account from the journal to each respective account. Posting to the ledger and calculating an account balance is the only way that you can determine the balance in any account. You cannot look at the journal and determine the account balance for Cash. This can only be determined by going to the ledger and reviewing the Cash account.

> Helpful Hint: Review Exhibit 2-9 in your text for a detailed illustration of journalizing and posting. Remember we are using the T-account as an abbreviated version of the ledger.

Objective 5 - Prepare and use a trial balance.

The **trial balance** is taken from the ledger and represents a listing of all accounts with their balances. The accounts are listed in the order in which they appear in the ledger. The trial balance tests whether the total debits equal the total credits. If total debits do not equal the total credits, an error has been made. Review Exhibit 2-8 in your text for an example of a trial balance.

Keep in mind that the trial balance is an internal document used by the business to make sure that the debits and credits are equal. The trial balance is NOT the same thing as the balance sheet. The balance sheet is a financial statement that is prepared to present to external users.

> <u>Study Tip</u>: Spend some time reading and thinking about the decision guidelines in your text. These should help you place the recording process in the proper context.

Objective 7 - Analyze transactions without a journal.

In general, the ledger is more useful than the journal in providing an overall model of a business. Therefore, when time is of the essence, decision-makers frequently skip the journal and go directly to the ledger in order to compress transaction analysis, journalizing, and posting into a single step.

TEST YOURSELF

All the self-testing materials in this chapter focus on information and procedures that your instructor is likely to test in quizzes and examinations.

I. Matching   *Match each numbered term with its lettered definition.*

_____ 1.   Account
_____ 2.   Capital
_____ 3.   Chart of accounts
_____ 4.   Compound entry
_____ 5.   Credit
_____ 6.   Debit
_____ 7.   Double-entry system
_____ 8.   Journal

_____ 9.   Ledger
_____ 10. Normal balance
_____ 11. Posting
_____ 12. Post reference
_____ 13. Trial balance
_____ 14. Withdrawals
_____ 15. Revenues

A. Detailed record of changes in a particular asset, liability, or owner's equity during a period of time.
B. Increases in owner's equity that result from delivering goods or services to customers or clients.
C. A way of cross-referencing amounts between the journal and ledger.
D. Left side of an account.
E. List of all the accounts in the ledger and their account numbers.
F. Copying information from the journal to the ledger.
G. A list of all the accounts with their balances which tests whether total debits equals total credits.
H. The book of accounts.
I. Right side of an account.
J. Provides a chronological record of an entity's transactions.
K. The type of balance an account usually carries.
L. The account that shows the owner's claim to the business's assets.
M. The account that summarizes the removal of cash by the owner.
N. When more than two accounts are affected by a transaction.
O. Recording the dual effects of transactions.

II. Multiple Choice   *Circle the best answer.*

1. An attorney performs services for which he receives cash. The correct entry for this transaction is:

A.   Service Revenue
          Accounts Payable

B.   Service Revenue
          Cash

C.   Accounts Receivable
          Service Revenue

D.   Cash
          Service Revenue

2. An accountant debited Insurance Expense $1,500 and credited Cash $1,500 in error. The correct entry should have been to debit Prepaid Insurance for $1,500 and credit Cash for $1,500. As a result of this error:

A. assets are overstated by $1,500.
B. expenses are understated by $1,500.

C. the trial balance will not balance.
D. expenses are overstated by $1,500.

3. Accounts Receivable had total debits for the month of $3,500 and total credits for the month of $2,700. The beginning balance in Accounts Receivable was $3,200. What was the net change in Accounts Receivable?

A. A decrease of $800
B. An increase of $4,000

C. An increase of $800
D. A decrease of $4,000

4. Accounts Payable had a balance of $4,000 on April 1. During April, $2,750 of equipment was purchased on account. The April 30 balance was a credit of $3,850. How much were payments on Accounts Payable during April?

A. $ 6,750
B. $ 7,850

C. $ 2,900
D. $ 6,600

5. Income statement accounts are:

A. assets and liabilities.
B. revenues and withdrawals.

C. revenues and expenses.
D. assets and withdrawals.

6. The posting reference in the ledger tells:

A. the page of the ledger on which the account is found.
B. the explanation of the transaction.

C. whether it is a debit or a credit entry.
D. the page of the journal where the original entry can be found.

7. The list of accounts and their account numbers is called the:

A. chart of accounts.
B. trial balance.

C. ledger.
D. accountants reference.

8. The revenue earned by lending money is called:

A. advertising expense.
B. loan revenue.

C. interest revenue.
D. prepaid expense.

9. When the owner of a business withdraws cash, the journal entry should include a:

A. debit to Accounts Payable.
B. credit to Capital.

C. debit to Cash.
D. debit to Withdrawals.

10. When cash was received on account in payment for services previously rendered, the accountant recorded the transaction by debiting Cash and crediting Service Revenue. As a result there was:

A. an overstatement of Cash and Service Revenue.
B. an understatement of assets and overstatement of revenues .
C. an overstatement of assets and an overstatement of revenues.
D. no over- or understatement of any accounts. This is the correct entry.

III. Completion *Complete each of the following statements.*

1. Put the following in proper sequence by numbering them from 1 to 3.

    _____ a. Post to ledger
    _____ b. Trial balance
    _____ c. Journal entry

2. Indicate whether the following accounts would be increased or decreased with a debit.

		Increase	**Decrease**
a.	Land	_____	_____
b.	Capital	_____	_____
c.	Prepaid Insurance	_____	_____
d.	Interest Payable	_____	_____
e.	Service Revenue	_____	_____
f.	Rent Expense	_____	_____
g.	Interest Revenue	_____	_____
h.	Accounts Payable	_____	_____
i.	Withdrawals	_____	_____
j.	Advertising Expense	_____	_____

3. Indicate the normal balance for each of the following.

		Debit	**Credit**
a.	Notes Receivable	_____	_____
b.	Accounts Payable	_____	_____
c.	Prepaid Advertising	_____	_____
d.	Building	_____	_____
e.	Capital	_____	_____
f.	Accounts Receivable	_____	_____
g.	Rent Expense	_____	_____
h.	Interest Revenue	_____	_____
i.	Land	_____	_____
j.	Withdrawals	_____	_____

IV. Daily Exercises

1. Classify each of the following accounts as asset, liability, capital, withdrawals, revenue, or expense.

Account	Classification
a. Salaries Payable	_____
b. Supplies	_____
c. Fees Receivable	_____
d. Computer Equipment	_____
e. Fees Earned	_____
f. Insurance Expense	_____
g. James Brown, Capital	_____
h. Sales Revenue	_____
i. Notes Payable	_____
j. James Brown, Withdrawals	_____

2. Review the list of accounts in #1 above and indicate the normal balance of each account.

a. _____		f. _____	
b. _____		g. _____	
c. _____		h. _____	
d. _____		i. _____	
e. _____		j. _____	

2. Prepare a trial balance from the following list of accounts and balances. List the accounts in their proper order. All accounts reflect normal balances.

Accounts Payable	$ 830
Accounts Receivable	1,050
Capital	2,700
Cash	1,350
Fees Earned	3,700
Furniture and Fixtures	4,500
Insurance Expense	500
Notes Payable	1,700
Rent Expense	950
Supplies	380
Withdrawals	200

Accounts	Debit	Credit

V. Exercises

1. Walker Smith opened a financial planning firm on June, 20X6. During the first month of operations, the following transactions occurred:

6/1   Walker invested $7,500 cash in the business.

6/2   Purchased used office equipment for $3,000. He made an $800 cash down payment and gave the seller a note payable due in 90 days.

6/3   Paid $500 for a month's rent.

6/15   Walker provided financial planning services, $6,000 during the first fifteen days of the month. The fees for these services were collected from clients at the time the services were provided. Walker made one deposit in the business checking account.

6/17   Withdrew $1,275 to pay the rent on his apartment.

6/19   Purchased $250 of supplies on account.

6/19   Paid the phone bill for the month, $130.

6/21   Received the utility bill for July, $225. The utility bill is not due until next month.

6/25   Paid his secretary a salary of $1,350.

6/28   Paid for the supplies purchased on 6/19.

6/30   Performed $10,500 in services for the last half of June. Clients paid for $4,000 of these services at the time the services were performed.

Prepare the journal entries for each of these transactions, omitting the explanations. Use the following accounts: Cash; Accounts Receivable; Supplies; Equipment; Accounts Payable; Notes Payable; Walker Smith, Capital; Walker Smith, Withdrawals; Service Revenue; Rent Expense; Salary Expense; Telephone Expense; Utilities Expense.

Date	Accounts	PR	Debit	Credit

2. The following are normal balances for the accounts of Kevin's Landscaping & Lawn Service on August 31, 20X7.

Accounts Payable	$ 375
Accounts Receivable	5,370
Advertising Expense	700
Equipment	7,500
Cash	10,000
Gasoline Expense	1,200
Interest Payable	85
Lawn Care Supplies	875
Rent Expense	425
Prepaid Insurance	250
Salary Expense	3,125
Notes Payable	1,500
Kevin, Capital	?
Service Revenue	5,500
Kevin, Withdrawals	1,500

a. Prepare a trial balance based on the account balances above. List the accounts in their proper order and calculate the correct balance for the Kevin, Capital account.

Accounts	Debit	Credit

b. How much net income (loss) did Kevin's Landscaping & Lawn Service generate for the month of August? _____

3. Tommy's Totally Taxi Service had the following trial balance on October 31, 20X7:

Accounts	Debit	Credit
Cash	$ 36,000	
Accounts Receivable	18,000	
Notes Receivable	6,000	
Supplies	700	
Vehicles	40,000	
Accounts Payable		$ 1,400
Tommy, Capital		68,100
Service Revenue		34,000
Salary Expense		7,000
Insurance Expense		1,500
	$100,700	$ 106,000

The following errors caused the trial balance not to balance:

a. Tommy recorded a $1,500 note payable as a note receivable.
b. He posted a $3,000 credit to Accounts Payable as $300.
c. He recorded Prepaid Insurance of $1,500 as Insurance Expense.
d. He recorded a cash revenue transaction by debiting Cash for $3,000 and crediting Accounts Receivable for $3,000.

Prepare a corrected trial balance as of October 31, 20X7:

Tommy's Totally Taxi Service
Trial Balance
October 31, 20X7

Accounts	Debit	Credit

VI. Beyond the Numbers

The following errors occurred in posting transactions from the journal to the ledger.

1. A payment of $170 for advertising was posted as a $170 debit to Advertising Expense and a $710 credit to Cash.
2. The receipt of $300 from a customer on account was posted as a $300 debit to Cash and a $300 credit to Fees Earned.
3. The purchase of Supplies on account for $140 was posted twice as a debit to Supplies and once as a credit to Accounts Payable.
4. The payment of $220 to a creditor on account was posted as a credit to Accounts Payable for $220 and a credit to Cash for $220.

For each of these errors, determine the following:
- A. Is the trial balance out of balance, yes or no?
- B. If you answer "yes" to A., by what amount will the debits and credits be out of balance?
- C. Which column total, debit or credit, is larger as a result of the error?
- D. Which column total, debit or credit, reflects the correct total?

Error	Out of balance?	Column difference	Larger column amount	Correct column total
1.				
2.				
3.				
4.				

VII. Demonstration Problems

Demonstration Problem #1

Joe's Adventures Unlimited rents canoes to customers who want to spend a day canoeing down the Bluewater River. Joe Davidson established the business in 20X6.

During the month of May, the business performed the following transactions:

a. Joe Davidson borrowed $125,000 from a local bank signing a note payable in the name of the business.
b. A small parcel of land was acquired for $30,000 cash.
c. Canoe trips were provided for customers. Cash totaling $6,000 was received for these trips at the time the rentals were provided.
d. Supplies costing $1,800 were purchased on account.
e. Joe contracted with one of the local youth groups and canoe trips were provided for this group on account. The total amount of revenue earned on account, $4,500.
f. The following expenses were paid in cash:
>   Salary Expense, $3,000
>   Rent Expense, $1,700
>   Advertising Expense, $650
>   Interest Expense, $350

   Record these expenses using one compound entry.
g. Joe Davidson withdrew $2,800 for personal use.
h. Paid $3,800 owed on account.
i. Received $2,750 cash on account for services previously rendered.

Required:

1. Using the T-account format, open the following ledger accounts for Joe's Adventure's Unlimited with the beginning account balances as indicated.

ASSETS
Cash, $10,000
Accounts receivable, no balance
Supplies, no balance
Equipment, $26,000
Land, no balance
LIABILITIES
Accounts Payable, $7,000
Notes Payable, no balance

OWNER'S EQUITY
Joe Davidson, Capital, $29,000
Joe Davidson, Withdrawals, no balance

REVENUE
Rental Revenue, no balance

EXPENSES
Salary Expense, no balance
Rent Expense, no balance
Interest Expense, no balance
Advertising Expense, no balance

2. Journalize the transactions using the format illustrated in Exhibit 2-4 on page 45. Key each journal entry by its transaction letter. Omit explanations.
3. Post to the T-accounts on the next two pages. Key all amounts by letter and compute a balance for each account.
4. Prepare the trial balance as of May 31, 20X6 using the format illustrated in Exhibit 2-8 on page 49.

Requirements 1 and 3: (Open ledger accounts and post journal entries)

ASSETS

LIABILITIES

OWNER'S EQUITY

REVENUE

EXPENSES

Requirement 2 (Journal entries)

Date	Accounts and Explanation	PR	Debit	Credit

Requirement 4 (Trial balance)

Accounts	Debits	Credits

Demonstration Problem #2

Using the information from the Trial Balance in Demonstration Problem # 1, prepare an Income Statement, Statement of Owner's Equity, and Balance Sheet. Use proper headings.

Income Statement

Statement of Owner's Equity

Balance Sheet

SOLUTIONS

I. Matching

1. A	4. N	7. O	10. K	13. G
2. L	5. I	8. J	11. F	14. M
3. E	6. D	9. H	12. C	15. B

II. Multiple Choice

1. D The receipt of cash for the performance of services causes an increase in assets and an increase in owner's equity. This increase in owner's equity from providing services is called revenue. Cash is increased with a debit and revenue is increased with a credit.

2. D The recorded entry incorrectly increased expenses by $1,500. Accordingly, expenses are overstated. Since the entry should have debited the Prepaid Insurance account, and did not, assets are *understated*. To correct this error, Insurance Expense should be credited (or decreased) by $1,500 and Prepaid Insurance should be debited (or increased) by $1,500.

3. C The $3,500 of debits to Accounts Receivable increased the balance, while the $2,700 of credits to Accounts Receivable decreased the balance. The net effect of the debits and the credits is $3,500 - $2,700 = $800 increase.

4. C The following equation is used to solve this problem:

    Beginning balance
    + Increase (new purchases on account)
    - Decrease (payments on account)
    = Ending balance

    Rearranged to solve for the payments on account, the equation is:
    Payments = beginning balance + new accounts - ending balance
    Payments = $4,000 + 2,750 - $3,850 = $2,900

5. C Only "Revenues and Expenses" appear on the income statement and are referred to as "income statement accounts". The other three responses include at least one account that would appear on the balance sheet account.

6. D The posting reference provides a "trail" through the accounting records for future reference. The post reference appears in the ledger and "refers" back to the location in the journal from which the entry was posted.

7. A A list of accounts and account numbers is called a chart of accounts.

8. C An entity may have as many revenue accounts as it has sources of revenue. Each account title should be descriptive of the source of the revenue. Since the revenue earned from lending money is "interest," interest revenue is the appropriate account title, just as the revenue earned from providing services to customers is called "service revenue".

9. D Withdrawals of cash from a business by the owner decreases the cash account balance and

increases the balance in the withdrawals account. To decrease the cash balance it is necessary to credit the cash account; to increase the withdrawals account balance it is necessary to debit the withdrawals account. (Remember that the debit to the Withdrawals account has the affect of decreasing overall Owner's Equity.)

10. C   The journal entry incorrectly credited (increased) the service revenue account balance. The correct entry should have been to credit (decrease) accounts receivable. As a result, assets (accounts receivable) are overstated and revenue (service revenue) is overstated.

III. Completion

1. a. 2; b. 3; c. 1. Journal entries are recorded first and then are posted to the ledger. The trial balance is prepared from ledger balances.

2. Increase: a; c; f; i; j
   Decrease: b; d; e; g; h

Debits increase accounts with a normal debit balance and decrease accounts with a normal credit balance. Assets, expenses and withdrawals have normal debit balances, while liabilities, capital, and revenue have normal credit balances.

3. A. debit   F. debit
   B. credit   G. debit
   C. debit   H. credit
   D. debit   I. debit
   E. credit   J. debit

Assets, expenses, and withdrawals have normal debit balances. Liabilities, capital, and revenue have normal credit balances.

IV. Daily Exercises

1. a. liability   g. capital
   b. asset   h. revenue
   c. asset   i. liabilities
   d. asset   j. withdrawals
   e. revenue
   f. expense

2. a. credit   g. credit
   b. debit   h. credit
   c. debit   i. credit
   d. debit   j. debit
   e. credit
   f. debit

3.

	Debit	Credit
Cash	$1,350	
Accounts Receivable	1,050	
Supplies	380	
Furniture and Fixtures	4,500	
Accounts Payable		$ 830
Notes Payable		1,700
Capital		2,700
Withdrawals	200	
Fees Earned		3,700
Rent Expense	950	
Insurance Expense	500	
Total	$8,930	$8,930

V. Exercises

1.

Date	Accounts	PR	Debit	Credit
6/1	Cash		7,500	
	Walker Smith, Capital			7,500
6/2	Equipment		3,000	
	Cash			800
	Notes Payable			2,200
6/3	Rent Expense		500	
	Cash			500
6/15	Cash		6,000	
	Service Revenue			6,000
6/17	Walker Smith, Withdrawals		1,275	
	Cash			1,275
6/19	Supplies		250	
	Accounts Payable			250
	Telephone Expense		130	
	Cash			130
6/21	Utility Expense		225	
	Accounts Payable			225
6/25	Salary Expense		1,350	
	Cash			1,350

			Debit	Credit
6/28	Accounts Payable		250	
	Cash			250
6/31	Cash		4,000	
	Accounts Receivable		6,500	
	Service Revenue			10,500

2. a.

Kevin's Landscaping & Lawn Service
Trial Balance
August 31, 20X7

	Debit	Credit
Cash	$ 10,000	
Accounts Receivable	5,370	
Lawn Care Supplies	875	
Prepaid Insurance	250	
Equipment	7,500	
Accounts Payable		$ 375
Interest Payable		85
Notes Payable		1,500
Kevin, Capital		23,485
Kevin, Withdrawals	1,500	
Service Revenue		5,500
Salary expense	3,125	
Gasoline Expense	1,200	
Advertising Expense	700	
Rent Expense	425	
Total	$30,945	30,945

b. Net income = Revenues – Expenses or
    $5,500-3,125-1,200-700-425 = $50

3.

Tommy's Totally Taxi Service
Trial Balance
October 31, 20X7

	Debit	Credit
Cash	$ 36,000	
Accounts Receivable	21,000	
Notes Receivable	4,500	
Prepaid Insurance	1,500	
Supplies	700	
Vehicles	40,000	
Accounts Payable		$ 4,100
Notes Payable		1,500
Tommy, Capital		68,100
Service Revenue		37,000
Salary Expense	7,000	
Insurance Expense	0	
Total	$110,700	$110,700

VI. Beyond the Numbers

Error	Out of balance?	Column total difference	Larger column total	Correct column total
1.	yes	$540	credit	credit
2.	no			
3.	yes	$140	debit	credit
4.	yes	$440	credit	debit

VII. Demonstration Problems

Demonstration Problem #1 Solved and Explained

Requirement 1 (Open ledger accounts)

ASSETS

Cash		Accounts Receivable	
Bal. 10,000			

Supplies		Equipment	
		Bal. 26,000	

Land	

LIABILITIES

Accounts Payable		Notes Payable	
	Bal. 7,000		

OWNER'S EQUITY

Joe Davidson, Capital		Joe Davidson, Withdrawals	
	Bal. 29,000		

REVENUE

Rental Revenue	

EXPENSES

Salary Expense		Rent Expense	

Interest Expense		Advertising Expense	

Requirement 2 (Journal entries)

Date	Accounts and Explanation		Debit	Credit
a.	Cash		125,000	
	Notes Payable			125,000
	Borrowed cash and signed note payable.			
b.	Land		30,000	
	Cash			30,000
	Purchased land for future office location.			
c.	Cash		6,000	
	Rental Revenue			6,000
	Revenue earned and collected.			
d.	Supplies		1,800	
	Accounts Payable			1,800
	Purchased supplies on account.			
e.	Account Receivable		4,500	
	Rental Revenue			4,500
	Performed services on account.			
f.	Salary Expense		3,000	
	Rent Expense		1,700	
	Advertising Expense		650	
	Interest Expense		350	
	Cash			5,700
	Paid cash expenses.			
g.	Joe Davidson, Withdrawals		2,800	
	Cash			2,800
	Owner withdrawal for personal use.			
h.	Accounts Payable		3,800	
	Cash			3,800
	Paid on account			
i.	Cash		2,750	
	Accounts Receivable.			2,750
	Received on account.			

Requirement 3 (Posting)

ASSETS

Cash			
Bal. 10,000			
(a) 125,000	(b) 30,000		
(c) 6,000	(f) 5,700		
(i) 2,750	(g) 2,800		
	(h) 3,800		
Bal. 101,450			

Accounts Receivable	
(e) 4,500	(i) 2,750
Bal. 1,750	

Supplies	
(d) 1,800	
Bal. 1,800	

Equipment	
Bal. 26,000	
Bal. 26,000	

Land	
(b) 30,000	
Bal. 30,000	

LIABILITIES

Accounts Payable	
	Bal. 7,000
(h) 3,800	(d) 1,800
	Bal. 5,000

Notes Payable	
	(a) 125,000
	Bal. 125,000

OWNER'S EQUITY

Joe Davidson, Capital	
	Bal. 29,000
	Bal. 29,000

Joe Davidson, Withdrawals	
(g) 2,800	
Bal. 2,800	

REVENUE

Rental Revenue	
	(c) 6,000
	(e) 4,500
	Bal. 10,500

EXPENSES

Salary Expense	
(f) 3,000	
Bal. 3,000	

Rent Expense	
(f) 1,700	
Bal. 1,700	

Interest Expense	
(f) 350	
Bal. 350	

Advertising Expense	
(f) 650	
Bal. 650	

Requirement 4 (Trial Balance)

Accounts	Debits	Credits
Cash	$ 101,450	
Accounts Receivable	1,750	
Supplies	1,800	
Equipment	26,000	
Land	30,000	
Accounts Payable		$ 5,000
Notes Payable		125,000
Joe Davidson, Capital		29,000
Joe Davidson, Withdrawals	2,800	
Rental revenue		10,500
Salary expense	3,000	
Rent expense	1,700	
Interest expense	350	
Advertising expense	650	
Total	$169,500	$169,500

Total debits = total credits. The accounts appear to be in balance. If the trial balance did not balance, we would look for an error in recording or posting.

Demonstration Problem #2 Solved

Joe's Adventures Unlimited
Income Statement
For the Month Ended May 31, 20X6

Revenues:		
Rental Revenues		$10,500
Expenses:		
Salary Expense	$3,000	
Rent Expense	1,700	
Interest Expense	350	
Advertising Expense	650	
Total Expenses		5,700
Net Income		$4,800

Joe's Adventures Unlimited
Statement of Owner's Equity
For the Month Ended May 31, 20X6

Joe Davidson, Capital 5/1/X6	$29,000
Add: Net Income	4,800
	33,800
Less: Withdrawals	2,800
Joe Davidson, Capital 5/31/X6	$31,000

Joe's Adventures Unlimited
Balance Sheet
May 31, 20X6

ASSETS		LIABILITIES	
Cash	$ 101,450	Accounts Payable	$ 5,000
Accounts Receivable	1,750	Notes Payable	125,000
Supplies	1,800	Total Liabilities	130,000
Equipment	26,000		
Land	30,000	OWNER'S EQUITY	
		Joe Davidson, Capital	31,000
		Total Liabilities and	
Total Assets	$161,000	Owner's Equity	$161,000

Chapter 3—The Adjusting Process

CHAPTER OVERVIEW

Chapter Three extends the discussion begun in Chapter Two concerning the recording of business transactions using debit and credit analysis. Therefore you should feel comfortable with the debit and credit rules when you begin this chapter. The learning objectives for Chapter 3 are to:

1. Distinguish accrual accounting from cash-basis accounting.
2. Apply the revenue and matching principles.
3. Make adjusting entries.
4. Prepare an adjusted trial balance.
5. Prepare the financial statements from the adjusted trial balance.

Appendix to Chapter 3: Alternative Treatment of Prepaid Expenses and Unearned Revenues

CHAPTER REVIEW

Objective 1 - Distinguish accrual accounting from cash-basis accounting.

There are two methods used to do accounting:

- **Cash-basis accounting**: A business records revenues only when cash is received and expenses only when cash is paid.
- **Accrual accounting:** A business records revenues as they are earned and expenses as they are incurred. This means that with respect to the recognition of revenue under accrual accounting, the exchange of cash is irrelevant. Revenues are considered earned when services have been performed or merchandise is sold because the provider of the services or merchandise has a legal right to receive payment. Expenses are considered incurred when something has been used such as merchandise, services, or assets.

GAAP requires that businesses use accrual accounting so that financial statements will not be misleading. Financial statements would understate revenue if they did not include all revenues earned during the accounting period and would understate expenses if they did not include all expenses incurred during the accounting period.

Accountants prepare financial statements at specific intervals called accounting periods. The basic interval is a year, and nearly all businesses prepare annual financial statements. Usually, however, businesses need financial statements more frequently, at quarterly or monthly intervals. Statements prepared at intervals other than the one-year interval are called **interim statements**.

Whether financial statements are prepared on an annual basis or on an interim basis, they are prepared at the end of each accounting period. The cutoff date is the last day of the time interval for which financial statements are prepared. All transactions that occur up to the cutoff date should be included in the accounts. Thus, if financial statements are prepared for January, all transactions occurring on or before January 31 should be recorded.

Objective 2 - Apply the revenue and matching principles.

The **revenue principle** guides the accountant on 1) when to record revenue and 2) the amount of revenue to record. Revenue is recorded when it is earned; that is, when a business has delivered goods to the customer or provided a service to the customer. The amount of revenue to record is generally the cash value of the goods delivered or the services performed. When revenue is recorded, we would say that we are recognizing the revenue. This accounting language means that the revenue will appear on the income statement for the current accounting period.

The **matching principle** guides the accountant on when to record or recognize expenses. The objectives of the matching principle are 1) to identify the expenses that have been incurred in an accounting period; 2) to determine the amount of the expenses and 3) to match them against revenues earned during the same period. There is a natural relationship between revenues and some types of expenses. For example, if a business pays its salespeople commissions based on amounts sold, there is a direct relationship between sales revenue and commission expense. Other expenses, such as rent and utilities, do not have such an obvious relationship with revenues. However, we recognize that a business must pay the rent and the utility bill to operate the business. So, we typically assign these types of expenses to the accounting period (a month, quarter or year) in which the rent or utilities were used. When expenses are recognized, it means that they will appear on the income statement of the current accounting period, and subtracted from revenues to determine net income.

The **time-period concept** interacts with the revenue and the matching principles. It states that accounting information must be reported at regular intervals, which we refer to as accounting periods, and that income must be measured accurately each period.

Objective 3 - Make adjusting entries.

In order to accurately measure all of the revenues that have been earned and all of the expenses that have been incurred, accountants must make adjusting entries at the end of each accounting period. The purpose of adjusting entries is to obtain an accurate measure of the net income (loss) for the accounting period by bringing certain asset, liability, revenue, and expense accounts up to date prior to the preparation of financial statements. Adjusting entries also enable accountants to properly record the effect of transactions that span more than one accounting period. End-of-period processing begins with the preparation of a trial balance (from Chapter 2), which is sometimes referred to as an unadjusted trial balance. There are two broad categories of adjusting entries: deferrals and accruals. **Deferrals** can refer to deferred expenses or deferred revenues. In either case, with deferrals, the cash transaction occurs first, and the recognition of the expense or revenue is deferred to a later time when it is determined that the expense has been incurred or the revenue has been earned. **Accruals** can refer to accrued expenses or accrued revenues. In either case, with an accrual, the recognition of the expense or revenue occurs first when it is determined that the expense has been incurred and the revenue has been earned, and the cash transaction occurs later.

Adjusting entries fall into five categories:

1) **Prepaid expenses (prepaid assets)** refer to deferred expenses that are paid in advance. It is important to understand that at the time prepaid expenses are acquired, they are first recorded as assets because the future benefits are expected to extend beyond the present accounting period, and they become expenses later when they are used or have expired, thus, the term prepaid expenses.

For example, if on December 31 the business pays three months rent in advance in the amount of $3,000 ($1,000 per month for January, February, and March), then on December 31 the business will record Prepaid Rent (asset) of $3,000. None of the $3,000 payment is an expense for the month of December because the payment benefits future periods, specifically January, February, and March of the following year. At the end of each subsequent month, Rent Expense of $1,000 will be recorded as one-third of the Prepaid Rent expires.

Date	Accounts	Debit	Credit
Dec 31	Prepaid Rent	3,000	
	Cash		3,000
	Paid three months rent in advance		
Jan. 31	Rent Expense	1,000	
	Prepaid Rent		1,000
	To adjust for expired rent		
Feb. 28	Rent Expense	1,000	
	Prepaid Rent		1,000
	To adjust for expired rent		
Mar. 31	Rent Expense	1,000	
	Prepaid Rent		1,000
	To adjust for expired rent		

Prepaid Rent
12/31	3,000	Adj. 1/31	1,000
Bal.1/31	2,000	Adj. 2/28	1,000
Bal.2/28	1,000	Adj. 3/31	1,000
Bal. 3/31	0		

Balance Sheet

Rent Expense
Adj. 1/31	1,000	
Adj. 2/28	1,000	
Adj. 3/31	1,000	

Income Statement

Keep in mind, the amount of the adjusting entry for prepaid expenses represents the amount of expense recognized on the income statement and will always reflect the portion of the prepaid asset that has expired or has been used up. Thus, the accountant takes a portion of the cost of the asset and shifts it off of the balance sheet and onto the income statement as expense because the asset no longer has future benefit because it has expired or has been used. Other examples of prepaid expenses are supplies, prepaid insurance, and sometimes advertising fees may be paid for in advance. The adjusting entry for a prepaid expense always credits (decreases) the asset account and debits (increases) an expense account.

2) **Depreciation** is another deferred expense that results from the decline in usefulness over time related to long-lived, or plant assets. Plant assets are distinguished from other prepaid items due to the fact that plant assets are useful for longer periods of time. Examples of plant assets include buildings, office equipment, and office furniture. Compare these to the prepaid expenses described above such as supplies, rent, insurance and advertising which are usually used up or expire within one year. Buildings, office equipment and office furniture usually remain useful to a business for several years. Land is the only plant asset that does not depreciate because land does not decline in usefulness over time.

In an accounting context, depreciation does not refer to the decline in market value of an asset, but rather the decline in usefulness to the business. When making the adjusting entry for depreciation, the accountant systematically allocates a portion of the asset's cost as an expense over the asset's estimated useful life. In essence, the accountant is shifting a portion of the cost of the asset off of the balance sheet and onto the income statement as depreciation expense.

How we record depreciation is also different from the way in which we account for other prepaid expenses because the reduction in the usefulness of plant assets is not reflected in the specific plant asset account. The portion of the cost of the asset that is recognized as depreciation is recorded in a contra account called Accumulated Depreciation. Using the Accumulated Depreciation account allows the accountant to record the reduction in usefulness of the asset without changing the historical cost of the asset. A **contra accounts** has two unique characteristics:

1.) It always has a companion account.
2.) The normal balance of a contra account is opposite from the normal balance of its companion account.

For accumulated depreciation, the companion account is a plant asset account. For example, the plant asset account Building would have a contra account titled Accumulated Depreciation—Building. The plant asset account holds the original cost of the asset and has a normal debit balance. The contra account, Accumulated Depreciation, holds the portion of the cost of the asset that has been depreciated and has a normal credit balance. The difference between these two amounts is called the asset's **book value**. The adjusting entry for depreciation always debits (increases) the depreciation expense account and credits (increases) the Accumulated Depreciation account. The different methods of determining how much depreciation expense is recognized will be discussed in a later chapter. Let's look at an example, where Travis's Travel Center owns a building that cost $100,000 and has an estimated useful life of 20 years. This means that Travis is going to expense the cost of this building over a 20-year period. Let's take a look at the first three years:

Building		Accumulated Depreciation--Building		
100,000 (cost)			5,000 Yr 1 Adj.	Balance Sheet
			5,000 Yr. 2 Adj.	
			5,000 Yr. 3 Adj.	
			15,000 Bal.	

Depreciation Expense --Building			
Adj. Yr. 1	5,000		Income Statement
Adj. Yr. 2	5,000		
Adj. Yr. 3	5,000		

Take note of the following:

> ➤ As the Building is depreciated, the original cost of the asset is not affected.
> ➤ Each year the balance in the Accumulated Depreciation account increases by the amount of depreciation expense that is recognized each year. At the end of the third year, the balance in the Accumulated Depreciation account is $15,000. The balance in the Accumulated Depreciation account is subtracted from the cost in the Building account to determine the asset's book value of $85,000 or ($100,000 - $15,000). The book value represents the portion of the cost of the asset that has not been depreciated and is the amount reported on the balance sheet. See Exhibit 3-5 for the proper presentation of plant assets and their related accumulated depreciation accounts on the balance sheet.
> ➤ The amount of depreciation expense each year is determined by taking the cost of the asset, $100,000 and dividing it by the 20 year estimated useful life.

3) An **accrued expense** is an expense that a business has incurred but has not yet paid. Accrued expenses always create liabilities. Remember all liability accounts represent amounts owed in the future. A business's most common accrued expense is salary expense for employees. If you have worked a summer job, then you know that there may be an interval of several days or even a week between the end of your pay period and the date that you receive your paycheck. If an accounting period ends during such an interval, then your employer's salary expense would be accrued for the salary that you have earned but have not yet been paid. The adjusting entry for an accrued expense always debits (increases) an expense account and credits (increases) a liability account. Other examples of accrued expenses are interest and sales commissions.

4) **Accrued revenues** have been earned, but payment in cash has not been collected. For example, Bob Bush's Appliance Repair completed $75 of repairs on a VCR on January 28, the last business day of the month, but did not receive payment until February 3. The adjusting entry for accrued revenue of $75 would be recorded on January 31 because the service was performed in the month of January. The adjusting entry is recorded for January because the revenue was earned in the accounting period in which the service was performed. The adjusting entry for accrued revenue always debits (increases) a receivable account and credits (increases) a revenue account. Another example of an accrued revenue is interest revenue.

5) **Unearned revenues** are deferred revenues that result when cash is received from a customer before work is performed. Suppose that on March 15 you pay $80 for two tickets to a concert scheduled for April 7. The concert hall will not earn the $80 until April 7. Therefore, on March 15, the concert hall will debit (increase) Cash and credit (increase) Unearned Revenue. Unearned revenue is a liability account that indicates that the concert hall now owes the concert to the ticket holders. In April, when the concert occurs, the concert hall earns the revenue and will debit Unearned Revenue and credit Revenue. Since adjusting entries are recorded on the last day of the accounting period prior to the preparation of the financial statements, even though the concert hall officially earns the revenue on April 7, it is not recorded in the accounting records until the end of the month along with all the other adjusting entries. The adjusting entry to recognize unearned revenue that has been earned will always debit (decrease) the unearned revenue account and credit (increase) a revenue account.

Date	Accounts	Debit	Credit
Mar 15	Cash	80	
	Unearned Revenue		80
	Collected revenue in advance		
Apr. 30	Unearned Revenue	80	
	Ticket Revenue		80
	To adjust for earned ticket revenue		

Unearned Revenue

	3/15 80
Adj. 4/30 80	
	4/30 Bal. 0

Balance Sheet

Ticket Revenue

	Adj. 4/30 80

Income Statement

Note:
- ➢ Each type of adjusting entry affects at least one income statement account and at least one balance sheet account.
- ➢ Adjusting entries never affect the Cash account. Adjusting entries are noncash transactions required by accrual accounting.

Helpful Hint: See Exhibit 3-8 for a summary of adjusting entries.

Objective 4 - Prepare an adjusted trial balance.

The general sequence for preparing an adjusted trial balance is:

1. **Record** business transactions in the journal as they occur. (Chapter 2)
2. **Post** transactions from the journal to the ledger. (Chapter 2)
3. **Prepare** an unadjusted trial balance. (Chapter 2)
4. **Record** adjusting entries in the journal at the end of the accounting period. (Chapter 3)
5. **Post** adjusting entries from the journal to the ledger. (Chapter 3)
6. **Prepare** the adjusted trial balance and the financial statements. (Chapter 3)

Helpful Hint: Study Exhibits 3-9 through 3-13 in your text carefully to become familiar with the process that brings you to the adjusted trial balance and the preparation of the financial statements.

Objective 5 - Prepare the financial statements from the adjusted trial balance.

The **adjusted trial balance** provides the data needed to prepare the financial statements. The financial statements should always be prepared in the following order:

1. Income Statement
2. Statement of Owner's Equity
3. Balance Sheet

The reason for this order is quite simple. The income statement computes the amount of net income. Net income is needed for the statement of owner's equity. The statement of owner's equity computes the amount of ending capital. Ending capital is needed for the balance sheet. Exhibits 3-11, 3-12 and 3-13 in your text illustrate the flow of data from the income statement to the statement of owner's equity to the balance sheet.

The income statement starts with revenues for the period and subtracts total expenses for the period. A positive result is net income; a negative result is net loss.

The statement of owner's equity starts with the amount of capital at the beginning of the period, adds any owner investments for the period, adds net income or subtracts net loss, and subtracts withdrawals. The result is the ending capital balance.

The balance sheet uses the asset and liability balances from the adjusted trial balance and the capital balance from the statement of owner's equity.

Note that none of the financial statements will balance back to the total debits and total credits on the adjusted trial balance. This is because the financial statements group accounts differently from the debit and credit totals listed on the adjusted trial balance. For example, the new balance for Capital on the balance sheet is a summary of the beginning Capital balance, any investments made by the owner during the period, the revenue and expense accounts used to obtain net income, and owner's withdrawals during the period.

Helpful Hints: What if the balance sheet does not balance?

1. Make sure that the balance sheet contains all asset and liability accounts with the correct balances. Check your math.
2. Be sure that you correctly transferred ending capital from the statement of owner's equity to the owner's equity section of the balance sheet.
3. Check to be sure that the statement of owner's equity is correct.
4. Check the income statement to be sure that all revenue and expense accounts have been recorded at the correct amounts. Check your math.

Objective A1 - Account for a prepaid expense recorded initially as an expense.

An alternative treatment for recording prepaid expenses into asset accounts (Prepaid Insurance, Supplies, Prepaid Rent, etc.) is to record them initially into an expense account (Insurance Expense, Supplies Expense, Rent Expense, etc.) If the accountant initially recorded the prepaid expense into an expense account rather than an asset account, the adjusting entry will reduce the expense account by the amount of **unexpired** insurance and create a prepaid insurance (asset) account. As an example, assume the company pays $2,400 for a one-year insurance policy on March 1. If the payment is recorded initially as an expense, the entry is

Mar. 1	Insurance Expense	2,400	
	Cash		2,400
	Purchased a one-year insurance policy		

Assuming the accounts are adjusted on December 31, the adjusting entry is

Dec. 31	Prepaid Insurance	400	
	Insurance Expense		400
	To adjust for unexpired insurance		

After the adjusting entry is posted, the accounts would appear as follows:

Insurance Expense			
3/1	2,400	Adj. 12/31	400
Balance	2,000		

Prepaid Insurance		
Adj. 12/31	400	
Balance	400	

The $2,000 balance in the Insurance Expense account will appear on the Income Statement, while the $400 balance in Prepaid Insurance will be listed in the asset section of the Balance Sheet. Notice the adjusting entry still affects one income statement and one balance sheet account.

Objective A2 - Account for an unearned (deferred) revenue recorded initially as a revenue.

An alternative treatment for recording unearned (deferred) revenue into a liability account (Unearned Revenue) is to record it as revenue (Fees Earned) when received. If the accountant records the unearned revenue into a revenue account when received, the adjusting entry will reduce the revenue account by the amount of unearned revenue for the period and create an unearned revenue account. As an example, assume a delivery service company receives $50,000 on December 30 for packages to be delivered on December 31 and January 2 and 3. As of the close of business on December 31, the company has earned $45,000 for packages delivered that day. If the $50,000 is recorded initially as revenue, the entry is

Dec. 30	Cash	50,000	
	Fees Earned		50,000
	Collected revenue in advance		

Assuming the accounts are adjusted on December 31, the adjusting entry is

Dec. 31	Fees Earned	5,000	
	Unearned Revenue		5,000
	To adjust for unearned fees		

After the adjusting entry is posted, the accounts appear as follows:

Fees Earned		Unearned Fees	
Adj. 12/31 5,000	50,000 12/30		Adj. 12/31 5,000
	45,000 Balance		Balance 5,000

The $5,000 balance in Unearned Fees would be listed in the liability section of the Balance Sheet while the $45,000 balance in Fees Earned would appear on the Income Statement.

TEST YOURSELF

All the self-testing materials in this chapter focus on information and procedures that your instructor is likely to test in quizzes and examinations. Those questions followed by an * refer to information contained in the Appendix to the chapter.

I. Matching   *Match each numbered term with its lettered definition.*

_____	1. Contra asset	_____	9. Deferrals
_____	2. Matching principle	_____	10. Accruals
_____	3. Prepaid expenses	_____	11. Accumulated depreciation
_____	4. Unearned revenue	_____	12. Adjusting entries
_____	5. Depreciation	_____	13. Accrued expenses
_____	6. Plant asset	_____	14. Liquidation
_____	7. Revenue principle	_____	15. Accrued revenues
_____	8. Book value	_____	16. Cash-basis accounting

A. A category of assets that typically expire or are used up in the near future.

B. A liability created when a business collects cash from customers in advance of providing services for the customer.

C. A type of asset account with a normal credit balance and a companion account.

D. Expense associated with spreading (allocating) the cost of a plant asset over its useful life.

E. Long-lived assets, such as land, buildings, and equipment that are used in the operations of the business.

F. The basis for recording revenues that tells accountants when to record revenues and the amount of revenue to record.

G. The guidelines for recording expenses that direct accountants to identify all expenses incurred during the period, to measure the expenses, and to match them against the revenues earned during that same period.

H. A process of discontinuing operations and going out of business.

I. Revenues that have been earned but not recorded and paid.

J. Recorded at the end of the accounting period that updates assets, liabilities, revenues and expenses.

K. A collective term for accrued expenses and accrued revenues.

L. Expenses that have been incurred but not yet recorded.

M. A balance sheet account that is credited when adjusting for depreciation.

N. The difference between a plant asset account balance and its companion account balance.

O. A collective term for prepaid expenses and unearned revenues.

P. Accounting that records transactions only when cash is received or paid.

II. Multiple Choice *Circle the best answer.*

1. An accountant who does not recognize the impact of a business event as it occurs is probably using:

   A. accrual accounting.

   B. cash-basis accounting.

   C. income tax accounting.

   D. actual-basis accounting.

2. An example of accrual accounting is:

   A. recording the purchase of land for cash

   B. recording utility expense when the bill is paid

   C. recording revenue when merchandise is sold on account

   D. recording salary expense when wages are paid

3. Which of the following is considered an adjusting entry category?

   A. Accrued expenses

   B. Accrued revenues

   C. Depreciation

   D. All of the above

4. All of the following have normal credit balances <u>except</u>:

   A. Accumulated Depreciation.

   B. Accounts Receivable.

   C. Unearned Rent.

   D. Wages Payable.

5. The first financial statement prepared from the adjusted trial balance is the:

   A. income statement.

   B. balance sheet.

   C. statement of owner's equity.

   D. order does not matter.

6. Which of the following statements regarding the link between the financial statements is correct?

   A. Net income from the income statement goes to the balance sheet.

   B. Owner's equity from the balance sheet goes to the statement of owner's equity.

   C. Net income from the balance sheet goes to the income statement.

   D. Owner's equity from the statement of owner's equity goes to the balance sheet.

7. Bell Co. paid one year's rent on January 1 and debited Prepaid Rent for $14,400. On January 31, Bell should:

   A. credit Prepaid Rent for $13,200.

   B. debit Rent Expense for $1,200.

   C. debit Rent Expense for $13,200.

   D. credit Cash for $14,400.

8. A company has a beginning balance in Supplies $4,100. It purchases $4,200 of supplies during the period and uses $3,800 of supplies. If the accountant does not make an adjusting entry for supplies at the end of the period, then:

   A. assets will be understated by $4,500.

   B. assets will be overstated by $3,800.

   C. expenses will be overstated by $3,800.

   D. expenses will be understated by $4,500.

9. During September, a company received $10,000 cash for services rendered. In September, the company also performed $4,000 of services on account and received $3,000 cash in advance for services to be performed in October. The amount of revenue to be included on the September income statement is:

A. $10,000.
B. $14,000.

C. $13,000.
D. $17,000

10. A company correctly made an adjusting entry on December 31, 20X6 and credited Prepaid Insurance for $2,800. During 20X6 it paid $5,500 for insurance. The December 31, 20X6 balance in Prepaid Insurance was $4,000. What was the balance in the Prepaid Insurance account on January 1, 20X6?

A. $6,800
B. $1,300

C. $9,500
D. $3,300

11. Bell Co. paid one year's rent on January 1 and debited Rent Expense for $14,400. On January 31, Bell should:

A. credit Prepaid Rent for $13,200.
B. debit Rent Expense for $13,200.

C. debit Prepaid Rent for $1,200.
D. credit Rent Expense for $13,200.

12. On December 1, 20X6 Fees Earned was credited for $12,000, representing six months of revenue for the period December 1, 20X6 to June 1, 20X7. On December 31, 20X6 the company should:

A. credit Fees Earned for $10,000
B. debit Unearned Fees for $10,000

C. debit Fees Earned for $10,000
D. credit Unearned Fees for $2,000

III. Completion   *Complete each of the following statements.*

1. _____ accounting recognizes revenue when it is earned and expenses when they are incurred.

2. Adjusting entries categories include _____ , _____ ,
   _____ , _____ , and _____ .

3. The end-of-period process of updating the accounts is called the _____ .

4. Accumulated depreciation is an example of a(n) _____ account.

5. An amount that has been earned but not yet received in cash is a(n) _____ .

6. The revenue principle provides guidance to accountants as to _____ and
   _____ .

7. The objectives of the matching principle are: _____ ,
   _____ and _____ .

8. Financial statements should be prepared in the following order: 1) _____ , 2)
   _____ , and 3) _____ .

9. The basic time period for financial statements is _____ , while statements prepared at other times and for shorter intervals of time are called
   _____ .

10. What is the difference between prepaid expense and unearned revenue? _____
    _____ .

IV. Daily Exercises

1. Review the information provided in Multiple Choice question #9, but assume the bookkeeper was following cash-basis accounting. What amount would appear on the income statement as revenue for the month of September?

2. List the following in correct sequence: trial balance, statement of owner's equity, record adjusting entries, income statement, adjusted trial balance, balance sheet, post the adjustments.

   a. _____
   b. _____
   c. _____
   d. _____
   e. _____
   f. _____
   g. _____

3. Record the following transactions in the space provided. The company has a five-day workweek.

   Friday, December 27   Paid the weekly wages, $4,000
   Tuesday, December 31 Adjusted for two days accrued wages
   Friday, January 3   Paid the weekly wages, $4,000

Date:	Accounts	Debit	Credit

4. Classify each of the following as (a) prepaid expense, (b) accrued expense, (c) unearned revenue or (d) accrued revenue.

1. _____ AJ's Advertising Agency performed advertising design services that have not yet been recorded and collected.
2. _____ A customer paid $5,000 in advance for advertising design services to be performed.
3. _____ AJ's Advertising Agency purchased $300 of office supplies.
4. _____ Fly With Us Airlines sold airline tickets for flights that will take place next month, $3,000.
5. _____ AJ's Advertising Agency's employees have not yet been paid for hours worked.
6. _____ Fly With US Airlines recently purchased a two-year insurance policy.

V. Exercises

1. The accounting records of Jose's Southwestern Interiors include the following unadjusted normal balances on July 31:

Accounts Receivable	$ 2,000
Supplies	525
Salary Payable	0
Unearned Revenue	1,500
Service Revenue	8,000
Salary Expense	1,575
Supplies Expense	0
Depreciation Expense	0
Accumulated Depreciation	800

The following information is available for the July 31 adjusting entries:

a. Supplies on hand, $300
b. Salaries owed to employees, $275
c. Service revenue earned but not billed, $1,100
d. Services performed which had been paid for in advance, $125
e. Depreciation, $400

Required:

1. Open the T-accounts.
2. Record the adjustments directly to the T-accounts. (Key each entry by letter.)
3. Compute the adjusted balance for each account.

Accounts Receivable	Supplies	Salary Payable

Unearned Revenue	Service Revenue	Salary Expense

Supplies Expense	Depreciation Expense	Accumulated Depreciation

2. The balance sheets for Brown's Photo Studio had the following balances after adjusting entries: (The ending balances that appear on the previous year's balance sheet become the beginning balances for the current year.)

	20X7	20X8
Supplies	$1,700	$1,075
Prepaid rent	2,400	800
Interest payable	1,100	200
Unearned revenue	3,150	4,100

Cash payments and receipts for 20X8 included

Payments for supplies	$2,500
Payments for rent	3,000
Payments of interest	1,400
Receipts from customers	81,000

How much supplies expense, rent expense, interest expense, and revenue were reported on the 20X8 income statement?

Supplies Expense _____

Rent Expense _____

Interest Expense _____

Revenue _____

3. Antonio Carlini, owner of Treat Your Feet, a shoe repair shop, began the year with capital of $25,000. During the year, the owner invested $10,000 cash in his business and transferred to the business repair equipment valued at $23,500. During the year the business earned $74,000 and the owner withdrew $3,000 each month for his personal use. Prepare a statement of owner's equity for Treat Your Feet for the year ended December 31, 20X7.

Statement of Owner's Equity

VI. Beyond the Numbers

If a business is using cash-basis accounting, what is the amount listed on the Balance Sheet for Accounts Receivable and on the Income Statement for Revenue, assuming clients have been billed $118,500 during the year and sent in payments totaling $93,000 by the end of the year?

VII. Demonstration Problems

Demonstration Problem #1

Family Movie Center is in the business of renting VHS movies and DVD's. The trial balance for Family Movie Center at December 31, 20X9 and the data needed for year-end adjustments are as follows:

Family Movie Center
Trial Balance
December 31, 20X9

Cash	$19,415	
Accounts Receivable	90	
Prepaid Rent	1,200	
Supplies	400	
Movie Library	24,000	
Accumulated Depreciation—Movie Library		$12,000
Furniture	9,500	
Accumulated Depreciation—Furniture		3,800
Accounts Payable		1,450
Salary Payable		
Unearned Movie Rental Revenue		1,300
Jayne Gold, Capital		22,150
Jayne Gold, Withdrawals	3,000	
Movie Rental Revenue		43,365
Salary Expense	14,400	
Rent Expense	6,600	
Utilities Expense	2,800	
Depreciation Expense—Movie Library		
Depreciation Expense—Furniture		
Advertising Expense	2,660	
Supplies Expense		
Total	$84,065	$84,065

Adjustment data:

   a. Depreciation for the year:
      - on the movie library, $6,000
      - on the furniture, $1,900
   b. Accrued salary expense at December 31, $120.
   c. Prepaid rent expired, $600.
   d. Unearned movie rental revenues which remain unearned as of December 31, $625.
   e. Supplies on hand at December 31, $230
   f. Accrued advertising expense at December 31, $115. (Credit Accounts Payable)

Required:

1. Prepare T-accounts for those accounts listed on the trial balance that are affected by the adjusting entries. First, enter the December 31 unadjusted balances, then prepare and post the adjusting journal entries in the accounts. Key adjustment amounts by letter as shown in the text.
2. Using the form provided, enter the adjusting entries in the Adjustment columns, and prepare an adjusted trial balance, as shown in exhibit 3-10 of the text. Be sure that each account balance affected by an adjusting entry agrees with the adjusted T-account balances as calculated in Requirement 1.

Requirement 1 (T-accounts; adjusting journal entries; posting to ledger)

a.

Date	Accounts	PR	Debit	Credit
Dec. 31				

b.

Date	Accounts	PR	Debit	Credit
Dec. 31				

c.

Date	Accounts	PR	Debit	Credit
Dec. 31				

d.

Date	Accounts	PR	Debit	Credit
Dec. 31				

e.

Date	Accounts	PR	Debit	Credit
Dec. 31				

f.

Date	Accounts	PR	Debit	Credit
Dec. 31				

Requirement 2 (Adjusted trial balance)

Family Movie Center
Preparation of Adjusted Trial Balance
December 31, 20X9

Accounts	Trial Balance Debit	Trial Balance Credit	Adjustments Debit	Adjustments Credit	Adjusted Trial Balance Debit	Adjusted Trial Balance Credit
Cash	$19,415					
Accounts Receivable	90					
Prepaid Rent	1,200					
Supplies	400					
Movie library	24,000					
Accumulated Depreciation—Movie Library		$12,000				
Furniture	9,500					
Accumulated Depreciation—Furniture		3,800				
Accounts Payable		1,450				
Salary Payable						
Unearned Movie Rental Revenue		1,300				
Jayne Gold, Capital		22,150				
Jayne Gold, Withdrawals	3,000					
Movie Rental Revenue		43,365				
Salary Expense	14,400					
Rent Expense	6,600					
Utilities Expense	2,800					
Depreciation Expense—Movie Library						
Depreciation Expense— Furniture						
Advertising Expense	2,660					
Supplies Expense						
	$84,065	$84,065				

Demonstration Problem #2

Refer to the adjusted trial balance in Demonstration Problem #1 and complete the following:

1. An income statement
2. A statement of owner's equity
3. A balance sheet

Income Statement

Statement of Owner's Equity

Balance Sheet

SOLUTIONS

I. Matching

1. C	5. D	9. O	13. L
2. G	6. E	10. K	14. H
3. A	7. F	11. M	15. I
4. B	8. N	12. J	16. P

II. Multiple Choice

1. B   In cash-basis accounting the accountant does not record a transaction until cash is received or paid. In accrual accounting, the accountant records transactions when they occur. Income tax accounting is appropriate for the preparation of income tax returns not financial statements and there is no such thing as actual-basis accounting.

2. C   Recording revenue when the merchandise is sold is the only event listed that does not involve the receipt or payment of cash. Accordingly, it would not be recorded using cash-basis accounting and is the only item that would be recorded under accrual-basis accounting.

3. D   Adjusting entries assign revenues to the period in which they are earned and expenses to the period in which they are incurred. The five categories of adjusting entries are 1) prepaid expenses, 2) depreciation, 3) accrued expenses, 4) accrued revenues, and 5) unearned revenues

4. B   Accounts Receivable is an asset account with a normal debit balance. Accumulated Depreciation is a contra-asset account with a normal credit balance. Unearned Rent and Wages Payable are both liability accounts with normal credit balances.

5. A   Since net income is required to prepare the statement of owner's equity, the income statement should be prepared first.

6. D   The correct sequence is:
    1) Net income from the income statement goes to the statement of owner's equity.
    2) The ending Owner's equity from the statement of owner's equity goes to the balance sheet.

7. B   One month of rent will expire during January. Therefore an adjusting entry to expense for 1/12 x $14,400, or $1,200 will be recorded with the following journal entry:

Rent Expense	1,200	
Prepaid Rent		1,200

8. B   The adjusting entry that should be made at the end of the period is:

Supplies Expense	3,800	
Supplies		3,800

Failure to credit the Supplies account for $3,800 means that assets will be overstated by $3,800.

9. B With accrual accounting, total revenues in September will be $10,000 of revenues received in cash plus $4,000 of revenues that have been billed but not received. The $3,000 cash received for services to be performed in October represent unearned revenues that will sit on the balance sheet as a liability until the services are rendered in October.

10. B This problem requires you to work backward to find the solution.

Adjusted balance (given)	$4,000
Adjustment (given)	2,800
Unadjusted balance	$6,800

The unadjusted trial balance amount of $6,800 consists of the beginning balance and purchases made during the year. Since the purchases were $5,500 (given), the beginning balance must have been $1,300.

11. D Because the entire prepayment was placed in an expense account, and at the end of January, only one month of the rent had expired, the adjusting entry must adjust the expense account for the amount of **unexpired** rent and place that amount into a Prepaid Rent account on the balance sheet:

Prepaid Rent	13,200	
Rent Expense		13,200

> Study Tip: When prepaid expenses are initially recorded into expense accounts, the adjusting entry will credit (reduce) the expense account and debit (increase) the asset account.

12. C Because the $12,000 was placed into a revenue account on December 1, 20X6 the following adjusting entry is required on December 31, 20X6 to adjust the revenue account for the amount of **unearned** revenue and place that amount into the Unearned Fees account on the balance sheet:

Fees Earned	10,000	
Unearned Fees		10,000

> Study Tip: When unearned revenue is initially recorded into a revenue account, the adjusting entry will debit (reduce) the revenue account and credit (increase) a liability (unearned) account.

III. Completion

1. Accrual
2. prepaid expenses, depreciation, accrued expenses, unearned revenue, accrued revenues (order not important)
3. adjusting the accounts
4. contra asset (A contra account has two distinguishing characteristics: (1) it always has a companion account, and (2) its normal balance is opposite that of the companion account. Accumulated depreciation's companion account is property, plant and equipment.)
5. accrued revenue
6. when to record revenue, the amount of revenue to record
7. to identify expenses which have been incurred, to measure the expenses, to match the expenses with revenues earned during the same time period
8. income statement, statement of owner's equity, balance sheet (order is important)
9. one year, interim statements
10. Prepaid expense is an asset of the business that become an expense when the asset has expired or been used. Unearned revenue represents a liability for the business to perform services or deliver goods in the future and become revenue when it is earned.

IV. Daily Exercises

1. $13,000 - representing all the cash received during September.
2.
   1. trial balance
   2. record adjusting entries
   3. post adjusting entries
   4. adjusted trial balance
   5. income statement
   6. statement of owner's equity
   7. balance sheet

3.

Dec. 27	Wages Expense	4,000	
	Cash		4,000
Dec. 31	Wages Expense	1,600	
	Wages Payable		1,600
	($4,000/5 = $800/ day x 2 days)		
Jan. 3	Wages Expense	2,400	
	($4,000/5 = $800/day x 3 days)		
	Wages Payable	1,600	
	Cash		4,000

On Jan. 3, note that $1,600 of the week's wages was already recorded (accrued) on Dec. 31; therefore only $2,400 of the weekly payroll remains an expense on Jan. 3.

4.
1. (d) Accrued revenue results when services have been performed but not yet collected.
2. (c) Unearned revenue results because the cash was collected in advance of the design services being performed.
3. (a) Supplies represent a prepaid expense, an asset, that will become an expense once the supplies are used.
4. (c) Selling the tickets has created an obligation for the airline to provide the future transportation services.
5. (b) AJ's Advertising Agency has an accrued expense for the employees' wages. This reflects that the business has incurred the expense because the employees worked, but just have not been paid yet.
6. (a) An insurance policy represents a prepaid expense, an asset, that will be expensed as the policy expires.

V. Exercises

1.

Accounts Receivable	
Bal. 2,000	
(c) 1,100	
Bal. 3,100	

Supplies	
Bal. 525	
	(a) 225
Bal. 300	

Salary Payable	
	(b) 275
	Bal. 275

Unearned Revenue	
	Bal. 1,500
(d) 125	
	Bal. 1,375

Service Revenue	
	Bal. 8,000
	(c) 1,100
	(d) 125
	Bal. 9,225

Salary Expense	
Bal. 1,575	
(b) 275	
Bal. 1,850	

Supplies Expense	
(a) 225	
Bal. 225	

Depreciation Expense	
(e) 400	
Bal. 400	

Accumulated Depreciation	
	Bal. 800
	(e) 400
	Bal. 1,200

84

2. Remember that Beginning balance + Additions - Reductions = Ending balance

Account analyzed:

Supplies:

	Beginning balance	+	Supplies purchased for cash	-	Supplies expense	=	Ending balance
	$1,700	+	$2,500	-	?	=	$1,075

Supplies expense = $3,125

Prepaid Rent:

	Beginning balance	+	Rent paid	-	Rent expense	=	Ending balance
	$2,400	+	$,3000	-	?	=	$800

Rent expense = $4,600

Interest Payable:

	Beginning balance	+	Interest expense	-	Cash paid for interest	=	Ending balance
	$1,100	+	?	-	$1,400	=	$200

Interest expense = $500

Unearned Revenue:

	Beginning balance	+	Receipts from customers	-	Revenue earned	=	Ending balance
	$3,150	+	$81,000	-	?	=	$4,100

Revenue = $80,050

3.

Treat Your Feet
Statement of Owner's Equity
For the Year Ended December 31, 20X7

Carlini, Capital, 1/1/X7	$25,000
Add: Cash invested	10,000
Equipment transferred	23,500
Net income	74,000
	132,500
Less: Carlini, Withdrawals	36,000
Capital, 12/31/X7	$96,500

VI. Beyond the Numbers

The balance in Accounts Receivable would be zero. Why? Because cash-basis accounting does not record revenue when a client is billed, only when the business receives payment. Therefore, while the business may send bills to clients, they are not recorded as receivables. Since the customers sent in payments totaling $93,000, that would be the amount of revenue reported on the Income Statement for the year.

VII. Demonstration Problems

Demonstration Problem #1 Solved and Explained

Requirement 1 (T-accounts; adjusting entries; posting to ledger)

a.

Depreciation Expense—Movie Library

(a) 6,000	
Bal. 6,000	

Accumulated Depreciation—Movie Library

	Bal. 12,000
	(a) 6,000
	Bal. 18,000

Depreciation Expense—Furniture

(a) 1,900	
Bal. 1,900	

Accumulated Depreciation—Furniture

	Bal. 3,800
	(a) 1,900
	Bal. 5,700

Date	Accounts	PR	Debit	Credit
Dec. 31	Depreciation Expense—Movie Library		6,000	
	Accumulated Depreciation—Movie Library			6,000
	To record depreciation expense on movie library			
	Depreciation Expense—Furniture		1,900	
	Accumulated Depreciation—Furniture			1,900
	To record depreciation expense on furniture			

Explanation of Adjustment (a)

As a long-lived plant asset (such as building, furniture, machinery, equipment) becomes less useful, its cost is systematically transferred from the asset account to a depreciation expense account. Note that the original cost of the asset remains unchanged on the books of Family Movie Center. The reduction in book value of each asset is accomplished by increasing the asset's accumulated depreciation account.

Example: Change in book value of furniture.

Plant Assets	Before Adjustment	Change	After Adjustment
Furniture	$9,500	0	$9,500
Less accumulated depreciation	3,800	+1,900	5,700
Book value	$5,700	-$1,900	$3,800

b.

Salary Expense		Salary Payable	
Bal. 14,400			(b) 120
(b) 120			
Bal. 14,520			Bal. 120

Dec. 31	Salary Expense	120	
	Salary Payable		120
	To accrue salary expense		

Explanation of Adjustment (b)

Amounts owed employees for salary and wages unpaid as of the close of an accounting period must be accrued. The facts indicate that $120 must be accrued to record salary expense and the related liability. As a result, Salary Expense is debited $120 (expenses are increased by debits), and Salary Payable is credited $120 (liabilities are increased by credits).

c.

Rent Expense			Prepaid Rent		
Bal. 6,600			Bal. 1,200	(c)	600
(c) 600					
Bal. 7,200			Bal. 600		

Dec. 31	Rent Expense		600	
	Prepaid Rent			600
	To record rent expense			

Explanation of Adjustment (c)

Family Movie Center must adjust the Prepaid Rent account for the portion of the rent that has expired, $600. Thus, $600 is transferred to the Rent Expense account by crediting the Prepaid Rent account (assets are reduced by credits) and debiting (expenses are recorded as debits) the Rent Expense account. The balance in the Prepaid Rent account represents the amount of prepaid rent still in force.

d.

Movie Rental Revenue			Unearned Movie Rental Revenue		
	Bal. 43,365			Bal. 1,300	
	(d) 675		(d) 675		
	Bal. 44,040			Bal. 625	

Dec. 31	Unearned Movie Rental Revenue		675	
	Movie Rental Revenue			675
	To record revenue collected in advance.			

Explanation of Adjustment (d)

When cash is collected from customers before the agreed-upon product or service is provided, a liability is created. If $675 of the $1,300 of Unearned Movie Rental Revenue remains unearned, then $675 has been earned. The liability account Unearned Rental Revenue should be debited (a liability is reduced by a debit) and Movie Rental Revenue should be credited (a revenue is increased by a credit).

e.

Supplies Expense			Supplies			
(e)	170		Bal.	400	(e)	170
Bal.	170		Bal.	230		

Dec. 31	Supplies Expense		170	
	Supplies			170
	To record supplies expense.			

Explanation of Adjustment (e)

Supplies purchased for business use represent an asset until they are used. The Supplies account must be adjusted periodically to reflect supplies no longer on hand. Supplies of $230 remain on hand at December 31. Since $400 of supplies were on hand initially, it is clear that $170 of supplies have been used up ($400 - $230 = $170). Reduce the Supplies account by crediting it $170 (assets are decreased by credits) and record the $170 supplies expense by debiting Supplies Expense (expenses are increased by debits).

f.

Advertising Expense			Accounts Payable			
Bal.	2,660				Bal.	1,450
(f)	115				(f)	115
Bal.	2,775				Bal.	1,565

Date	Accounts	PR	Debit	Credit
Dec. 31	Advertising Expense		115	
	Accounts Payable			115
	To record accrued advertising expense.			

Explanation of Adjustment (f)

The rationale for this entry is similar to that for the adjusting entry for accrued salary expense in (b.). Advertising Expense is increased by debiting the account (expenses are recorded by debits) and Accounts Payable is credited (liabilities are recorded by credits) to reflect the amount owed for advertising by Family Movie Center.

Requirement 2 (Adjusted trial balance)

Family Movie Center
Preparation of Adjusted Trial Balance
December 31, 20X9

Accounts	Trial Balance Debit	Trial Balance Credit	Adjustments Debit	Adjustments Credit	Adjusted Trial Balance Debit	Adjusted Trial Balance Credit
Cash	$19,415				$19,415	
Accounts Receivable	90				90	
Prepaid Rent	1,200			(c) 600	600	
Supplies	400			(e) 170	230	
Movie Library	24,000				24,000	
Accumulated depreciation—Movie Library		$12,000		(a) 6,000		$18,000
Furniture	9,500				9,500	
Accumulated Depreciation—Furniture		3,800		(a) 1,900		5,700
Accounts Payable		1,450		(f) 115		1,565
Salary Payable				(b) 120		120
Unearned Movie Rental Revenue		1,300	(d) 675			625
Jayne Gold, Capital		22,150				22,150
Jayne Gold, Withdrawals	3,000				3,000	
Movie Rental Revenue		43,365		(d) 675		44,040
Salary Expense	14,400		(b) 120		14,520	
Rent Expense	6,600		(c) 600		7,200	
Utilities Expense	2,800				2,800	
Depreciation Expense—Movie Library			(a) 6,000		6,000	
Depreciation Expense—Furniture			(a) 1,900		1,900	
Advertising Expense	2,660		(f) 115		2,775	
Supplies Expense			(e) 170		170	
	$84,065	$84,065	$9,580	$9,580	$92,200	$92,200

Demonstration Problem #2 Solved

Requirement 1

Family Movie Center
Income Statement
For the Year Ended December 31, 20X9

Revenues:		
Movie Rental revenue		$44,040
Expenses:		
Salary Expense	14,520	
Rent Expense	7,200	
Utilities Expense	2,800	
Depreciation Expense	7,900	
Advertising Expense	2,775	
Supplies Expense	170	
Total expenses		35,365
Net Income		$ 8,675

Requirement 2

Family Movie Center
Statement of Owner's Equity
For the Year Ended December 31, 20X9

Owner's Equity 1/1/X9	$ 22,150
Add: Net Income	8,675
	30,825
Less: Withdrawals	3,000
Jayne Gold, Capital 12/31/X9	$27,825

Requirement 3

Family Movie Center
Balance Sheet
December 31, 20X9

ASSETS			LIABILITIES	
Cash		$19,415	Accounts Payable	$ 1,565
Accounts Receivable		90	Salary Payable	120
Prepaid Rent		600	Unearned Movie Rental	
Supplies		230	Revenue	625
Movie Rental Library	24,000		Total Liabilities	2,310
Less: Acc. Dep.—Library	18,000	6,000	**OWNER'S EQUITY**	
Furniture	9,500		Jayne Gold, Capital	
Less: Acc. Dep.—Furniture	5,700	3,800	Total Liabilities and	27,825
			Owner's Equity	
Total Assets		$30,135		$30,135

Chapter 4—Completing the Accounting Cycle

CHAPTER OVERVIEW

Chapter Four introduces you to the final steps in the accounting cycle. Using the information you learned in the previous three chapters you are now ready to complete the accounting cycle, thereby preparing the financial records for the next accounting period. The learning objectives for this chapter are to

1. Prepare an accounting work sheet.
2. Use the work sheet to complete the accounting cycle.
3. Close the revenue, expense, and withdrawal accounts.
4. Classify assets and liabilities as current or long-term.
5. Use the current ratio and the debt ratio to evaluate a company.

CHAPTER REVIEW

OVERVIEW OF THE ACCOUNTING CYCLE

The **accounting cycle** is the process by which companies produce financial statements for a specific period.

The accounting cycle can be subdivided into two categories:

- Work performed during the period includes:
  1. Starting with the ledger account balances at the beginning of the period.
  2. Analyzing and journalizing daily business transactions as they occur.
  3. Posting journal entries to the accounts in the ledger.

- Work performed at the end of the period includes:
  4. Computing the unadjusted balance in each account at the end of the period.
  5. Entering the unadjusted trial balance on the work sheet, and completing the worksheet.
  6. Using the adjusted trial balance or the full work sheet as a guide, a) record and post adjusting entries, b) prepare financial statements, and c) record and post-closing entries.
  7. Preparing the post-closing trial balance.

Objective 1 - Prepare an accounting work sheet.

A **work sheet** is an optional tool the accountant often uses to prepare financial statements. It is not part of a formal accounting system. Remember that in Chapter 3 you learned how to prepare an adjusted trial balance. To complete the worksheet you use basically the same steps:

1. Prepare the unadjusted trial balance from the ledger accounts. Make sure the debits equals the credits.
2. Enter the necessary adjustments in the Adjustments column. Use lower case letters to denote each adjustment. Make sure the debits equal the credits.
3. Calculate the adjusted account balances. Make sure the debits equal the credits.

The work sheet is completed using the following steps:

1. Extend only the adjusted revenue and expense account balances to the Income Statement columns, which are located to the right of the Adjusted Trial Balance columns. **The debits will not equal the credits.** The difference between the two columns will be the total net income (loss) for the period.
2. Extend the adjusted asset, liability, and owner's equity (Capital and Withdrawals) account balances to the Balance Sheet columns, which are located to the right of the Income Statement columns. **The debits will not equal the credits.** The difference between the two columns will be the total net income (loss) for the period.
3. Enter net income (loss) as a balancing amount on both the Income Statement and the Balance Sheet columns, and compute the adjusted column totals. **The debits should now equal the credits.**

You should review Exhibits 4-2 through 4-6 in your text to be sure you understand the preparation of the worksheet.

Exhibits 4-2, 4-3, and 4-4 illustrate how to determine the adjusted trial balance using the work sheet. Once the adjusted trial balance has been prepared, Exhibit 4-5 illustrates how the adjusted revenue and expense account balances are transferred to the Income Statement columns and the adjusted asset, liability, and owner's equity account balances are transferred to the Balance Sheet columns. Note that every account from the adjusted trial balance will appear in either the Income Statement columns, or the Balance Sheet columns, but not both. At this point the debit and credit column totals are not equal in either the Income Statement or the Balance Sheet columns.

Exhibit 4-6 illustrates the final step in completing the work sheet, which is to calculate the difference between the debit and credit columns of the Income Statement and the Balance Sheet columns on the worksheet. This difference is the net income (loss) for the period and is entered as a balancing amount at the bottom of the Income Statement and Balance Sheet columns. If the transactions for the period result in net income, then the Income Statement column is debited and the Balance Sheet column is credited. If the result is a net loss, the Income Statement column is credited and the Balance Sheet column is debited. This balancing amount will bring the columns totals into equality meaning the debits will equal the credits.

Helpful Hint: Recall that net income increases owner's equity. On the work sheet, the capital account is recorded in the credit column of the balance sheet, which is consistent with the account's normal balance. Adding net income to the credit column of the balance sheet illustrates the increase in owner's equity that results from net income. Similar logic applies to a net loss, which appears on the work sheet in the debit column of the balance sheet, because a net loss decreases owner's equity, and decreases in owner's equity are recorded with a debit.

Objective 2 - Use the work sheet to complete the accounting cycle.

Once the work sheet has been completed, financial statements must be prepared, adjusting entries must be recorded, and the accounts must be closed.

Exhibit 4-7 in your text illustrates financial statements prepared from a completed work sheet. (Remember that the work sheet is an optional tool, and that the financial statements can be prepared directly from the adjusted trial balance, as you learned in Chapter 3.)

Next, it is necessary to record the adjusting entries. Since the work sheet is not a journal or a ledger, the adjustments entered on the work sheet do not adjust the accounts. Adjusting journal entries must be recorded in the journal and posted to the accounts, as shown in Exhibit 4-8 of your text. Companies often do not record adjusting entries until after the work sheet is completed.

Objective 3 - Close the revenue, expense, and withdrawal accounts.

Closing the accounts refers to the process of preparing certain accounts for the next accounting period. Closing involves journalizing and posting **closing entries** that set the balances of revenues, expenses, and owner's withdrawals to zero. Remember that when the balance sheet is prepared, the owner's equity balance that is carried forward from the statement of owner's equity includes the summary effect of the revenue, expense, and owner's withdrawal accounts. These accounts are referred to as **temporary accounts**—they measure the effect on owner's equity for a single accounting period and are set to zero at the end of each accounting period. This is in contrast to balance sheet accounts: assets, liabilities, and capital accounts, which are **permanent accounts** whose account balance carries forward into the next accounting period.

The closing process uses a special, temporary holding account called **Income Summary**. Turn to Exhibit 4-10 in your text to follow the four steps taken to close the accounts at the end of the accounting period:

1. Close the revenue accounts to the Income Summary account. The revenue accounts are the accounts that appear in the Income Statement credit column of the work sheet. Debit each revenue account for the amount of its balance (to zero it out), and credit Income Summary for the total amount of the revenues (total debits).
2. Close the expense accounts to the Income Summary account. The expense accounts are the accounts that appear in the Income Statement debit column of the work sheet. Credit each expense account for the amount of its balance (to zero it out), and debit Income Summary for the total amount of the expenses (total credits).
3. Calculate a balance in the Income Summary account and close the Income Summary account to the Capital account. Income Summary has no normal balance. It can have either a debit or credit balance.
    *   If Income Summary has a credit balance, then the company has generated a net income. To close Income Summary when it has a credit balance, debit it for that amount (to zero it out) and credit the owner's capital account.
    *   If Income Summary has a debit balance, then the company has generated a net loss. To close Income Summary when it has a debit balance, credit it for that amount (to zero it out) and debit the owner's capital account.

The amount of this third closing entry should agree with the net income (or loss) reported for the period on the Income Statement. It should also correlate with the balancing amounts for the Income Statement and Balance Sheet columns on the work sheet.

4. Close the Withdrawals account to the owner's capital account. The Withdrawals account is found in the Balance Sheet debit column of the work sheet. To close the owner's withdrawals account, credit it for the amount of its debit balance and debit the Capital account. Note that the Withdrawals account is neither a revenue nor an expense account, and thus is not closed to Income Summary.

Exhibits 4-9 and 4-10 in your text illustrate the closing process. Note that after the closing entries are posted, the balance in the owner's capital account in the ledger should be the same as the amount reported as the ending balance on the statement of owner's equity and the balance sheet.

The accounting cycle ends with the **post-closing trial balance**. It should contain only the ending balances of the permanent, balance sheet accounts, assets, liabilities, and capital. Exhibit 4-11 in your text illustrates a post-closing trial balance. Notice there are no revenue, expense, or withdrawals accounts on the post-closing trial balance. This is because each of these account balances is zero after the closing entries have been posted.

Reversing entries are an optional step in the accounting cycle completed after the post-closing trial balance has been prepared. Reversing entries literally reverse any previous accrual adjusting entries. (Deferrals are not reversed.) Doing so allows the accountant to record a subsequent cash payment (for a previously accrued expense) or cash receipt (for a previously accrued revenue) in a routine manner.

Study Tip: If a business uses reversing entries, you can identify the adjusting entries that need to be reversed by tracing the effect of the adjustment to the balance sheet. If the adjustment increases total assets or total liabilities on the balance sheet, the adjusting entry should be reversed.

Using a work sheet, the complete **accounting cycle** can now be summarized as follows:

1. Analyze the transaction
2. Record and post the journal entry
3. Complete an unadjusted trial balance and enter on worksheet
4. Analyze the adjustments and enter on work sheet
5. Complete the adjusted trial balance columns on the work sheet
6. Complete the work sheet by extending the account balances to the appropriate Income Statement or Balance Sheet columns.
7. Prepare the financial statements
8. Journalize and post the adjusting entries
9. Journalize and post the closing entries
10. Prepare a post-closing trial balance
11. Journalize and post the reversing entries (optional)

Objective 4 - Classify assets and liabilities as current or long term.

Assets and liabilities are classified according to their liquidity. **Liquidity** is a measure of how quickly an item can be converted into cash. The balance sheet lists assets and liabilities in the order of their relative liquidity, with Cash, as the most liquid asset, listed first.

Current assets are those assets expected to be converted into cash, sold, or consumed within a year, or within the business's normal operating cycle if longer than a year. Current assets include: 1) Cash, 2) Accounts Receivable, 3) Notes Receivable, 4) Inventory, and 5) Prepaid Expenses.

Long-term assets are all assets that are not current assets. Long-term assets include plant assets such as: 1) Land, 2) Buildings, and 3) Equipment. It should make sense to you that land, buildings and equipment would be considered long-term assets because these items typically will benefit the business for more than one year, which also supports the concept of depreciation that was discussed in Chapter 3.

Current liabilities are obligations that are due within one year or the normal operating cycle if the cycle is longer than one year. Current liabilities include: 1) Accounts Payable, 2) Notes Payable due within one year, 3) Salary Payable, 4) Unearned Revenue, and 5) Interest Payable.

Long-term liabilities are obligations that are not classified as current and are due in future years. Long-term liabilities include: 1) Notes Payable (the portion due beyond the current year) 2) Bonds Payable, and 3) Mortgages Payable.

Helpful hint: Review Exhibits 4-12 and 4-13 in your text for examples of a classified (detailed) balance sheet. When you prepare a balance sheet from this point forward, it should use the classified presentation.

Objective 5 - Use the current ratio and the debt ratio to evaluate a company.

The primary purpose of accounting is to provide reliable information for decision-making. Lenders need to be able to evaluate a company's financial information to determine whether a borrower has the ability to repay a loan before the loan is actually made. Analyzing ratios of various items drawn from a company's financial statements can help creditors assess the likelihood that a loan can be repaid. Two of the most widely used decision aids in business are the:

1. **Current ratio** measures the ability of a company to pay current liabilities (short-term debt) with current assets.

$$\text{Current ratio} = \frac{\text{Total current assets}}{\text{Total current liabilities}}$$

A strong current ratio typically will be 1.50 or greater indicating that the current assets in the numerator are significantly greater than the current liabilities in the denominator. If a company has a current ratio of 1.60, for example, this means that for every $1.00 of current liabilities, the company has $1.60 in current assets. Since current assets are those assets that can be converted into cash quickly, then it can reasonably be assumed that the company could pay its current liabilities if they all came due immediately. If a company has a current ratio of .80, this means that for every $1.00 of current liabilities, the company has $.80 in current assets. A current ratio of .80 would indicate that the company would not have the ability to pay its current liabilities should they all come due immediately.

2. **Debt ratio** measures how much of a company's total assets it has financed with debt. The debt ratio evaluates the relationship of total liabilities to total assets, and is an indication of a company's overall ability to pay its debt, both current and long-term.

$$\text{Debt ratio} = \frac{\text{Total Liabilities}}{\text{Total Assets}}$$

A strong debt ratio typically should be something less than .60 or 60%. Therefore, a company wants to show a high current ratio, but overall, it wants a low debt ratio.

TEST YOURSELF

All the self-testing materials in this chapter focus on information and procedures that your instructor is likely to test in quizzes and examinations.

I. Matching   *Match each numbered term with its lettered definition.*

_____ 1. Account format
_____ 2. Closing the accounts
_____ 3. Current liability
_____ 4. Liquidity
_____ 5. Long-term asset
_____ 6. Report format
_____ 7. Debt ratio
_____ 8. Work sheet

_____ 9. Post-closing trial balance
_____ 10. Accounting cycle
_____ 11. Closing entries
_____ 12. Income Summary
_____ 13. Long-term liability
_____ 14. Permanent accounts
_____ 15. Temporary accounts
_____ 16. Reversing entries

A. A columnar document that is designed to help move data from the trial balance to the finished financial statements
B. A debt due to be paid within one year or within the entity's normal operating cycle, whichever is longer
C. A liability other than a current liability
D. A measure of how quickly an item may be converted to cash
E. A temporary holding account into which revenues and expenses are transferred prior to their final transfer to the Capital account
F. Accounts that are not closed at the end of the accounting period
G. An asset other than a current asset
H. Ratio that measures a company's overall ability to pay its debts
I. Entries that transfer the revenue, expense and owner withdrawal balances to the Capital account
J. Balance sheet format that lists the assets at the top, with the liabilities and owner's equity below
K. Balance sheet format that lists the assets at the left, with the liabilities and owner's equity at the right
L. List of the ledger accounts and their balances at the end of the period after journalizing and posting the closing entries
M. Process by which accountants produce an entity's financial statements for a specific period
N. Revenue accounts, expense accounts, and withdrawals
O. Step in the accounting cycle that prepares the accounts for recording the transactions of the next period
P. An optional entry after the books are closed.

II. Multiple Choice *Circle the best answer.*

1. Which of the following accounts will *not* appear on the post-closing trial balance?

   A. Cash
   B. Rent Expense
   C. Capital
   D. Interest Receivable

2. On a work sheet, which of the following is *not* extended from the adjusted trial balance to the balance sheet columns?

   A. Liabilities
   B. Capital
   C. Assets
   D. Revenues

3. What effect will adjusting entries usually have on the balance of the Accumulated Depreciation account?

   A. Increase
   B. Decrease
   C. No effect
   D. Cannot be determined

4. What effect will adjusting entries have on the balance of the companion plant asset account?

   A. Increase
   B. Decrease
   C. No effect
   D. Cannot be determined

5. A company has a $10,000 net loss for 20X7. This amount is entered on the work sheet as:

   A. a debit on the income statement column.
   B. a credit on the balance sheet column.
   C. a debit on the balance sheet column.
   D. both A and B.

6. Suppose a company has posted its closing entries to the Income Summary account. The account now has a debit balance. This means that the company had:

   A. net income.
   B. a net loss.
   C. net income only if there were no owner withdrawals.
   D. a net loss only if there were no owner withdrawals.

7. The DeRienzo, Withdrawals account has a balance of $3,000 before closing. What is the correct entry to close the Withdrawals account?

   A. Debit Capital and credit Withdrawals, $3,000
   B. Debit Withdrawals and credit Income Summary, $3,000
   C. Debit Withdrawals and credit Capital, $3,000
   D. Debit Income Summary and credit Withdrawals, $3,000

8. Which of the following accounts would be classified as a current asset?

   A. Accounts Payable
   B. Unearned Revenue
   C. Equipment
   D. Accounts Receivable

9. The current ratio measures:

A. the company's ability to pay all of its debt as it comes due.
B. the company's ability to pay its current liabilities with current assets.
C. the proportion of current liabilities to long-term liabilities.
D. the relationship of total liabilities to total assets.

10. The Income Summary has debits of $50,000 and credits of $67,000. This means that the company had:

A. $17,000 net income.
B. $17,000 net loss.
C. $117,000 net income.
D. $117,000 net loss.

III. Completion   *Complete each of the following statements.*

1. The accounting cycle starts with _____.
2. Revenue, expense, and the withdrawals accounts are called _____ accounts.
3. The optional summary device used for convenience in preparing financial statements is the _____.
4. The accounts that are never closed at the end of an accounting period are called _____ accounts.
5. Revenue and expense accounts are usually closed to the _____ account.
6. The Withdrawals account is closed to _____.
7. _____ refers to how quickly an asset can be converted into cash.
8. The accounting cycle ends with the _____.
9. _____ and _____ decrease owner's equity.
10. The debt ratio compares _____ to _____.
11. The_____ is a measure of short-term liquidity.

IV. Daily Exercises

1. From the following list of account balances as of December 31, 20X8, present the current assets and total assets that would appear on the balance sheet.

Accounts Payable	$ 6,000
Accounts Receivable	9,000
Inventory	11,000
Notes Receivable (due in 120 days)	8,500
Notes Payable (due in 60 days)	6,500
Rent Expense	12,000
Jones, Withdrawals	3,200
Unearned Revenue	3,500
Cash	4,500
Utilities Expense	2,400
Notes Payable (due in 2 years)	18,000
Prepaid Insurance	1,200
Salaries Payable	2,400
Supplies	350
Interest Payable	1,280
Jones, Capital	37,020
Equipment	14,000
Accumulated Depreciation-Equipment	4,000
Service Revenue	20,250
Advertising Expense	1,800
Salaries Expense	6,000
Land	25,000

Balance Sheet

2. Using the information in #1 above, calculate the current ratio.

3. Using the information in #1 above, calculate the debt ratio.

4. Using the information in #1 above, calculate whether the company generated net income or net loss and how much.

5. On a work sheet, the asset and liability amounts appearing in the balance sheet columns are the same amounts listed on the financial statement; however, the amount for Capital on the work sheet is not the same figure listed on the financial statement. Why are the two amounts different?

_____
_____
_____
_____
_____
_____
_____
_____

V. Exercises

1.

The Design Company
Trial Balance
December 31, 20X7

Cash	$ 13,500	
Accounts Receivable	2,500	
Prepaid Advertising	1,600	
Supplies	1,700	
Unearned Revenue		$ 1,200
Notes Payable		10,000
Tyler, Capital		5,975
Tyler, Withdrawals	1,000	
Fees Earned		8,500
Salary Expense	3,000	
Rent Expense	1,750	
Utilities Expense	625	
	$25,675	$25,675

Additional information:
- a. Supplies at year-end totaled $1,200.
- b. $1,100 of the Prepaid Advertising was expired at year-end.
- c. Unearned revenues total $700 as of December 31.
- d. Accrued salary expense, $250

Required:

1. Prepare the appropriate adjusting entries.
2. Prepare closing entries.

Requirement 1 (Adjusting entries)
GENERAL JOURNAL

Date	Accounts and Explanation	PR	Debit	Credit

Requirement 2 (Closing entries)

GENERAL JOURNAL

Date	Accounts and Explanation	PR	Debit	Credit

2. Using the information in Exercise 1, calculate the ending Tyler, Capital balance.

	$
	$

3. Using the information in Exercises 1 and 2, prepare a post-closing trial balance.

The Design Company
Post-Closing Trial Balance
December 31, 20X7

	$	$
	$	$

104

4. List the accounting cycle in the correct sequence.

VI. Beyond the Numbers

Given the following information, answer the following questions:

	Income Summary					Capital	
12/31	82,000	12/31	96,000		Bal.	106,000
					5/5	9,000
					10/1	4,000

	Withdrawals	
3/10	5,000	
7/15	8,000	
11/2	4,000	

1. Where did the credits to the Capital account on 5/5 and 10/1 come from?

2. Did the company generate net income or net loss? How much?

3. Has the value of the company increased or decreased for the year? Explain.

VII. Demonstration Problems

Demonstration Problem #1

1. Below are the trial balance columns of the work sheet of Thai Production Company for the year ended November 30, 20X6. Using this trial balance, prepare the journal entries necessary to adjust the accounts of Thai Productions The additional data needed are provided below:

   a. Supplies on hand at November 30, 20X6, $1,095
   b. Depreciation expense, $2,350
   c. Accrued interest expense, $750
   d. Prepaid rent as of November 30, $6,700
   e. On November 30, Thai had accrued ticket revenue, $3,225.
   f. All but $20,450 of the unearned ticket revenue was earned at year end

Thai Production Company
Trial Balance
November 30, 20X6

Accounts	Debit	Credit
Cash	$ 21,325	
Accounts Receivable	1,555	
Prepaid Rent	11,000	
Supplies	7,395	
Equipment	78,000	
Accumulated Depreciation		$ 18,415
Accounts Payable		4,925
Note Payable		5,000
Interest Payable		
Unearned Ticket Revenue		52,560
Sujan Pradesh, Capital		88,510
Sujan Pradesh, Withdrawals	13,000	
Ticket Revenue		58,700
Salary Expense	19,900	
Rent Expense	37,000	
Interest Expense	9,225	
Depreciation Expense		
Advertising Expense	29,710	
Supplies Expense		
Total	$228,110	$ 228,110

2. Place each adjusting entry directly into the Adjustments columns of the work sheet and key each entry by letter. Complete the work sheet on page 95 using Exhibit 4-6 in your text as a guide.
3. Prepare the journal entries needed to close the accounts.

Requirement 1 (adjusting entries)

GENERAL JOURNAL

Date	Accounts and Explanation	PR	Debit	Credit

Requirement 2 (work sheet)

Thai Production Company
Work sheet
For the Year Ended November 30, 20X6

Accounts	Trial Balance Debit	Trial Balance Credit	Adjustments Debit	Adjustments Credit	Adjusted Trial Balance Debit	Adjusted Trial Balance Credit	Income Statement Debit	Income Statement Credit	Balance Sheet Debit	Balance Sheet Credit
Cash	21,325									
Accounts Receivable	1,555									
Prepaid Rent	11,000									
Supplies	7,395									
Equipment	78,000									
Accumulated Depreciation		18,415								
Accounts Payable		4,925								
Note Payable		5,000								
Interest Payable										
Unearned Ticket Revenue		52,560								
Sujan Pradesh, Capital		88,510								
Sujan Pradesh, Withdrawals	13,000									
Ticket Revenue		58,700								
Salary Expense	19,900									
Rent Expense	37,000									
Interest Expense	9,225									
Depreciation Expense										
Advertising Expense	29,710									
Supplies Expense										
Total	228,110	228,110								
Net Income (Loss)										

108

Requirement 3 (closing entries)

GENERAL JOURNAL

Date	Accounts and Explanation	PR	Debit	Credit

Demonstration Problem #2

Refer to the completed work sheet in Demonstration Problem #1.

1. Prepare the income statement for the year ended November 30, 20X6.
2. Prepare the statement of owner's equity for the year ended November 30, 20X6. Draw the arrow that links the income statement to the statement of owner's equity.
3. Prepare a classified balance sheet at November 30, 20X6 using the report format. All liabilities are current.
4. Using the balance sheet, calculate the current ratio and the debt ratio.
5. Prepare the post-closing trial balance.

Requirement 1 (Income Statement)

Thai Production Company
Income Statement
For the Year Ended November 30, 20X6

Requirement 2 (Statement of Owner's Equity)

Thai Production Company
Statement of Owner's Equity
For the Year Ended November 30, 20X6

Requirement 3 (Balance Sheet)

Thai Production Company
Balance Sheet
November 30, 20X6

Requirement 4 (current and debt ratios)

Current ratio:

Debt ratio:

Requirement 5 (post-closing trial balance)

Thai Production Company
Post-Closing Trial Balance
November 30, 20X6

SOLUTIONS

I. Matching

1. K	4. D	7. H	10. M	13. C	16. P
2. O	5. G	8. A	11. I	14. F	
3. B	6. J	9. L	12. E	15. N	

II. Multiple Choice

1. B The post-closing trial balance contains the ending balances of the permanent accounts only. The temporary accounts (revenues, expenses and withdrawals) have been closed, and therefore, have no balances and are not listed.

2. D Revenues are extended to the income statement columns. Assets, liabilities, capital, and withdrawals are extended to the balance sheet columns.

3. A The adjusting entry for depreciation is
    Depreciation Expense   XX
        Accumulated Depreciation   XX
    The credit to accumulated depreciation increases the account balance.

4. C The adjusting entry for depreciation does not affect the balance in the plant asset account. The adjusting entry for depreciation increases Depreciation Expense and increases the balance in the Accumulated Depreciation account. The increase in Accumulated Depreciation has the effect of decreasing the total assets without modifying the historical cost of the asset.

5. C A net loss is entered as a credit on the income statement column of the work sheet and as a debit on the balance sheet column of the work sheet. Net income is entered as a debit on the income statement column of the income statement and as a credit on the balance sheet column of the work sheet.

6. B Closing has the effect of transferring all revenues to the credit side of Income Summary and all expenses to the debit side. If revenues are larger than expenses, income summary will have a credit balance that reflects net income. If expenses are greater than revenue, Income Summary will have a debit balance that reflects a net loss.

7. A The entry to close withdrawals is
    Capital   XX
        Withdrawals   XX
    Note that Withdrawals is closed directly to Capital and is not closed through Income Summary.

8. D Current assets are assets that are expected to be converted to cash, sold, or consumed during the next 12 months or within the business's normal operating cycle if longer than a year. Equipment is a long-term asset. Accounts Payable and Unearned Revenues are current liability accounts.

9. B The current ratio measures the company's ability to pay its current liabilities as they come due.

10. A Closing has the effect of transferring all revenues to the credit side of Income Summary and all expenses to the debit side. If revenues are larger than expenses, income summary will have a credit balance that reflects net income. If expenses are greater than revenues, Income Summary will have a debit balance that reflects a net loss.

III. Completion

1. account balances at the beginning of the period (The accounting cycle is the process by which accountants produce the financial statements for a specific period of time. The cycle starts with the beginning account balances.)
2. temporary (Revenue, expenses and withdrawals are temporary accounts. They are closed at the end of each accounting period.)
3. work sheet. (The work sheet is a columnar document that is designed to help move data from the trial balance to the finished financial statements.)
4. permanent (Permanent accounts, i.e., assets, liabilities and capital, are not used to measure income for a period and are not closed at the end of the period.)
5. Income Summary (Closing has the effect of transferring all revenues to the credit side of Income Summary and all expenses to the debit side. If revenues are larger than expenses, Income Summary will have a credit balance that reflects net income. If expenses are greater than revenue, Income Summary will have a debit balance that reflects a net loss.)
6. Capital (The entry to close withdrawals is always:

     Capital   XX
         Withdrawals   XX

Note that Withdrawals is closed directly to Capital and is *not* closed through Income Summary.)
7. Liquidity (Balance Sheets list assets and liabilities in the order of their relative liquidity.)
8. post-closing trial balance
9. Net losses, withdrawals
10. total liabilities, total assets
11. current ratio (current assets ÷ current liabilities)

IV. Daily Exercises

1. From the following list of account balances as of December 31, 20X8, present the current assets and total assets that would appear on the balance sheet.

Current Assets:		
Cash		$ 4,500
Accounts Receivable		9,000
Notes Receivable		8,500
Inventory		11,000
Prepaid Insurance		1,200
Supplies		350
Total current assets		$34,550
Fixed Assets:		
Land		25,000
Equipment	$14,000	
Less: Accumulated Depreciation	(4,000)	10,000
Total Assets		$69,550

2. Current ratio = current assets ÷ current liabilities
   Current assets = $34,550 (from #1 above)
   Current liabilities =

Accounts Payable	$ 6,000
Notes Payable	6,500
Unearned Revenue	3,500
Salaries Payable	2,400
Interest Payable	1,280
	$19,680

   Current ratio = $34,550 ÷ $19,680 = 1.76. This means that for every $1.00 of current liabilities, the company has $1.76 in current assets.

3. Debt ratio = Total liabilities ÷ Total assets.
   Current liabilities = $19,680 (from #2 above)
   Long-term liabilities = $18,000 (Note payable due in 2 years)
   Total liabilities -= $37,680
   Total assets = $69,550 (from #1 above)
   Debt ratio = $37,680 ÷$69,550 = .54. This means that 54% of the company's assets are financed with debt.

4. The company has generated a net loss, $1,950. If Total Revenues = $20,250 and Total Expenses = $22,200, then $20,250-$22,200= ($1,950) net loss.

5. The Capital figure appearing on the work sheet has not been updated to reflect the effects of the income statement and withdrawals. Most account balances are updated when they are adjusted; however, the capital account is updated through the closing process. Remember, net income (from the income statement) is added to Capital on the Owner's Equity Statement. The ending balance amount from the Owner's Equity Statement is the updated amount listed on the Balance Sheet.

V. Exercises

1.

The Design Company

Trial Balance
December 31, 20X7

Cash	$ 13,500	
Accounts Receivable	2,500	
Prepaid Advertising	1,600	
Supplies	1,700	
Unearned Revenue		$ 1,200
Notes Payable		10,000
Tyler, Capital		5,975
Tyler, Withdrawals	1,000	
Fees Earned		8,500
Salary Expense	3,000	
Rent Expense	1,750	
Utilities Expense	625	
	$25,675	$25,675

Additional information:
- e. Supplies at year-end totaled $1,200.
- f. $1,100 of the Prepaid Advertising was expired at year-end.
- g. Unearned revenues total $700 as of December 31.
- h. Accrued salary expense, $250

Requirement 1

Date		Accounts and Explanation	PR	Debit	Credit
	a.	Supplies Expense ($1,700- $1,200)		500	
		Supplies			500
		To record supplies used			
	b.	Advertising Expense		1,100	
		Prepaid advertising			1,100
		To record expired advertising.			
	c.	Unearned Revenues		500	
		Fees Earned ($1,200 - $700)			500
		To record fees earned			
	d.	Salary Expense		250	
		Salary Payable			250
		To record accrued salary expense			

Requirement 2

Date	Accounts and Explanation	PR	Debit	Credit
	Fees Earned ($8,500 + $500)		9,000	
	Income Summary			9,000
	Income Summary		7,225	
	Salary Expense ($3,000 + $250)			3,250
	Rent Expense			1,750
	Utilities Expense			625
	Supplies Expense			500
	Advertising Expense			1,100
	Supplies Expense and Advertising Expense from the adjusting entries must be included.			
	Income Summary		1,775	
	Tyler, Capital			1,775
	Income Summary had a credit balance of $1,775 before this entry ($9,000 credit - $7,225 debit).			
	Tyler, Capital		1,000	
	Tyler, Withdrawals			1,000

2.

Beginning Capital	$5,975
Plus: Net Income	1,775
	7,750
Less: Withdrawals	(1,000)
Ending Capital	$6,750

3.

The Design Company
Post-closing Trial Balance
December 31, 20X7

Cash	$13,500	
Accounts receivable	2,500	
Prepaid advertising	500	
Supplies	1,200	
Salary Payable		$ 250
Unearned revenue		700
Notes payable		10,000
Tyler, Capital		6,750
Totals	$17,700	$17,700

4.
1. Start with the balances in the ledger at the beginning of the period.
2. Analyze and journalize transactions as they occur.
3. Post entries to the ledger accounts.
4. Compute the unadjusted balance in each account at the end of the period.
5. Enter the trial balance on the work sheet, and complete the work sheet.
6. Prepare the financial statements.
7. Journalize and post the adjusting entries and the closing entries.
8. Prepare a post-closing trial balance.

VI. Beyond the Numbers

Income Summary			
12/31	82,000	12/31	96,000
12/31	14,000		
	-0-		

Capital			
12/31	17,000	Bal.	106,000
		5/5	9,000
		10/1	4,000
		12/31	14,000
		Bal.	116,000

Net increase $10,000

Withdrawals			
3/10	5,000	12/31	17,000
7/15	8,000		
11/2	4,000		
	-0-		

1. Where did the credits to the Capital account on 5/5 and 10/1 come from?
   Credits that appear in the Capital account during an accounting period represent additional capital contributions by the owner.

4. Did the company generate net income or net loss? How much?
   The company generated net income in the amount of $14,000. This is determined by evaluating the Income Summary account. The credit represents the total revenues, $96,000 and the debit represents total expenses, $82,000.

5. Has the value of the company increased or decreased for the year? Explain.
   The value of the company has increased by $10,000. This increase is determined by analyzing the overall change in the owner's Capital account, or owner's equity.

VII. Demonstration Problems

Demonstration Problem #1 Solved and Explained

Requirement 1

(a) Nov. 30   Supplies Expense   6,300
                    Supplies   6,300
    To record supplies expense.

Calculation:

Supplies at the beginning of accounting period	$7,395
Supplies at the end of the accounting period	1,095
Supplies Expense (used up)	$6,300

A business must adjust its Supplies account to reflect supplies used up during each accounting period. Supplies are assets that are used to operate the business. When supplies are used in the business, the amount used up during the period must be transferred from the asset account, Supplies to the expense account, Supplies Expense. To decrease the asset, credit Supplies. To record the expense, debit Supplies Expense.

(b) Nov. 30   Depreciation Expense   2,350
                    Accumulated Depreciation - Equipment   2,350
    To record depreciation expense.

To reflect the decline in usefulness of long-lived assets, a portion of the asset's cost is systematically transferred from the asset to expense. Depreciation Expense is debited (expenses are recorded with debits) and the contra asset account Accumulated Depreciation - Equipment is credited (decreases in assets are recorded by credits).

(c) Nov. 30   Interest Expense   750
                    Interest Payable   750
    To record accrued interest expense.

Accrued interest is interest that is owed but will not be paid within the current accounting period. An adjusting entry must be made to reflect the fact that the company owes money for interest, thereby updating the interest payable account, and to properly match the expense to revenues in the period when the expense was incurred. Credit Interest Payable to reflect the increase in the liability account, and debit Interest Expense to record the increase in expense.

(d) Nov. 30   Rent Expense   4,300
                    Prepaid Rent   4,300
    To record rent expense.

Prepaid rent must be decreased to adjust its balance for the amount of rent that has expired. Decrease the asset account, Prepaid Rent by crediting it, and increase Rent Expense by debiting the account.

Calculation:

Prepaid Rent at the beginning of accounting period	$11,000
Prepaid Rent at the end of the accounting period	6,700
Rent Expense (used up)	$4,300

119

(e) Nov. 30 Accounts Receivable   3,225
                     Ticket Revenue   3,225
         To record admissions revenue.

Tickets sold on account in the last day or two of the month are occasionally not recorded for several days. To recognize this revenue in the proper accounting period, an adjusting entry must be made to increase the Ticket Revenue account (by crediting it) and increase the Accounts Receivable (by debiting it). This is an example of accrued revenue.

(f) Nov. 30 Unearned Ticket Revenue   32,110
                     Ticket Revenue   32,110
         To record ticket revenue.

Advance payment is a liability because the business owes the customer a service or product. The business records the liability in an unearned revenue account. This account must be adjusted at the close of each accounting period to reflect amounts earned during the period. Note that the liability Unearned Ticket Revenue is decreased by transferring $32,110 to the Ticket Revenue account. The unearned revenue, a liability, became revenue once the agreed-on service was performed.

Calculation:

Unearned ticket revenue at the beginning of the period	$52,560
Unearned ticket revenue at the end of the period	20,450
Revenue Earned	$32,110

Work Sheet:

If the adjusting entries are prepared correctly, completion of an accurate work sheet is relatively straightforward. The work sheet makes preparation of the financial statements fast and easy. The work sheet also provides a summary of all information needed to prepare the closing entries.

Errors made in the footing of individual columns of the work sheet are revealed and, of course, corrected prior to the formal preparation of the financial statements. As a result, the work sheet is a time saver. "Cross-footing" mistakes will occur less frequently if you use a ruler. Starting at the top of the work sheet and working from left to right, cross-foot and extend one column at a time. Working methodically, and slowly if necessary, saves time in the long run. You will become more efficient with practice.

Requirement 2

Thai Production Company
Work Sheet
For the Year Ended November 30, 20X6

Accounts	Trial Balance Debit	Trial Balance Credit	Adjustments Debit	Adjustments Credit	Adjusted Trial Balance Debit	Adjusted Trial Balance Credit	Income Statement Debit	Income Statement Credit	Balance Sheet Debit	Balance Sheet Credit
Cash	21,325				21,325				21,325	
Accounts receivable	1,555		(e) 3,225		4,780				4,780	
Prepaid Rent	11,000			(d) 4,300	6,700				6,700	
Supplies	7,395			(a) 6,300	1,095				1,095	
Equipment	78,000				78,000				78,000	
Accumulated Depreciation		18,415		(b) 2,350		20,765				20,765
Accounts Payable		4,925				4,925				4,925
Note Payable		5,000				5,000				5,000
Interest Payable				(c) 750		750				750
Unearned Ticket Revenue		52,560	(f) 32,110			20,450				20450
Sujan Pradesh, Capital		88,510				88,510				88,510
Sujan Pradesh, Withdrawals	13,000				13,000				13,000	
Ticket Revenue		58,700		(e) 3,225 (f) 32,110		94,035		94,035		
Salary Expense	19,900				19,900		19,900			
Rent Expense	37,000		(d) 4,300		41,300		41,300			
Interest Expense	9,225		(c) 750		9,975		9,975			
Depreciation Expense			(b) 2,350		2,350		2,350			
Advertising Expense	29,710				29,710		29,710			
Supplies Expense			(a) 6,300		6,300		6,300			
Total	228,110	228,110	49,035	49,035	234,435	234,435	109,535	94,035	124,900	140,400
Net Income (Loss)								15,500	15,550	
							109,535	109,535	140,400	140,400

121

Requirement 3

GENERAL JOURNAL

Date	Accounts and Explanation	PR	Debit	Credit
Nov. 30	Ticket Revenue		94,035	
	Income Summary			94,035
	Income Summary		109,535	
	Salary Expense			19,900
	Rent Expense			41,300
	Interest Expense			9,975
	Depreciation Expense			2,350
	Advertising Expense			29,710
	Supplies Expense			6,300
	Sujan Pradesh, Capital		15,500	
	Income Summary			15,500
	Sujan Pradesh, Capital		13,000	
	Sujan Pradesh, Withdrawals			13,000

Closing entries zero out revenue, expense, and withdrawal accounts by transferring their amounts to the capital account. Revenues and expenses undergo the intermediate step of being transferred to a "holding" account called Income Summary.

The closing procedure can be broken down into four steps:
1. Close Revenues to Income Summary
2. Close Expenses to Income Summary
3. Close Income Summary to Capital
4. Close Withdrawals to Capital

Note how the above closing entries follow this sequence.

All information required for the first three closing entries can be taken directly from the Income Statement columns of the work sheet. Look at the Income Statement columns. Compare the revenue and expense figures with the first two closing entries, and compare the net loss figure with the third entry.

Demonstration Problem #2 Solved and Explained

Requirement 1

Thai Production Company
Income Statement
For the Year Ended November 30, 20X6

Revenues:		
Ticket Revenue		$94,035
Expenses:		
Salary Expense	$19,900	
Rent Expense	41,300	
Interest Expense	9,975	
Depreciation Expense	2,350	
Advertising Expense	29,710	
Supplies Expense	6,300	
Total Expenses		109,375
Net Income (Loss)		($ 15,500)

All the information for the Income Statement can be taken directly from the Income Statement columns of the work sheet.

Requirement 2 (Statement of Owner's Equity)

Thai Production Company
Statement of Owner's Equity
For the Year Ended November 30, 20X6

Sujan Pradesh, Capital 11/30/X5	$ 88,510
Less: Net Loss	(15,500)
	73,010
Less: Withdrawals	13,000
Sujan Pradesh, Capital 11/30/X6	$ 60,010

Beginning capital and withdrawals can be taken directly from the Balance Sheet columns of the work sheet. Net income can be taken from the Income Statement. Ending capital is then calculated. The ending capital for this period will appear as the beginning capital on next year's work sheet and statement of owner's equity.

Requirement 3 (Balance Sheet)

Thai Production Company
Balance Sheet
November 30, 20X6

ASSETS

Current Assets:

Cash	$21,325	
Accounts Receivable	4,780	
Prepaid Rent	6,700	
Supplies	1,095	
Total Current Assets		$33,900
Plant Assets:		
Equipment	78,000	
Less: Accumulated Depreciation	(20,765)	57,235
Total Assets		$91,135

LIABILITIES

Current Liabilities:

Accounts Payable	$4,925
Notes Payable	5,000
Interest Payable	750
Unearned Ticket Revenue	20,450
Total Liabilities	31,125

OWNER'S EQUITY

Sujan Pradesh, Capital	60,010
Total Liabilities and Owner's Equity	$91,135

Requirement 4

Current ratio = current assets ÷ current liabilities
= $33,900 ÷ $31,125 = 1.09 (rounded)

Debt ratio = total liabilities ÷ total assets
= $31,125 ÷ $91,135 = 0.34 (rounded)

Requirement 5

Thai Production Company
Post-closing Trial Balance
November 30, 20X6

Accounts	Debit	Credit
Cash	$ 21,325	
Accounts Receivable	4,780	
Prepaid Rent	6,700	
Supplies	1,095	
Equipment	78,000	
Accumulated Depreciation		$ 20,765
Accounts Payable		4,925
Note Payable		5,000
Interest Payable		750
Unearned Ticket Revenue		20,450
Sujan Pradesh, Capital		60,010
	$111,900	$111,900

Preparing a post-closing trial balance performs a final check of the closing process. If any temporary account balances (Revenue, Expense, Income Summary, or Withdrawals) appear in the post-closing trial balance, a mistake has been made in closing the accounts. On a post-closing trial balance, the only accounts you should see are the balance sheet (permanent) accounts.

Chapter 5—Merchandising Operations

CHAPTER OVERVIEW

Throughout the previous four chapters, you learned about the accounting cycle as it applies to a service business. In Chapter Five, the emphasis changes from a service business to a **merchandising business**—one that earns its revenue by selling a product, rather than a service, to its customers. Accounting for a merchandising business is a bit more complex because the merchandiser must obtain inventory, pay for it, sell it to customers, collect from customers, and then obtain more inventory. This process is referred to as the **operating cycle**. Understanding this chapter will make subsequent chapters, particularly Chapters 6 and 9 easier to comprehend. The learning objectives for this chapter are to

1. Account for the purchase of inventory.
2. Account for the sale of inventory.
3. Use sales and gross profit to evaluate a company.
4. Adjust and close the accounts of a merchandising business.
5. Prepare a merchandiser's financial statements.
6. Use the gross margin percentage and inventory turnover to evaluate a business.

CHAPTER REVIEW

Objective 1 - Account for the purchase of inventory.

The difference between a service business and a merchandising business is a merchandiser sells a product referred to as inventory, where a service business provides, or sells, a service. For merchandising businesses, inventory is one of the largest and most important assets. When inventory is purchased, the merchandiser acquires the asset—inventory—and holds it until it is sold to customers.

When a merchandiser decides to purchase inventory, it sends a purchase order to its supplier. The supplier ships the merchandise and sends an invoice, or bill, to the merchandiser. After the inventory has been received and inspected, the merchandiser pays the supplier.

There are two types of discounts a supplier might extend to the buyer:

- **A quantity discount** offers a buyer the option of purchasing a larger number of units and, by doing so, obtaining a lower per unit cost. The amount of a quantity discount is never recorded in the accounting records. Quantity discounts are offered and deducted prior to the purchase and establish the purchase price for the order.

- **A purchase discount** offers the buyer the option of paying an invoice early and, by doing so, takes advantage of the offered reduction in the total price paid for the merchandise. Purchase discounts are offered after the purchase and are only recorded when the purchaser takes advantage of the discount within the allowed discount period. A purchase discount would be expressed as a part of the credit terms of the sale. The terms might be 2/10, n/30. This means that the purchaser may take a 2% discount on the amount owed if the invoice is paid within 10 days of the invoice date, excluding freight charges, if any. If the invoice is not paid within 10 days of the invoice date, then the purchaser has not taken advantage of the discount, the option expires, and the buyer must pay the invoice in full within 30 days of the invoice date. If a discount is offered, it is always advantageous for the buyer to take the discount because the discount represents a savings of 2% over a period of 20 days (assuming a 30 day month). This savings represents an effective annual rate of 36.5%, calculated as follows:

# of days in a year / # of days outside of discount period x discount = annual rate
or, 365 days in a year / 20 days of savings x 2% = 36.5% annual rate

This means that over a year's time, if the buyer takes advantage of the discount every month, the business will save approximately 36.5% on the total cost of its inventory. While 2% does not look like much each month, as you can see, it represents a significant savings over a year.

If the terms of the sales are n/30, then no discount is offered and the buyer must pay the invoice within 30 days of the invoice date.

Review the following sequence of transactions and explanations:

Purchase of inventory on account:

Inventory	500	
Accounts Payable		500
Purchased inventory on account, terms 1/15, n/30		

If the amount owed is paid within discount period:

Accounts Payable	500	
Cash [$500-($500 x .01)]		495
Inventory ($500 x .01)		5

If paid after discount period:

Accounts Payable	500	
Cash		500

Anytime a supplier ships goods to the merchandiser, someone must pay for the shipping costs that may also be referred to as freight charges. The entity responsible for paying the freight charges is determined by the shipping terms at the time the purchase is made.

- If the shipping terms are **FOB shipping point**, then the buyer is responsible for paying the freight charges. FOB shipping point indicates that title to the goods transfers to the buyer at the shipping point and therefore, the buyer must pay the shipping charges. Shipping costs incurred by the buyer are termed **freight-in** and are debited to the inventory account. Freight charges paid by the buyer represent an additional cost to the buyer for the inventory and are added to the cost of the asset that appears on the balance sheet.
- If the shipping terms are **FOB destination**, then the seller is responsible for paying the freight charges since title to the goods will not transfer until the goods reach the destination, or the buyer's warehouse. Shipping costs incurred by the supplier are called freight-out and accounted for as delivery expense that appears on the income statement.

Sometimes the buyer will need to return a portion of the purchase to the seller or the buyer may request an allowance for goods that are defective, damaged, or the wrong item. **Purchase returns and allowances** are credited directly to the inventory account and reflect a reduction in the cost of merchandise acquired. A purchase return is where the buyer actually returns the goods to the supplier. A purchase allowance is where the buyer keeps the merchandise, and the supplier gives the buyer an allowance, or cost reduction for the merchandise.

The two main accounting systems used for keeping track of merchandise inventory within the accounting records are the **periodic system** and the **perpetual system**. The major difference between the two is the availability, within the accounting records, of an up-to-date value for merchandise inventory on hand. When a perpetual system is used, this value is available continuously, whereas the periodic system can only determine a value when an actual physical count is made. Taking a physical count called taking inventory can be time consuming and expensive for a business to perform. With the increasing use of computers, more and more businesses have changed their systems from periodic to perpetual. For this reason, we use the perpetual system in our discussion of merchandise businesses and cover the periodic system in the chapter supplement.

Objective 2 - Account for the sale of inventory.

After a company buys its inventory, the next step is to sell the goods. The merchandiser now shifts into the role of the seller. When inventory is sold to customers, the amount of the sale is referred to as Sales Revenue, or simply Sales. Remember, revenue is generated when the business does what it is in the business of doing, which, in this case, is selling goods. Keep in mind that when a merchandiser purchases inventory, it is an asset. Once the inventory is sold to customers, it is no longer held by the merchandiser for sale, so it is no longer an asset. The cost of the inventory that has been sold to customers becomes Cost of Goods Sold, an expense. When merchandise is sold and a perpetual inventory system is in use, two entries are required, as follows:

Sale of inventory on account:

1)	Accounts Receivable	700	
	Sales		700
	Sold inventory on account, terms 2/15, n/30		
2)	Cost of Goods Sold	500	
	Inventory		500
	Recorded the cost of goods sold		

- Entry 1 records the sale at the selling price. The selling price will be some amount greater than the cost of the goods that are sold.
- Entry 2 transfers the cost of the items sold from the Inventory account (an asset) to the Cost of Goods Sold account (an expense).

As mentioned earlier, sellers offer discounts to encourage prompt payment. By offering the sales discount, the seller is willing to accept less cash to entice its customer to pay for the goods within 10 days, in this example. If the customer chooses to take advantage of the sales discount, then on the seller's books, the entry to record the collection within the discount period is

If the amount owed by the customer is collected
within the discount period:

Cash [$700-($700 x .02)]	686	
Sales Discount ($700 x .02)	14	
Accounts Receivable		700

If collected after discount period:

Cash	700	
Accounts Receivable		700

The seller may also have to accept a return or grant an allowance. The entries to record a return of merchandise is:

Sales Return and Allowances	XX	
Accounts Receivable		XX
Inventory	XX	
Cost of Goods Sold		XX

The entry to record the granting of an allowance is:

Sales Return and Allowances	XX	
Accounts Receivable		XX

Sellers rarely debit either discounts or returns and allowances directly to the Sales account. The use of a Sales Discount account and a Sales Returns and Allowances account allows a merchandiser to track how much of the business's overall sales are reduced by extending sales discounts, and from returns or allowances. Sales Discount and Sales Returns and Allowances are contra-revenue accounts that are contra to the Sales account.

Objective 3 – Use sales and gross profit to evaluate a company.

Managers and investors evaluate a business's profitability by analyzing net sales revenue, cost of goods sold, and gross profit. **Net Sales,** the amount that appears on the income statement, is computed as follows:

> Sales Revenues (credit balance)
> - Sales Discounts (debit balance)
> <u>- Sales Returns and Allowances (debit balance)</u>
> = Net Sales (a calculation, not an account)

The difference between the amount of the sale (determined by the selling price) and the cost of the inventory sold, called Cost of Goods Sold is called the **Gross Profit** or Gross Margin.

Gross Profit = Sales - Cost of Goods Sold

Helpful Hint: Review page 177 in your textbook.

Gross profit is a measure of how successful a business is at selling its inventory to generate a profit. A merchandising business must sell its inventory at a selling price that is greater than it's cost to generate gross profit. And, the gross profit must be sufficient to also cover the business's operating expenses in order to generate net income. This is illustrated in Exhibit 5-1 in your textbook where the income statement of a service company is compared to the income statement of a merchandising company.

Objective 4 - Adjust and close the accounts of a merchandising business.

Adjusting entries for a merchandiser are the same as those for a service business, except there is one additional adjusting entry for any discrepancy between the accounting records for inventory and the physical count for the inventory.

The general form of the **closing entries** for a merchandiser is basically the same as for a service business except now there are some additional accounts that must be closed.

When a difference exists between the balance in the Inventory account and the result of a physical count of merchandise still on hand, the inventory account will need to be adjusted so its balance agrees with the physical count. In most cases, this adjusting entry will always affect the Inventory and the Cost of Goods Sold accounts and appear as follows:

When the physical count of the inventory reports less inventory on hand than the Inventory account reports in the accounting records:

Cost of Goods Sold	XX	
Inventory		XX
To decrease the Inventory account to match the physical count		

When the physical count of the inventory reports more inventory on hand than the Inventory account reports in the accounting records:

Inventory	XX	
Cost of Goods Sold		XX
To increase the Inventory account to match the physical count		

The format for the **work sheet** is identical to the one introduced in Chapter 4, and the steps in completing the work sheet are the same. The closing process also remains unchanged, as follows:

1. Income Statement credit balances are transferred to the Income Summary account.

2. Income Statement debit balances are transferred to the Income Summary account. The debit balances will now include the Cost of Goods Sold account, Sales Discounts account, and Sales Returns and Allowances account. (Remember: Sales Discounts and Sales Returns and Allowances are contra-revenue account, not expense accounts.)
3. The Income Summary account is closed to the Capital account. (Remember, the amount of this third closing entry must agree with net income or net loss.)
4. The Withdrawals account is closed to the Capital account.

Objective 5 - Prepare a merchandiser's financial statements.

The major difference between the financial statements of a merchandiser and those of a service business is the presence of Inventory on the merchandiser's balance sheet and Cost of Goods Sold on the merchandiser's income statement.

For many businesses, Inventory will be the largest current asset on the Balance Sheet. Cost of Goods Sold will be the largest expense item on the Income Statement. In addition, the Income Statement will generally report operating expenses in two categories:

- **Selling Expenses.** Those costs directly related to marketing the company's products.
- **General Expenses**. Other operating costs incurred in the major line of business, and are not directly related to selling the products.

Finally, non-operating revenues and expenses (called Other revenues and expenses) are listed separately. Other revenues and expenses result from activities that a business might encounter in the normal course of doing business, but they do not result from the entity's main line of business. These distinctions allow the user of the financial statements to clearly differentiate between operating income, the income generated from the entity's main line of business, and net income, the bottom line income generated from all sources.

The Income Statement can be presented in either a **multiple-step format** or a **single-step format**. The multiple-step format clearly establishes significant relationships within the statement. Exhibit 5-7 is an example of a multiple-step income statement. The single-step format groups together all revenues, then groups together all expenses and, in a single computation, deducts the expenses from the revenues. Exhibit 5-8 is an example of a single-step format. You should also notice that the single-step format is similar to the income statements you have studied throughout Chapters 1-4.

Objective 6 - Use the gross margin percentage and inventory turnover ratios to evaluate a business.

A key measure of profitability for a merchandiser is the **gross margin percentage**. The gross profit percentage measures how much gross profit is generated by every dollar of sales revenue.

$$\textbf{Gross profit percentage} \quad = \quad \frac{\textbf{Gross profit}}{\textbf{Net Sales Revenues}}$$

Inventory turnover measures the number of times a company sells its average level of inventory during a year.

$$\textbf{Inventory turnover} \quad = \quad \underline{\textbf{Cost of goods sold}}$$

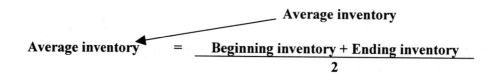

Average inventory

Average inventory = $\dfrac{\text{Beginning inventory} + \text{Ending inventory}}{2}$

Helpful hint: Review Exhibits 5-9 and 5-10 in your text.

TEST YOURSELF

All the self-testing materials in this chapter focus on information and procedures that your instructor is likely to test in quizzes and examinations. Those questions followed by an *S* refer to information contained in the Appendix to the chapter.

I. Matching   *Match each numbered term with its lettered definition.*

_____ 1. Cost of Goods Sold

_____ 2. Income from operations

_____ 3. Multiple-step income statement

_____ 4. Operating expenses

_____ 5. Sales returns and allowances

_____ 6. Single-step income statement

_____ 7. Purchase returns & allowances

_____ 8. Purchase discount

_____ 9. Sales discount

_____ 10. Gross profit

_____ 11. Invoice

_____ 12. Net sales

_____ 13. Net purchases

_____ 14. Other expense

_____ 15. Sales revenue

_____ 16. Quantity discount

A. A discount from supplier to merchandiser that lowers the price per item for volume purchases

B. A reduction in the amount receivable from a customer that is offered by the seller as an incentive for the customer to pay promptly

C. A reduction in the cost of inventory that is offered by a seller as an incentive for the customer to pay promptly

D. A seller's request for payment of a purchase

E. Amount that a merchandiser earns from selling inventory

F. Decreases in a buyer's debt that result from returning merchandise to the seller or receiving an allowance on the amount owed

G. Decreases in the seller's revenue from a customer's return of merchandise or from granting to the customer an allowance from the amount the customer owes

H. Excess of sales revenue over cost of goods sold

I. Expense that is outside the main operations of a business

J. Expenses, other than cost of goods sold, that are incurred in the entity's main line of business

K. Format that contains only two sections, revenues and expenses

L. Gross profit less operating expenses

M. Income statement format that lists the figures within subsections and presents intermediate subtotals, such as gross profit and income from operations

N. Purchases less purchase discounts and purchases returns & allowances

O. Sales revenue less sales discounts and sales returns & allowances

P. An account in the perpetual system; a calculation in the periodic system that represents the cost of inventory that the business sold to its customers.

II. Multiple Choice   *Circle the best answer.*

1. Which of the following companies would *not* be considered a merchandising entity?

    A. The Gap
    B. A Ford dealership

    C. Sears
    D. Alltel

2. A company will have a net loss if:

    A. cost of goods sold exceeds operating expenses.
    B. operating expenses exceed gross profit.

    C. sales exceed gross profit.
    D. sales exceed operating expenses.

3. Which of the following is classified as an operating expense?

    A. Cost of Goods Sold
    B. Rent Expense

    C. Sales Discount
    D. Interest Expense

4. A debit to Sales Returns and Allowances will:

    A. increase Inventory.
    B. increase Net Purchases.

    C. increase Net Sales.
    D. decrease Net Sales.

5. When using a perpetual inventory system, which account will capture all costs associated with the purchase of inventory?

    A. Purchases
    B. Purchase Discounts

    C. Inventory
    D. Purchase Returns and Allowances

6. A company purchases 30 DVD players systems that sell for $500 each. There is a $300 freight charge added to the invoice. The supplier also offers a 1% discount if the buyer pays the invoice within 10 days. The buyer takes advantage of all discounts offered. What will the total cost of this purchase be to the buyer?

    A. $15,000
    B. $15,147

    C. $15,150
    D. $15,000

7. A company sells merchandise on June 1 for $1,800 with terms 1/15, n/30. If it receives payment for the merchandise on June 8, the entry to record the receipt would:

    A. credit Accounts Receivable $1,800.
    B. credit Inventory $18.

    C. credit Cash $1,800.
    D. debit Inventory $1,782.

8. A company purchased merchandise for $3,200 on October 1 with terms 2/10, n/30. When it paid the account on October 13, the journal entry:

    A. debited Accounts Payable $3,136
    B. credited Inventory $64

    C. debited Inventory $3,200
    D. credited Cash $3,200

9. Which of the following accounts is *not* a contra account?

   A. Inventory
   B. Accumulated Depreciation
   C. Sales Returns and Allowances
   D. Sales Discounts

10. Gross Profit plus Cost of Goods Sold equals:

   A. Net Income.
   B. Cost of Goods Available for Sale.
   C. Net Sales.
   D. Operating Income.

III. Completion   *Complete each of the following statements.*

1. A merchandising entity earns its revenues by _____.
2. The largest single expense for most merchandisers is _____.
3. A seller's request for payment is called a(n) _____.
4. The major difference between a merchandiser's balance sheet and a service entity's balance sheet is

   _____.
5. The largest single current asset for most merchandisers is _____.
6. Sales minus Cost of Goods Sold is called _____.
7. A company credits the Inventory account when merchandise is sold. It is using a _____
   _____ inventory system.
8. The four sections found on a multiple-step income statement for a merchandising business are

   _____, _____, _____,

   and _____.
9. The gross margin percentage measures _____

   _____
10. Inventory turnover measures _____

   _____

IV. Daily Exercises

1. Record the following transactions in the space provided.

    7/4   Purchased merchandise on account from Traders, Inc., $1,500; term 2/10, n/60, FOB shipping point, freight of $75 added to the invoice.
    7/10   Returned $300 of merchandise to Traders, Inc.
    7/14   Sent a check to Traders, Inc. for the balance due.

Date	Accounts and Explanation	PR	Debit	Credit

2. Record the following transactions in the space provided.

    8/11   Sold merchandise on account to J. Starrs, $2,000; term 4/15, n/45. The cost of the sale was $750.
    8/16   Accepted a return of $400 from J. Starrs. The cost of the merchandise was $150.
    8/18   Granted an allowance of $75 for a portion of the order that was damaged during shipping.
    8/21   Received a check from J. Starrs for the amount due.

Date	Accounts and Explanation	PR	Debit	Credit

Date	Accounts and Explanation	PR	Debit	Credit

V. Exercises

1. The following information is available for Johnson's Jade Emporium for 20X7:

Beginning Inventory	$ 6,000
Ending Inventory	4,700
Operating Expenses	3,500
Cost of Goods Sold	31,500
Sales Discounts	600
Sales	43,000
Sales Returns and Allowances	200
Interest Expense	150

Required: Calculate the following for 20X7:

1. Net sales:

2. Gross profit:

3. Income from operations:

4. Net Income:

5. Gross profit percentage:

6. Inventory turnover:

2. Use the following information from Fedelina's Fedoras for 20X8 to prepare an income statement through gross profit on sales:

Depreciation Expense	$ 700
Interest Expense	1,100
Interest Revenue	1,000
Inventory	1,500
Cost of Goods Sold	7,790
Rent Expense	600
Sales Discounts	100
Sales Returns & Allowances	50
Sales Revenues	12,175
Withdrawals	250

3. Using the information in #2 above, prepare the necessary closing entries.

Date	Accounts and Explanation	PR	Debit	Credit

VI. Beyond the Numbers

A business is offered the purchase discount term 1/15, n/45. At the same time, the business can borrow money from its bank at 10% interest. Assuming the business does not have sufficient cash on hand to take advantage of the discount, which would be less expensive—to lose the discount or to borrow the needed cash from the bank and take the discount? Support your answer.

_____
_____
_____
_____
_____

VII. Demonstration Problems

Demonstration Problem #1

On March 1, Cronies & Fish, Inc. had the following account balances:

Cash	$ 20,000	
Accounts receivable	34,000	
Inventory	44,000	
Other current assets	15,000	
Property, plant, and equipment (net)	180,000	
Account payable		$ 37,000
Long-term liabilities		104,000
Capital		152,000
Totals	$293,000	$293,000

During March, the following merchandise purchase and sales transactions occurred:

a. Sold merchandise on account to Divas, $18,000; the cost of the merchandise was $8,400.
b. Purchased merchandise on account from Taylor, $9,600, terms 1/10, n/30, FOB shipping point.
c. Received a freight bill for the Taylor purchase, $275, terms n/10.
d. Sold merchandise on account to Lahni, $7,500; the cost of the merchandise was $1,650.
e. Paid the freight bill on the Taylor purchase (#c above).
f. Received payment from Divas (#a above) within the discount period.
g. Lahni returned $1,300 of merchandise; the cost of the merchandise was $450.
h. Paid Taylor (#b above) within the discount period.
i. Sold merchandise on account to Simmons, Inc., $10,200; the cost of the merchandise was $4,300.
j. Purchased merchandise on account from Carter Co., $11,240, terms 3/20, n/60.
k. Received payment from Lahni (#d and #g above) within the discount period.
l. Returned $1,400 of merchandise to Carter.
m. A $600 allowance was granted to Simmons (#i above).
n. Paid Carter (#j and #l above) within the discount period.
o. Simmons, Inc. paid the balance due (#i and #m above) but did not earn a discount.
p. Sold merchandise on account to Ferini Co., $12,750; the cost of the merchandise was $6,750.

Additional information:

1. The terms of all sales are 2/10, n/30, FOB destination.
2. Cronie & Fish, Inc. uses a perpetual inventory system.
3. Round amounts to the nearest dollar, where necessary.

Required:

1. Place the opening balances into the T-accounts, identifying each by date.
2. Record the transactions in the journal (omit explanations).
3. Post the entries to the T-accounts, identifying each by letter.
4. Balance the accounts and prepare a trial balance.
5. Calculate the gross margin percentage.

Requirements 1, 3, and 4

Cash	Accounts receivable	Inventory

Other current assets	Property, plant and equipment, net	Accounts payable

Long-term liabilities	Capital	Sales

Sales discount	Sales returns & allowance	Cost of goods sold

Requirement 2

Date	Accounts	PR	Debit	Credit

Date	Accounts	PR	Debit	Credit

Requirement 4

Accounts	Debit	Credit

Requirement 5

_____

_____

_____

Demonstration Problem #2

Using the completed work sheet for DuMont Company on the following page:

1. Prepare a multiple-step income statement, statement of owner's equity, and balance sheet.
2. Journalize the adjusting entries (identify each by letter) and closing entries.
3. Prepare a post-closing trial balance.
4. Prepare a single-step income statement.
5. Calculate the gross margin percentage.
6. Calculate the inventory turnover ratio. The beginning inventory was $36,000.

DuMont Company
Work Sheet
For the Year Ended December 31, 20X5

Accounts	Trial Balance Debit	Trial Balance Credit	Adjustments Debit	Adjustments Credit	Income Statement Debit	Income Statement Credit	Balance Sheet Debit	Balance Sheet Credit
Cash	18,250						18,250	
Accounts receivable	20,100						20,100	
Inventory	44,000			(g) 2,000			42,000	
Supplies	2,850			(a) 2,000			850	
Prepaid advertising	10,000			(b) 4,800			5,200	
Equipment	92,500						92,500	
Accumulated depreciation		43,500		(d) 8,300				51,800
Accounts payable		23,765						23,765
Salary payable				(e) 990				990
Interest payable				(f) 255				255
Unearned sales revenue		1,560	(c) 1,000					560
Note payable, long-term		75,000						75,000
Eric DuMont, Capital		38,100						38,100
Eric DuMont,	19,750						19,750	
Sales revenue		300,460		(c) 1,000		301,460		
Sales discounts	8,700				8,700			
Sales returns and allowances	2,610				2,610			
Cost of Goods Sold	146,410		(g) 2,000		148,410			
Salary expense	75,100		(e) 990		76,090			
Rent expense	19,000				19,000			
Depreciation expense			(d) 8,300		8,300			
Utilities expense	7,125				7,125			
Supplies expense			(a) 2,000		2,000			
Interest expense	2,750		(f) 255		3,005			
Advertising Expense	13,240		(b) 4,800		18,040			
Total	482,385	482,385	19,345	19,345	293,280	301,460	198,650	190,470
Net income (loss)					8,180			8,180
					301,460	301,460	198,650	198,650

144

Requirement 1 (Financial Statements)

Income Statement

Statement of Owner's Equity

Balance Sheet

ASSETS		LIABILITIES	
		OWNER'S EQUITY	

Requirement 2 (adjusting and closing entries)

Date	Accounts	PR	Debit	Credit

Date	Accounts	PR	Debit	Credit

Requirement 3 (Post-closing Trial Balance)

Post-closing Trial Balance

Requirement 4 (Single-step Income Statement)

Income Statement

Requirement 5 (Gross margin)

_____

_____

_____

Requirement 6 (Inventory turnover ratio)

_____

_____

_____

SOLUTIONS

I. Matching

1. P	5. G	9. B	13. N
2. L	6. K	10. H	14. I
3. M	7. F	11. D	15. E
4. J	8. C	12. O	16. A

II. Multiple Choice

1. D A merchandising entity earns its revenue by selling products. Of the entities listed, all sell products except the Alltel, the telephone company that sells a service.

2. B The basic income statement formula for a merchandising company is:

    Sales
    - Cost of goods sold
    = Gross margin
    - Operating expenses
    = Net income or (net loss)

    For a company to have a net loss, operating expenses must be greater than gross margin.

3. B Cost of goods sold is the cost of inventory that the company sold to customers. The account Sales Discounts is a contra-revenue account and interest expense is "other expense."

4. D Sales Returns and Allowances is a contra account to the Sales account. A credit to Sales Returns and Allowances increases its balance. Since it is contra to the Sales account, Sales Returns and Allowances will decrease net sales.

5. C When a perpetual inventory system is used, the inventory account will be updated for every transaction that has an effect on the overall cost of inventory. Freight-in will increase the cost of inventory, where purchase discounts, and purchase returns and allowances will decrease the cost of inventory. The individual Purchases, Purchase Discounts, and Purchase Returns and Allowances accounts are only used under a periodic inventory system.

6. C The total amount owed for the DVD players is $15,300:

30 DVD players x $500 each =	$15,000
+ Freight charges	300
Total cost of purchase prior to discount	$15,300
After discount is taken:	
Purchase price of DVD players	$15,000
Amount of discount: $15,000 x .01 =	(150)
Cost of DVD players after discount	$14,850
+Freight in	300
Total cost of purchase after discount	$15,150

7.   A   The terms 1/15, n/30 mean that a 1% discount is available if payment is received within fifteen days of the invoice date; otherwise the net amount of the invoice is due in 30 days. Since payment is received within the fifteen-day discount period, the journal entry to record the payment is:

Cash	1,782	
Inventory	18	
Accounts Receivable		1,800

8.   D   The terms 2/10,n/30 mean that a 2% discount is available if payment is made within ten days of the invoice date; otherwise the net amount of the invoice is due in 30 days. Since payment was not made within the ten-day discount period the net amount is due. The journal entry to record the payment is:

Accounts Payable	3,200	
Cash		3,200

9.   A   A contra account has two distinguishing characteristics: 1) it always has a companion account, and 2) its normal balance is opposite that of the companion account. Items B, C, and D are contra accounts. Only item A, Inventory, is not a contra account.

10.   C   You are required to work backwards. Since Net Sales - Cost of Goods Sold = Gross Margin; therefore, Net Sales = Gross Margin + Cost of Goods Sold.

III. Completion

1. selling products. This is in contrast to the entities studied through Chapter 4 that earned revenue by selling a service.
2. Cost of Goods Sold. Cost of goods sold represents the cost of the goods a business has sold to its customers.
3. invoice. To the seller, the invoice results in a sale being recorded. To the purchaser, the same invoice results in a purchase being recorded.
4. the Inventory account. The merchandiser earns revenue by selling a tangible product, inventory. The service entity earns its revenue by selling an intangible service.
5. Inventory.
6. Gross Profit or Gross Margin. The basic income statement formula for a merchandising company is:

> Sales
> - Cost of Goods Sold
> = Gross margin
> - Operating expenses
> = Net income (Net loss)

7. perpetual. Under the perpetual system, all merchandise is debited to the Inventory account when acquired and credited to the Inventory account when sold.
8. The four sections are: 1) Revenue from Sales, 2) Cost of Goods Sold, 3) Operating Expenses, 4) Other Revenue and Expenses
9. how much gross profit is generated by every dollar of sales revenue
10. the number of times a company sells its average level of inventory during a year.

IV. Daily Exercises

1.

7/4	Inventory	1,575	
	Accounts Payable		1,575
7/10	Accounts Payable	300	
	Inventory		300
7/14	Accounts Payable	1,275	
	Inventory		24
	Cash		1,251

Note: The cash discount applies only to the original purchase less the return. It does not apply to the freight charge.

2.

8/11	Accounts Receivable	2,000	
	Sales		2,000
	Cost of Goods Sold	750	
	Inventory		750
8/16	Sales Returns and Allowances	400	
	Accounts Receivable		400
	Inventory	150	
	Cost of Goods Sold		150
8/18	Sales Returns and Allowances	75	
	Accounts Receivable		75
8/21	Cash	1,464	
	Sales Discount	61	
	Accounts Receivable ($2,000-$400-$75)		1,525

With a perpetual inventory system, sales and sales returns require double entries—one to record the sale (or return) and a second entry to update the inventory account. Recording an allowance does not require a second entry to update the inventory, because no inventory is returned to the seller.

V. Exercises

1.

Requirement 1

Sales - Sales Returns & Allowances - Sales Discount = Net Sales
$43,000 - $200 - $600= $42,200

Requirement 2

Net Sales - Cost of Goods Sold = Gross Profit (or Gross Margin)
$42,200 - $31,500 = $10,700

Requirement 3

Gross Profit – Operating Expenses = Income from Operations
$10,700 - $3,500 = $7,200

Requirement 4

Income from Operations– Other Expenses = Net Income (Loss)
$7,200 - $150 = $7,050

Requirement 5

Gross Profit ÷ Net Sales
$10,700 ÷ $42,200 = 25.36%

Requirement 6

Cost of Goods Sold ÷ Average Inventory
Average Inventory = ($6,000+ $4,700) ÷ 2 = $5,350
$31,500 ÷ $5,350 = 5.9 times

2.

Revenues from Sales			
Sales		$12,175	
Less: Sales Discount	$100		
Sales Returns/Allowance	50	150	
Net Sales			$12,025
Less: Cost of Goods Sold			7,790
Gross Profit			$4,235

4.

Date	Accounts and Explanation	PR	Debit	Credit
	Sales Revenue		12,175	
	Interest Revenue		1,000	
	Income Summary			13,175
	Income Summary		10,340	
	Cost of Goods Sold			7,790
	Interest Expense			1,100
	Sales Discounts			100
	Rent Expense			600
	Depreciation Expense			700
	Sales Returns & Allowances			50
	Income Summary		2,835	
	Capital			2,835
	Capital		250	
	Withdrawals			250

VI. Beyond the Numbers

It would be more expensive to let the discount lapse compared than to borrow the money from the bank at 10% interest. The term 1/15, n/45 means you pay 1% for extending the payment period an additional 30 days. This computes to about 12% annual interest (365 days / 30 days x .01) or about 2% more than your bank is charging. Since it will cost the business more to forego the discount than to borrow the money, the business should borrow the money in order to take advantage of the discount.

VII. Demonstration Problems

Demonstration Problem #1 Solved and Explained

Requirements 1, 3, and 4

Cash		Accounts receivable		Inventory	
Bal. 20,000	275 (e)	Bal. 34,000	18,000 (f)	Bal. 44,000	8,400 (a)
(f) 17,640	9,504 (h)	(a) 18,000	1,300 (g)	(b) 9,600	1,650 (d)
(k) 6,076	9,545 (n)	(d) 7,500	6,200 (k)	(c) 275	96 (h)
(o) 9,600		(i) 10,200	600 m)	(g) 450	4,300 (i)
Bal. 33,992		(p) 12,750	9,600 (o)	(j) 11,240	1,400 (l)
		Bal. 46,750			295 (n)
					6,750 (p)
				Bal. 42,674	

Other current assets

Bal. 15,000	

Property, plant and equipment, net

Bal. 180,000	

Accounts payable

(e) 275	37,000 Bal.
(h) 9,600	9,600 (b)
(l) 1,400	275 (c)
(n) 9,840	11,240 (j)
	37,000 Bal.

Long-term liabilities

	104,000 Bal.

Capital

	152,000 Bal.

Sales

	18,000 (a)
	7,500 (d)
	10,200 (i)
	12,750(p)
	48,450 Bal.

Sales discount

(f) 360	
(k) 124	
Bal. 484	

Sales returns & allowance

(g) 1,300	
(m) 600	
Bal. 1,900	

Cost of goods sold

(a) 8,400	450 (g)
(d) 1,650	
(i) 4,300	
(p) 6,750	
Bal. 20,650	

Requirement 2

a.	Accounts Receivable (Divas)		18,000	
	Sales			18,000
	Cost of Goods Sold		8,400	
	Inventory			8,400
b.	Inventory		9,600	
	Accounts Payable (Taylor)			9,600
c.	Inventory		275	
	Accounts Payable			275
d.	Accounts Receivable (Lahni)		7,500	
	Sales			7,500
	Cost of Goods Sold		1,650	
	Inventory			1,650
e.	Accounts Payable		275	
	Cash			275

154

f.	Cash		17,640	
	Sales Discount		360	
	Accounts Receivable (Divas)			18,000
g.	Sales Returns & Allowance		1,300	
	Accounts Receivable (Lahni)			1,300
	Inventory		450	
	Cost of Goods Sold			450
h.	Accounts Payable (Taylor)		9,600	
	Inventory			96
	Cash			9,504
i.	Accounts Receivable (Simmons, Inc.)		10,200	
	Sales			10,200
	Cost of Goods Sold		4,300	
	Inventory			4,300
j.	Inventory		11,240	
	Accounts Payable (Carter Co.)			11,240
k.	Cash		6,076	
	Sales Discount		124	
	Accounts Receivable (Lahni)			6,200
l.	Accounts Payable (Carter)		1,400	
	Inventory			1,400
m.	Sales Returns & Allowance		600	
	Accounts Receivable (Simmons, Inc.)			600
n.	Accounts Payable (Carter)		9,840	
	Inventory			295
	Cash			9,545
o.	Cash		9,600	
	Accounts Receivable (Simmons, Inc.)			9,600
p.	Accounts Receivable (Ferini Co.)		12,750	
	Sales			12,750
	Cost of Goods Sold		6,750	
	Inventory			6,750

Requirement 4

Cash	$33,992	
Accounts receivable	46,750	
Inventory	42,674	
Other current assets	15,000	
Property, plants, and equipment (net)	180,000	
Account payable		$ 37,000
Long-term liabilities		104,000
Capital		152,000
Sales		48,450
Sales discount	484	
Sales returns & allowance	1,900	
Cost of goods sold	20,650	
Totals	$341,450	$341,450

Requirement 5

Gross margin percentage = Gross margin ÷ Net sales
Net Sales = $48,450 - $484- $1,900 = $46,066

Gross margin = Net sales - Cost of goods sold
$\quad\quad\quad\quad = \$46,066 - \$20,650$
$\quad\quad\quad\quad = \$25,416$

Gross margin percentage = $25416 ÷ $46,066 = 55.2% (rounded)

Points to remember:

1. When a company uses a perpetual inventory system and records a sale, two transactions are required. One transaction records the sales (at the selling price) while the second transfers the cost of the inventory sold from the Inventory account to the Cost of Goods Sold account.
2. Because of #1 above, a sales return also requires two entries. However, a sales allowance (transaction (m) in the problem) only requires one entry because no merchandise is being returned.

Demonstration Problem #2 Solved and Explained

Requirement 1

DuMont Company
Income Statement
For the Year Ended December 31, 20X5

Sales revenue		$301,460	
Less: Sales discounts	$8,700		
Sales returns & allowances	2,610	11,310	
Net Sales			$290,150
Cost of goods sold			148,410
Gross profit			141,740
Operating expenses:			
Salary Expense		76,090	
Rent Expense		19,000	
Depreciation Expense		8,300	
Utilities Expense		7,125	
Supplies Expense		2,000	
Advertising Expense		18,040	130,555
Income from operations			11,185
Other expenses:			
Interest Expense			3,005
Net income			$ 8,180

DuMont Company
Statement of Owner's Equity
For the Year Ended December 31, 20X5

Eric DuMont, Capital 1/1/20X5	$38,100
Add: Net Income	8,180
	46,280
Less: Withdrawals	19,750
Eric DuMont, Capital 12/31/20X5	$26,530

DuMont Company
Balance Sheet
December 31, 20X5

ASSETS			LIABILITIES		
Current:			Current:		
Cash	$18,250		Accounts payable	$23,765	
Accounts receivable	20,100		Salary payable	990	
Inventory	42,000		Interest payable	255	
Supplies	850		Unearned sales revenue	560	
Prepaid advertising	5,200		Total current liabilities		$ 25,570
Total current assets		$ 86,400	Long term:		
			Notes payable		75,000
Plant:			Total liabilities		100,570
Equipment	92,500				
Less: Accumulated			OWNER'S EQUITY		
Depreciation	51,800	40,700	Eric DuMont, Capital		26,530
			Total liabilities and owner's		
Total assets		$127,100	equity		$127,100

Requirement 2 (adjusting and closing entries)

	ADJUSTING ENTRIES		Debit	Credit
(a)	Supplies Expense		2,000	
	Supplies			2,000
(b)	Advertising Expense		4,800	
	Prepaid Advertising			4,800
(c)	Unearned Sales Revenue		1,000	
	Sales Revenue			1,000
(d)	Depreciation Expense		8,300	
	Accumulated Depreciation			8,300
(e)	Salary Expense		990	
	Salary Payable			990
(f)	Interest Expense		255	
	Interest Payable			255
(g)	Cost of Goods Sold		2,000	
	Inventory			2,000

	CLOSING ENTRIES			
12/31	Sales Revenue		301,460	
	Income Summary			301,460
	Close revenue to Income Summary.			
12/31	Income Summary		293,280	
	Sales Discounts			8,700
	Sales Returns and Allowances			2,610
	Cost of Goods Sold			148,410
	Salary Expense			76,090
	Rent Expense			19,000
	Depreciation Expense			8,300
	Utilities Expense			7,125
	Supplies Expense			2,000
	Interest Expense			3,005
	Advertising Expense			18,040
	Close all expenses to Income Summary.			
12/31	Income Summary ($301,460 - $293,280)		8,180	
	Eric Dumont, Capital			8,180
	Close Income Summary to capital.			
12/31	Eric DuMont, Capital		19,750	
	Eric DuMont, Withdrawals			19,750
	Close withdrawals to capital.			

Requirement 3

DuMont Company
Post-closing Trial Balance
December 31, 20X5

Cash	$ 18,250	
Accounts receivable	20,100	
Inventory	42,000	
Supplies	850	
Prepaid advertising	5,200	
Equipment	92,500	
Accumulated depreciation		$ 51,800
Accounts payable		23,765
Salary payable		990
Interest payable		255
Unearned sales revenue		560
Note payable, long-term		75,000
Eric DuMont, capital		26,530
	$178,900	$178,900

Requirement 4 (Single-step Income Statement)

DuMont Company
Income Statement
For the Year Ended December 31, 20X5

Net Sales		$290,150
Less:		
Cost of goods sold	$148,410	
Operating expenses	130,555	
Interest expense	3,005	281,970
Net income		$ 8,180

Requirement 5 (Gross margin)

Gross Profit Percentage = Gross Margin ÷ Net Sales
Gross Profit Percentage = 141,740 ÷ 290,150 = 48.9% (Rounded)

Requirement 6 (Inventory turnover ratio)

Inventory turnover ratio	=	Cost of goods sold ÷ Average inventory
	=	$148,410 ÷ [($36,000 + $42,000) ÷ 2]
	=	$148,410 ÷ $39,000
	=	3.8 times (Rounded)

Chapter 6—Merchandise Inventory

CHAPTER OVERVIEW

In Chapter 5 you learned about merchandising businesses—ones that purchase goods and resell them. When acquired, merchandise inventory (the goods) is a current asset that becomes an expense once the goods are sold. In this chapter the principles of internal control are applied to this very important asset. Specifically you will learn the techniques businesses use to determine the cost (i.e., value) of their ending inventory. The learning objectives for this chapter are to

1. Compute perpetual inventory amounts under FIFO, LIFO, and average cost.
2. Record perpetual inventory transactions.
3. Compare the effects of FIFO, LIFO, and average cost.
4. Compute periodic inventory amounts under FIFO, LIFO, and average cost.
5. Apply the lower-of-cost-or-market rule to inventory.
6. Measure the effects of inventory errors.
7. Estimate ending inventory by the gross profit method.

CHAPTER REVIEW

Objective 1 - Compute perpetual inventory amounts under FIFO, LIFO, and average cost.

Inventories are initially recorded at historical cost. Inventory cost is what the business pays to acquire the inventory. Inventory cost includes the invoice cost of the goods, less purchase discounts, plus taxes, tariffs, transportation, and insurance while in transit. The **perpetual inventory** system is used to keep a *continuous* record of each inventory item. With the perpetual system, the inventory item record shows quantities received, quantities sold, and the balance remaining on hand.

GAAP allows four different costing methods:

1. **Specific-unit-cost method** (also called the **specific identification method**) is used by businesses whose inventory items are expensive or have "one-of-a-kind" characteristics—such as automobiles, jewelry, and real estate. Using specific unit cost to determine ending inventory is not practical for many businesses. When this is the case, the accountant has to make an assumption concerning the flow of costs through the inventory. Why is an assumption necessary? Because the actual (i.e., specific) unit cost of each item cannot be determined.

2. Under the **First-In, First-Out (FIFO)** method, the cost related to the first goods purchased is the cost assigned to the first goods sold. As a result, the costs assigned to the units remaining in the ending inventory will be the costs related to the most recent (last) purchases. Therefore, ending inventory reflects unit costs most recently incurred. See Exhibit 6-4 in your text.

3. Under the **Last-In, First-Out (LIFO)** method, the cost related to the last goods purchased is the cost assigned to the first goods sold. As a result, the cost of the units remaining in the ending inventory will be the costs associated with the earliest (oldest) purchases. See Exhibit 6-5 in your text.

4. The **average-cost method** is based on the average cost of all inventory items available for sale during the period. When a business uses the average-cost flow assumption, an average unit cost is assigned to all units sold to determine the cost of goods sold that will appear on the income statement; and, also assigned to all unsold units to get a value for ending inventory that will appear on the balance sheet. This average unit cost is weighted because the number of units at each price is different.

    The average-cost method requires the following computation:

$$\text{Average Unit Cost} = \frac{\text{Cost of Goods Available for Sale}}{\text{Number of Units Available for Sale}}$$

Cost of Goods Available for Sale = Beginning Inventory + Net Purchases
Ending Inventory = Number of Units Remaining × Average Unit Cost
Cost of Goods Sold = Cost of Goods Available for Sale - Ending Inventory

    See Exhibit 6-6 in your text.

Objective 2 - Record perpetual inventory transactions.

To record purchases of inventory on account under the perpetual inventory system:

Inventory	XX	
Accounts Payable		XX

To record sales of inventory on account under the perpetual inventory system:

Accounts Receivable	XX	
Sales Revenues		XX
Cost of Goods Sold	XX	
Inventory		XX

When the perpetual system is used, Cost of Goods Sold is debited directly and Inventory is credited directly to transfer the cost of the unit sold from Inventory into Cost of Goods Sold. As a result, the balance in the Inventory account should approximate the actual goods on hand at any time.

Objective 3 - Compare the effects of FIFO, LIFO, and average cost.

The effects of using the different inventory costing methods will vary depending on whether costs are increasing or decreasing. Let's take a look at both scenarios:

When inventory costs are increasing:

	FIFO	Average-Cost	LIFO
Ending Inventory	Highest	Middle	Lowest
Cost of Goods Sold	Lowest	Middle	Highest
Gross Profit	Highest	Middle	Lowest

When inventory costs are decreasing:

	FIFO	Average-Cost	LIFO
Ending Inventory	Lowest	Middle	Highest
Cost of Goods Sold	Highest	Middle	Lowest
Gross Profit	Lowest	Middle	Highest

Although FIFO is the most widely used costing method, using LIFO to account for inventories has tax advantages when inventory costs are increasing. This is because using LIFO increases Cost of Goods Sold, and thus decreases Gross Profit and Operating Income. If Operating Income is smaller, then total tax payments will be smaller. However, the major disadvantage to using LIFO is that the company will report lower net income. LIFO matches the most recent inventory costs (last into inventory, first out to Cost of Goods Sold) to revenue, but can result in unrealistic valuations of ending inventory on the balance sheet. The FIFO method presents an accurate ending inventory on the balance sheet but does not match the current cost of inventory to revenue, since the current cost of inventory remains in ending inventory.

LIFO vs. FIFO—some additional considerations:

a. Because LIFO results in the most recent costs reported on the income statement (as cost of goods sold), it presents the most current expense/revenue relationship.
b. Because FIFO uses the most recent costs as ending inventory, it presents the most current value for the asset on the balance sheet.
c. Companies using LIFO can manage the income statement by timing inventory purchases at the end of the accounting period.

As mentioned earlier, the perpetual system records each addition (purchase) and deletion (sale) of inventory. By so doing, an accurate up-to-date value for goods on hand is continually available.

Objective 4 - Compute periodic inventory amounts under FIFO, LIFO, and average cost.

With a periodic system, the value of goods on hand cannot be determined by examining the ledger because additions of inventory have been recorded in the Purchases account; thus the Inventory account has *not* been updated. Therefore, actual goods on hand can only be determined by taking a physical count.

Under a perpetual inventory system, cost of goods sold is a general ledger account. However, under a periodic inventory system, cost of goods sold is a calculation. The formula to calculate Cost of Goods Sold is as follows:

$$
\begin{array}{l}
\quad \text{Beginning Inventory} \\
+ \ \text{Purchases} \\
\hline
= \ \text{Cost of Goods Available for Sale} \\
- \ \text{Ending Inventory} \\
\hline
\quad \text{Cost of Goods Sold} \\
\hline
\end{array}
$$

When applying the inventory costing methods under a periodic inventory system, you will use the Cost of Goods formula from above. The beginning inventory and purchases are recorded in chronological order and cost of goods available for sale is calculated. Then, to determine the cost of goods sold, you must work through the cost layers according to the specific costing method used.

FIFO:

Recall that FIFO means the cost related to the first goods purchased is the cost assigned to the first goods sold; therefore, the ending inventory will be the costs related to the most recent (last) purchases. For example, if beginning inventory is 10 units at $4 each, 60 units were bought at $5 each, 80 more units were bought at $6 each, then the company would have 150 units available for sale with a cost of $820. If there are 50 units left, then those 50 units in ending inventory would be assigned the $6 unit cost from the "last" cost layer therefore, ending inventory would be $300 and Cost of Goods Sold would be $520.

LIFO

Recall that LIFO means the cost related to the last goods purchased is the cost assigned to the first goods sold; therefore, the ending inventory will be the costs related to the oldest (first) purchases. For example, if beginning inventory is, again, 10 units at $4 each, 60 units were bought at $5 each, 80 more units were bought at $6 each, then the company would have 150 units available for sale with a cost of $820. If there are 50 units left, then the 10 remaining units from the "first" cost layer would be assigned the $4 unit cost and 40 from the "second" cost layer would be assigned the $5 unit cost. Ending inventory would be $240 (10 × $4 + 40 × $5) and Cost of Goods Sold would be $580.

Average-Cost:

The average-cost method begins the same as FIFO and LIFO with the calculation of Cost of Goods Available for Sale. In our example, this cost is $820. To calculate the average-cost per unit, divide the cost of goods available for sale by the number of units available for sale or $820 ÷ 150 units = $5.47 (rounded). Therefore the ending inventory will be 50 units × $5.47 or $237.50, and cost of goods sold would be $546.50.

Periodic System

To record purchases of inventory on account under the periodic inventory system:

Purchases   XX
    Accounts Payable   XX

To record sales of inventory on account under the periodic inventory system:

Accounts Receivable   XX
    Sales Revenues   XX

Four accounting concepts or principles directly impact accounting for merchandise inventory:

1. The **consistency principle** states that a business should use the same accounting method from period to period.
2. The **disclosure principle** holds that a business's financial statements must report enough information for outsiders to make knowledgeable decisions about the company.
3. The **materiality concept** states that a company must perform strictly proper accounting only for items that are significant to the business's financial statements.
4. **Conservatism** means that a business should report items in the financial statements at amounts that lead to the most cautious immediate results.

Objective 5 - Apply the lower-of-cost-or-market rule to inventory.

The **lower-of-cost-or-market** rule (LCM) is a direct application of conservatism. The LCM rule dictates that an asset should be reported in the financial statements at whichever is lower—its historical cost or its market value (current replacement cost). The application of LCM applies the principle of conservatism by ensuring that assets are not overstated on the balance sheet and net income is not overstated on the income statement.

Conservatism also directs accountants to decrease the reported value of assets that appear overvalued. The LCM rule requires that assets be reported on the financial statements at the lower of (1) historical cost or (2) market value (replacement cost). Thus, if the inventory's market value decreases below its historical cost, it should be written down to its market value. If ending inventory is written down, then cost of goods sold absorbs the impact of the write-down.

Once the value of inventory is written down to market, it is not written back up even if the market value subsequently increases.

Study Tip: When LCM is applied, the effect will always reduce asset value (on the balance sheet) and net income (on the income statement).

Objective 6 - Measure the effects of inventory errors.

If the value of ending inventory is misstated, then cost of goods sold and net income will be misstated. Since the ending inventory for the current period becomes the beginning inventory for the next period, the errors will offset each other and total gross profit and net income for the two periods will be correct. Nevertheless, gross profit and net income for the individual periods will be misstated.

If ending inventory is overstated, then cost of goods sold is understated and net income is overstated. If ending inventory is understated, then cost of goods sold is overstated and net income is understated.

Study Exhibits 6-9 and 6-10 in your text carefully to familiarize yourself with the effect of inventory errors on 1) ending inventory, 2) cost of goods sold, and 3) net income.

Objective 7 - Estimate ending inventory by the gross profit method.

When a company wants an estimate of ending inventory, the **gross profit method** will calculate the amount quickly.

The gross profit method uses the gross profit rate to estimate cost of goods sold. Using the Cost of Goods Sold formula, cost of goods sold is then subtracted from cost of goods available for sale to arrive at estimated ending inventory.

$$\text{Gross Profit Rate} \quad = \quad \frac{\text{Gross Profit}}{\text{Net Sales Revenue}}$$

To use the gross profit method, it is necessary to rearrange ending inventory and cost of goods sold in the cost of goods sold equation as follows:

$$
\begin{array}{l}
 \text{Beginning Inventory} \\
+ \text{ Purchases} \\
\hline
= \text{ Cost of Goods Available for Sale} \\
- \text{ Cost of Goods Sold} \\
\hline
 \text{Ending Inventory} \\
\hline
\end{array}
$$

Cost of goods sold will equal net sales minus the estimated gross profit (sales × gross profit rate) as illustrated in Exhibit 6-11 in your text.

TEST YOURSELF

All the self-testing materials in this chapter focus on information and procedures that your instructor is likely to test in quizzes and examinations.

I. Matching   *Match each numbered term with its lettered definition.*

_____ 1. Gross profit method
_____ 2. Materiality concept
_____ 3. Consistency principle
_____ 4. Gross profit percentage
_____ 5. Perpetual inventory system
_____ 6. Specific unit cost method

_____ 7. First-In, First-Out (FIFO)
_____ 8. Lower-of-cost-or-market rule
_____ 9. Average-cost method
_____ 10. Last-In, First-Out (LIFO)
_____ 11. Periodic inventory system
_____ 12. Conservatism

A. Inventory costing method in which the first costs into inventory are the first costs out to cost of goods sold
B. Requires a company to perform strictly proper accounting only for items and transactions that are significant to the business's financial statements
C. A way to estimate inventory based on the cost of goods sold model: Beginning Inventory + Net Purchases = Cost of Goods Available for Sale. Cost of Goods Available for Sale - Cost of Goods Sold = Ending Inventory
D. Requires companies to use the same accounting methods and procedures from period to period
E. Requires that inventory be reported in the financial statements at the lower of its historical cost or its current replacement cost
F. An inventory system in which the business does not keep a continuous record of the inventory on hand
G. An inventory system in which the business keeps a continuous record for each inventory item to show the inventory on hand at all times
H. Inventory costing method based on the average cost of inventory during the period
I. Inventory costing method in which the last costs into inventory are the first costs out to cost of goods sold
J. Inventory cost method based on the cost of particular units of inventory
K. Gross Profit divided by Net Sales Revenue
L. Reporting items in the financial statements at amounts that lead to the most cautious immediate financial results

II. Multiple Choice   *Circle the best answer.*

1. When using a _____ inventory system, Cost of Goods Sold is a general ledger account. When using a _____ inventory system, Cost of Goods Sold must be calculated.

   A. Periodic; perpetual
   B. Perpetual, periodic.
   C. LIFO; periodic
   D. Periodic, FIFO

2. An automobile dealer will value inventory using which method?

   A. Average-cost   C. LIFO
   B. FIFO   D. Specific unit cost

3. When prices are increasing, which inventory method will produce the highest ending inventory cost?

   A. Average-cost   C. LIFO
   B. FIFO   D. Cannot be determined

4. When prices are decreasing, which inventory method will produce the lowest cost of goods sold?

   A. Average-cost   C. LIFO
   B. FIFO   D. Cannot be determined

5. Which inventory method reports ending inventory costs on the balance sheet at a value that reflects the most current cost?

   A. Average-cost   C. LIFO
   B. FIFO   D. Cannot be determined

6. Which of the followings methods can be used to estimate ending inventory?

   A. Average-cost   C. LIFO
   B. FIFO   D. Gross profit

7. When prices are increasing, which inventory method will maximize net income?

   A. Average-cost   C. LIFO
   B. FIFO   D. Gross profit

8. Cost of Goods Sold is debited directly using:

   A. only the perpetual inventory system.   C. only the serial inventory system.
   B. only the periodic inventory system.   D. both the periodic and perpetual inventory
                                                    systems.

9. To which of the following does the lower-of-cost-or-market rule apply?

    A. Disclosure   C. Conservatism
    B. Materiality   D. Consistency

10. To calculate the average unit cost:

    A. divide goods available for sale by ending inventory units.
    B. divide goods available for sale by total units available for sale.
    C. divide cost of goods sold by number of units sold.
    D. divide cost of goods sold by number of units available for sale.

III. Completion   *Complete each of the following.*

1. The largest current asset for most retailers is _____.
2. The largest single expense for most merchandisers is _____.
3. The inventory system that maintains continuous records of items in the inventory is called _____.
4. Which inventory system(s) require(s) a physical count of inventory? _____.
5. To calculate the gross profit percentage, _____ is divided by _____.
6. The _____ method is used to estimate ending inventory.
7. _____ uses the most recent costs as ending inventory; therefore, it presents the most current value for the asset on the balance sheet.
8. During periods of increasing prices, _____ results in the highest cost of goods sold.
9. The _____ method would not be appropriate for a retailer selling a large number of units each with low prices.
10. During periods of falling prices, _____ results in the highest value for ending inventory.

IV. Daily Exercises

1. Through an error, the ending inventory was overstated by $3,000. Indicate the effect of this error on

    a. Cost of goods sold

    b. Gross profit

    c. Net income

    d. Total current assets

2. Assume the per unit cost of ending inventory is $11, and a current replacement cost per unit of $10. If the lower-of-cost-or-market rule is applied, indicate how the income statement and balance sheet will be affected.

3. A company purchases the following inventory and uses a periodic inventory system:

   200 units at $6.00 each
   400 units at $6.50 each
   400 units at $6.60 each
   300 units at $6.70 each

   If 900 units are sold during the period, at what amount should ending inventory be reported if the FIFO cost method is used?

4. Refer to the information in Daily Exercise #3 and use the LIFO cost method.

5. Refer to the information in Daily Exercise #3 and use the average-cost method.

6. Given your answers to #3, #4, and #5 above, which assumption results in the lowest net income for the period? Which method results in the most current value of the inventory on the balance sheet?

V. Exercises

1. The following information is given for Teresa's Tile Co. for the month of August:

	Lbs. of tiles	Unit Cost
8/1 Inventory	600	$1.00
8/7 Purchase	800	1.10
8/13 Purchase	1,400	1.20
8/22 Purchase	1,400	1.25
8/29 Purchase	400	1.15

During the month, 3,800 pounds of tiles were sold. Teresa's Tile uses a periodic inventory system

A. How many tiles should be in the inventory at the end of August?

B. Using the average-cost method, what are the cost of ending inventory and cost of goods sold?

C. Using the FIFO method, what are the cost of ending inventory and cost of goods sold?

D. Using the LIFO method, what are the cost of ending inventory and cost of goods sold?

2. A fire destroyed the Brunnel Co.'s inventory. The company's records show net sales of $360,000, beginning inventory of $80,000, net purchase of $300,000, and a gross profit rate of 40%. What is the estimated value of ending inventory?

3. Assume the following:

	X1	X2	X3
Beginning Inventory	$ 8,000	$15,000	$12,000
Net Purchases	45,000	50,000	55,000
Goods Available for Sale	53,000	65,000	67,000
Ending Inventory	15,000	12,000	8,000
Cost of Goods Sold	38,000	53,000	59,000

You discover the following errors:
   a. Ending inventory X1 was overstated by $6,000
   b. Ending inventory X2 was understated by $4,000

Considering these errors, recalculate cost of goods sold for all three years.

4. The following information is available for Gearty Co. for 20X9:

Beginning Inventory	$ 2,500
Ending Inventory	1,850
Operating Expenses	1,650
Cost of Goods Sold	15,975
Sales Discounts	255
Sales	21,500
Sales Returns and Allowances	165

Required:

1. What is net sales for 20X9?

2. What is gross profit for 20X9?

3. What is net income for 20X9?

4. What is the gross profit rate?

5. The following information is given for Diane's Design 20X8:

Beginning Inventory	$ 12,250
Gross Profit	7,500
Operating Expenses	3,100
Purchase Returns & Allowance	600
Purchase Discounts	550
Purchases	39,250
Sales Discounts	500
Sales	51,500
Sales Returns & Allowances	1,700

Required

1. Compute net sales.

2. Compute net purchases.

3. Compute cost of goods sold.

4. Compute ending inventory.

5. Compute net income.

6. What is the gross profit rate?

VI. Beyond the Numbers

Re-examine the facts presented in Exercise #1. A physical count was taken, and ending inventory was determined to be 700 pounds. In re-checking the sales, you verify that 3,800 pounds were sold. How would you explain the 100 pounds difference (800 pounds you expected to be on hand less the actual count of 700 pounds), and how would you "account" for it?

_____
_____
_____
_____
_____

VII. Demonstration Problems

Demonstration Problem #1

Universal's Beauty Supply has the following records relating to its August 20X9 inventory:

Date	Item	Quantity (units)	Unit Cost	Sale price
8/1	Beginning inventory	50	7	--
8/3	Purchase	80	8	--
8/9	Sale	90	--	14
8/11	Purchase	100	9	--
8/18	Sale	60	--	15
8/22	Purchase	40	10	--
8/28	Sale	60	--	18

Company accounting records indicate that the related operating expenses for the month of August was $1,250. All purchases of inventory and sales of inventory are on account.

Required:
1. Assume that Universal uses a periodic inventory system and a FIFO cost flow assumption, record the August 3 through August 28 transactions (omit explanations).
2. Assume Universal uses a perpetual inventory system and a FIFO cost flow assumption, record the August 3 through August 28 transactions (omit explanations).

Requirement 1 (Periodic Inventory System)

Date	Accounts and Explanation	PR	Debit	Credit

Requirement 2 (Perpetual Inventory System)

Date	Accounts and Explanation	PR	Debit	Credit

Demonstration Problem #2

Requirement 1

Refer to the information in Demonstration Problem #1. Assuming Universal uses a periodic system, complete the income statement columns below. (Round income statement figures to whole dollar amounts.)

Universal Beauty Supply

Income Statement

Month Ended August 31, 20X9

	LIFO	FIFO	Average Cost
Sales revenue			
Cost of goods sold:			
Beginning inventory			
Purchases			
Cost of goods available for sale			
Ending inventory			
Cost of goods sold			
Gross profit			
Operating expenses			
Operating income			

Requirement 2

Refer to Demonstration Problem #1, and assume the same facts in the problem *except* the company uses the perpetual inventory system. Complete the income statement below, through operating income. (Round income statement figures to whole dollar amounts.)

Universal Beauty Supply

Income Statement

Month Ended August 31, 20X9

	LIFO	FIFO	Average Cost
Sales revenue			
Cost of goods sold			
Gross profit			
Operating expenses			
Operating income			

(Helpful hint: Before starting, think carefully about which income statement figures will change as a result of using the perpetual inventory system rather than the periodic inventory system. Those amounts that do not change can simply be transferred from your solution to Requirement #1.)

SOLUTIONS

I. Matching

1. C	5. G	9. H
2. B	6. J	10. I
3. D	7. A	11. F
4. K	8. E	12. L

II. Multiple Choice

1. B When using a perpetual inventory system, Cost of Goods Sold is a general ledger account. When using a periodic inventory system, Cost of Goods Sold must be calculated using the following formula:

$$\begin{array}{ll} & \text{Beginning Inventory} \\ + & \text{Purchases} \\ \hline = & \text{Cost of Goods Available for Sale} \\ - & \text{Ending Inventory} \\ \hline & \text{Cost of Goods Sold} \end{array}$$

2. D Specific unit cost is appropriate for inventory items that may be identified individually like automobiles, jewels, and real estate.

3. B To obtain the highest ending inventory when prices are increasing it is necessary to have the most recent inventory costs on the balance sheet. This is accomplished when the FIFO method is used during a period of increasing prices.

4. C To obtain the lowest cost of goods sold when prices are decreasing it is necessary to have the newest inventory costs on the income statement. This is accomplished when the LIFO method is used during a period of decreasing prices.

5. B LIFO assigns the most recent inventory costs to the income statement and older inventory cost to the balance sheet. FIFO, on the other hand, assigns the most recent inventory costs to the balance sheet and older inventory costs to the income statement.

6. D Of the items listed, only gross profit is an estimation technique. FIFO, LIFO, and average-cost are techniques for establishing actual ending inventory amounts, not estimates.

7. B In a period of increasing prices, FIFO will maximize net income because this method assigns the "oldest", lower costs to cost of goods sold, which results in a higher net income.

8. A Under the periodic inventory system, there is no Cost of Goods Sold general ledger account. Rather, cost of goods sold is a calculated amount. Accordingly, no entries can be made to it. Under the perpetual inventory system Cost of Goods Sold is a general ledger account and inventory purchases are debited directly to it.

9. C LCM is an extension of the application of conservatism because it reduces the ending inventory value and therefore net income.

10. B The unit cost for the average-cost method is calculated by dividing the cost of goods available for sale (beginning inventory + purchases) by the total number of units available for sale.

III. Completion

1. Merchandise Inventory
2. Cost of Goods Sold
3. perpetual
4. Both systems require a physical count. In a perpetual inventory system this verifies that the inventory listed in the accounting records actually exists.
5. gross profit, net sales
6. gross profit method
7. FIFO (The oldest and therefore lower prices are sent to cost of goods sold, leaving the most current, higher prices to value ending inventory.)
8. LIFO (The oldest and therefore lower prices are used to value ending inventory.)
9. specific unit cost
10. LIFO (The oldest and therefore higher prices are used to value ending inventory.)

IV. Daily Exercises

1.
    a. If ending inventory is overstated, the cost of goods sold will be understated.
    b. If cost of goods sold is understated, the gross profit will be overstated.
    c. If the gross profit is overstated, then net income will be overstated.
    d. If ending inventory is overstated, then total current assets will also be overstated.

Study Tip: The direction of the error in ending inventory value will also be the direction of the error in gross profit and net income.

---

2. When the $11 value is replaced with $10, the ending inventory value will decrease; therefore, cost of goods sold will increase and the gross profit and net income will decrease. The balance sheet will be affected because total assets will also decrease.

3. If 900 units were sold, there are 400 units on hand. Applying FIFO, the 400 units would be valued as followed:

    300 units at $6.70 each = $2,010
    100 units at $6.60 each = $660
    Total = $2,670

4. Applying LIFO, the 400 units would be valued as follows:

    200 units at $6.00 each = $1,200
    200 units at $6.50 each = $1,300
    Total = $2,500

5. Applying the average-cost method, the 400 units would be valued as follows:

Cost of goods available for sale ÷ Total number of units available for sale
$8,450 ÷ 1,300 units = $6.50 per unit × 400 units = $2,600

6. The lowest net income will result if LIFO is used. Remember the Study Tip mentioned above—the lower the ending inventory, the lower the net income. The most current value of ending inventory is obtained with FIFO.

V. Exercises

1. A.

		Pounds
	Beginning inventory	600
+	Purchases*	4,000
	Pounds available for sale	4,600
-	Pounds sold	3,800
=	Ending inventory	800

*Sum of purchases on 8/7 (800), 8/13 (1,400), 8/22 (1,400), and 8/29 (400).

B.

	Pounds		Unit Cost	Total
8/1	600	@	$1.00	$ 600
8/7	800	@	1.10	880
8/13	1,400	@	1.20	1,680
8/22	1,400	@	1.25	1,750
8/29	400	@	1.15	460
Goods available	4,600			$5,370

Average unit cost = 5,370 ÷ 4,600 = $1.167 (rounded)
Ending inventory = 800 pounds × $1.167 = $934
Cost of goods sold = 3,800 pounds × $1.167 = $4,435

C. Ending inventory will be the last 800 pounds purchased.

8/29	400 pounds @ $1.15	$460
8/22	400 pounds @ $1.25	500
Ending inventory		$960

Cost of goods available for sale	$5,370
Less Ending inventory	(960)
Cost of goods sold	$4,410

180

D. Ending inventory will be the 800 pounds that have been in inventory the longest.

Beginning inventory	600 pounds @ $1.00	$600
8/7	200 pounds @ $1.10	220
Ending inventory		$820

Cost of goods available for sale	$5,370
Less Ending inventory	(820)
Cost of goods sold	$4,550

2.

	Beginning inventory	$ 80,000
+	Purchases	300,000
	Cost of goods available for sale	380,000
-	Cost of goods sold [$360,000 × (1-.40)]	216,000
=	Ending inventory	$164,000

3. For Xl, ending inventory decreases to $9,000, so cost of goods sold will increase to $44,000

For X2, beginning inventory decreases to $9,000, and ending inventory increases to $16,000, so:

	Beginning inventory	$ 9,000
+	Net purchases	50,000
	Goods available for sale	59,000
-	Ending inventory	16,000
=	Cost of goods sold	$43,000

For X3, beginning inventory increases to $16,000, so cost of goods sold increases to $63,000

4.

Requirement 1

Sales - Sales Returns & Allowances - Sales Discount = Net Sales
$21,500 - $165 - $255 = $21,080

Requirement 2

Net Sales - Cost of Goods Sold = Gross Profit
$21,080 - $15,975 = $5,105

Requirement 3

Gross Profit - Operating Expenses = Net Income
$5,105 - $1,650 = $3,455

Requirement 4

Gross Profit ÷ Net Sales
$5,105 ÷ $21,080 = 24.2%

5.
Requirement 1

Sales - Sales Discounts - Sales Returns & Allowances = Net Sales
$51,500 - $500 - $1,700 = $49,300

Requirement 2

Purchases - Purchase Discounts - Purchase Returns & Allowances = Net Purchases
$39,250 - $550 - $600 = $38,100

Requirement 3

Net Sales - Cost of Goods Sold = Gross Profit
Cost of Goods Sold = $49,300 - $7,500 = $41,800

Requirement 4

Beginning Inventory + Net Purchase - Ending Inventory = Cost of Goods Sold
Therefore, Ending Inventory = Beginning Inventory + Net Purchase - Cost of Goods Sold
Ending Inventory = $12,250 + $38,100 - $41,800 = $8,550

Requirement 5

Gross Profit - Operating Expenses = Net Income
$7,500 - $3,100 = $4,400

Requirement 6

Gross Profit Rate = Gross profit ÷ Net sales
Gross Profit Rate = $7,500 ÷ $49,300 = 15.2%

VI. Beyond the Numbers

The 100-pound difference is called inventory shrinkage. Since the figure that appears on the balance sheet for ending inventory must represent the actual amount on hand (700 pounds), the shrinkage is accounted for by a larger cost of goods sold figure on the income statement. Possible explanations for the shrinkage are errors in the physical count, theft, and/or errors in recording purchases during the period. Internal control requires that the cause of the difference be investigated and appropriate corrective procedures taken.

VII. Demonstration Problems

Demonstration Problem #1 Solved and Explained

Requirement 1 (Periodic Inventory System)

Date	Accounts and Explanation	PR	Debit	Credit
8/3	Purchases		640	
	Account Payable			640
8/9	Account Receivable		1,260	
	Sales			1,260
8/11	Purchases		900	
	Account Payable			900
8/18	Account Receivable		900	
	Sales			900
8/22	Purchases		400	
	Account Payable			400
8/28	Account Receivable		1,080	
	Sales			1,080

These six journal entries are pretty straightforward. With a periodic system, the Purchases account is debited as merchandise for resale is acquired, but is not affected when goods are sold.

Study Tip: In a periodic system, the cost flow assumption (in this case FIFO) is irrelevant as far as these transactions are concerned. It becomes important only when you need to determine the value of ending inventory.

Requirement 2 (Perpetual Inventory System)

Date	Accounts and Explanation	PR	Debit	Credit
8/3	Inventory		640	
	Account Payable			640
8/9	Account Receivable		1,260	
	Sales			1,260
	Cost of Goods Sold		670	
	Inventory			670
	(50 × $7 + 40 × $8)			
8/11	Inventory		900	
	Account Payable			900
8/18	Account Receivable		900	
	Sales			900
	Cost of Goods Sold		500	
	Inventory			500
	(40 × $8 + 20 × $9)			
8/22	Inventory		400	
	Account Payable			400
8/28	Account Receivable		1,080	
	Sales			1,080
	Cost of Goods Sold		540	
	Inventory			540
	(60 × $9)			

In a perpetual system, goods for resale are debited to the Inventory account. When a sale occurs, the entry is identical to those recorded in a periodic system. However, a second entry is required for each sale. This entry transfers the cost of the sale from the Inventory account to a Cost of Goods Sold account. The amount of the entry is determined by the cost flow assumption used. In this problem, FIFO is assumed. Therefore, the cost of each sale is assigned using the oldest costs in the inventory. For instance, the 8/9 sale was 90 units. How much did these units cost the business? Assuming FIFO, 50 of the units cost $7 each (these are the units from the beginning inventory, i.e., the first units (oldest) in the inventory), and the next 40 units (90 - 50) cost $8 each (the purchase on 8/3). This same analysis applies to the 8/18 and 8/28 sales. The details are provided following each entry.

Demonstration Problem #2

Requirement 1

Universal Beauty Supply
Income Statement
Month Ended August 31, 20X9

	LIFO		FIFO		Average-Cost	
Sales revenue		$3,240		$3,240		$3,240
Cost of goods sold:						
Beginning inventory	350		350		350	
Net purchases	1,940		1,940		1,940	
Cost of goods available for sale	2,290		2,290		2,290	
Ending inventory	430		580		509	
Cost of goods sold		1,860		1,710		1,781
Gross profit		1,380		1,530		1,459
Operating expenses		1,250		1,250		1,250
Operating income		$ 130		$ 280		$ 209

Computations:

Sales Revenue:

Sale Date	Quantity	Price	Total
8/9	90	$14	$1,260
8/18	60	15	900
8/28	60	18	1,080
	210		$3,240

Sales revenue is unaffected by the firm's method of accounting for inventory costs. Quantity × Price = Total.

Beginning inventory: 8/1 quantity (50 units) × unit cost ($7) = $350. Total cost of purchases are $1,940.

Purchase Date	Quantity	Price	Total
8/3	80	$8	$ 640
8/11	100	9	900
8/22	40	10	400
	220		$1,940

Computation for beginning inventory, purchases, and goods available for sale are identical under the three methods.

	Beginning inventory in units	50
+	Total August purchases in units	220
	Units available for sale	270
-	Units sold	210

185

| | = | Ending inventory in units | 60 |

Ending Inventory
Valued at LIFO:

Purchase Date	Quantity	Price	Total
Beginning inventory	50	$7	$350
8/3	10	8	80
	60		$430

LIFO attains the best matching of current expense with current revenue. The most recently acquired costs (the last items in) are deemed sold first (the first ones out). Logically, ending inventory should consist of the oldest layers of cost.

Ending Inventory
Valued at FIFO:

Purchase Date	Quantity	Price	Total
8/22	40	$10	$400
8/11	20	9	180
	60		$580

FIFO reports the ending inventory at its most recent cost. The oldest costs are expensed as cost of goods sold. Note that net income under FIFO is larger than that reported under LIFO. In a period of rising prices, LIFO will generally produce a lower net income. The potential tax savings achieved under a LIFO valuation has made it an increasingly popular valuation method in recent years.

Ending Inventory
Valued at average-cost:

Purchase Date	Quantity	Price	Total
Beginning inventory	50	$7	$ 350
Purchases in August	220	Various	1,940
	270		$2,290

$2,290 inventory cost / 270 units = $8.48 per unit (rounded)

60 ending inventory units × $8.48 average cost per unit = $508.80 (rounded to $509)

The average-cost method reports ending inventory and produces operating income that falls between the results of FIFO and LIFO. It is not used as a valuation method by as many firms as LIFO and FIFO.

Requirement 2

Universal Beauty Supply
Income Statement
Month Ended August 31, 20X9

	LIFO	FIFO	Average Cost
Sales revenue	$3,240	$3,240	$3,240
Cost of goods sold	1,830	1,710	1,746
Gross profit	1,410	1,530	1,494
Operating expenses	1,250	1,250	1,250
Operating income	$ 160	$ 280	$ 244

Computations:

Sales—same as Demonstration Problem #1

Cost of Goods Sold:
Remember, in a perpetual system cost of goods sold is an account balance, not a calculation. Therefore, to arrive at the correct amount, you have to trace through each purchase and sale to determine which cost figures have been transferred from Inventory to Cost of Goods Sold, as follows:

LIFO:

Date	Quantity	Price		Total
8/9 Sale	80	$8	$640	
	10	7	70	
				$ 710
8/18 Sale	60	9		540
8/28 Sale	40	10	400	
	20	9	180	
				580
		Cost of goods sold, LIFO		$1,830
	40	7	280	
	20	9	180	
		Ending inventory, LIFO		$ 460*

*Note that this amount is not the same as LIFO periodic.

FIFO:

Date	Quantity	Price		Total
8/9 Sale	50	$ 7	$350	
	40	8	320	
				670
8/18 Sale	40	8	320	
	20	9	180	
				500
8/28 Sale	60	9		540
		Cost of goods sold, FIFO		$1,710
	40	10	400	
	20	9	180	
		Ending inventory, FIFO		$580**

**Note that this is the same as FIFO periodic.

Average-cost:
This is even more complicated because it requires you to re-calculate a new average each time there is an addition to inventory (for this reason it is referred to as a moving average-cost system).

8/9   Sale
50 units at $7 per unit = $350
80 units at $8 per unit = 640
130                      $990
Average unit cost   = $990 = $7.615 per unit, therefore
130
                        90 units × $7.615 = $ 685.35

8/18   Sale
40 units at $7.615 per unit = $304.60 (from above)
100 units at $9 per unit   = 900.00
140                           $1,204.60
Average unit cost   = $1,204.60 = $8.604 per unit, therefore
140
                        60 units × $8.604 = $ 516.24

8/28   Sale
80 units at $8.604 per unit = $688.32 (from above)
40 units at $10 per unit   = 400.00
120                           $1,088.32

Average unit cost   = $1,088.32 = $9.069 per unit, therefore
120
                        60 units × $9.069 = $ 544.14

Cost of goods sold, average-cost $1,745.73

Ending inventory = 60 units × $9.069 = $544.14***

***Note that this amount is not the same as average-cost periodic.

Chapter 7—Accounting Information Systems

CHAPTER OVERVIEW

Chapters 1 through 6 covered the accounting cycle for both service businesses (Chapters 1-4) and merchandising businesses (Chapter 5-6). Throughout those chapters frequent reference was made to the use of computers at various steps in the accounting cycle. We now turn our attention to an accounting information system and a more in-depth discussion of computers in accounting. In addition, we introduce special journals and subsidiary ledgers. The learning objectives for this chapter are to

1. Describe an effective accounting information system.
2. Understand both computerized and manual accounting systems.
3. Understand how spreadsheets are used in accounting.
4. Use the sales journal, the cash receipts journal, and the accounts receivable ledger.
5. Use the purchases journal, the cash payments journal, and the accounts payable ledger.

CHAPTER REVIEW

Objective 1 - Describe an effective accounting information system.

An **accounting information system** is the combination of people, procedures, and business records that a company maintains to manage financial data. Because each business is unique, businesses develop an accounting information system to meet their individual needs.

An effective information system provides:

- **Internal controls** are methods and procedures that a business uses to safeguard assets, authorize transactions, and ensure accuracy of the accounting records.
- **Compatibility** means that the information system works smoothly with the business's other operations.
- **Flexibility** refers to how easily the system accommodates changes in the organization.
- **Good cost/benefit relationship** refers to a system that provides the most benefit for the least cost.

Computers process data with accuracy and speed. There are three basic components of a computerized accounting system:

- **Hardware** is the electronic equipment that makes up the system—the computers, disk drives, monitors, printers, and so on. Modern systems can share information through the use of networks.
- **Software** is the set of instructions that directs the computer to perform specific tasks. Some software packages operate independently from other activities while others, particularly in larger companies, are integrated into the company's overall database.
- **Personnel** are key to the success of all information systems, along with security measures to insure the confidentiality of the information contained within the system.

Objective 2 - Understand both computerized and manual accounting systems.

There are three stages of **information processing:**

- **Inputs** represent the business source documents—the things that represent transactions and therefore need to be entered into the system.
- **Processing** means getting the information from the source document into the accounting system. Manually, this means journalizing and posting. A computerized system does the same thing but considerably faster and much less formally.
- **Outputs** are the reports used for decision-making, including the financial statements.

Both systems require the accountant to classify transactions. In a computerized system, you select the proper processing environment from a **menu**, which is a list of options organized by function. Once an option has been selected, transactions are recorded. Then the transactions are posted in one of two ways:

- **On-line processing** posts information continuously.
- **Batch processing** "parks" the data in the computer to await posting.

Various accounting reports, the outputs, are displayed or printed automatically in a computerized system by simply selecting the appropriate options from a menu.

Objective 3 - Understand how spreadsheets are used in accounting.

Spreadsheets are computer programs that link data by means of formulas and functions. A spreadsheet looks like the manual work sheet introduced in Chapter 4. The **columns** are identified with letters while the **rows** are identified with numbers. The intersection of any particular row and column is called a cell. The **cell** is the place where information is stored. The information in the cell can be words, numbers or a formula. (See Exhibit 7-5 for an example of a simple spreadsheet.) The use of formulas allow for amounts to be changed with results changing automatically.

Objective 4 - Use the sales journal, the cash receipts journal, and the accounts receivable ledger.

Special journals are used by businesses to increase the efficiency of the accounting system. This is accomplished when specific types of transactions (for instance, those involving debits to the Cash account) are removed from the general journal and grouped together in a special journal (for instance, a Cash Receipts Journal) that has been designed for only that type of transaction. Four commonly used special journals are the **Sales Journal**, the **Cash Receipts Journal**, the **Purchases Journal** and the **Cash Disbursements Journal**. As you study the different special journals, make sure you focus on when it is appropriate to use each type of journal. This understanding will help you identify certain transactions, and help you learn which journal to use. Keep in mind that the general journal is not a special journal because it can accommodate any type of transactions.

The **sales journal** is used to record all sales on account, also called credit sales. If the company uses a perpetual inventory system the sales journal will also be used to record the cost of goods sold. As credit sales are recorded, the business keeps track of each customer's account balance by posting the transaction to the customer's individual account that is contained in the **accounts receivable subsidiary ledger**. It is important to understand that the subsidiary ledger and the general ledger are not the same record. When special journals are used, the subsidiary ledger is updated as the transactions occur. This is important to maintain up-to-date account balances for each customer. But the general ledger is not updated until the accountant posts from the special journal to the general ledger accounts. Credit sales from the sales journal are posted to both the Sales and Accounts Receivable accounts in the General Ledger. Because Accounts Receivable has a subsidiary ledger attached to it, it is called a **control account**. Therefore, the accounts receivable subsidiary ledger will contain all of the current balances for each customer while the control account, Accounts Receivable, appears in the general ledger with a balance that represents the total amount owed by all customers in the accounts receivable subsidiary ledger. Study Exhibit 7-8 in your text to understand the posting process when a sales journal is used.

A **cash receipts journal** is the second type of special journal. It contains all transactions that include a debit to cash, regardless of the account(s) for which the corresponding credit(s) are recorded. In other words, all receipts of cash are now recorded together, thus the name the "cash receipts" journal. The posting process for the cash receipts journal is similar to that of the sales journal. Receipts from customers are posted to their individual accounts in the accounts receivable subsidiary ledger daily, thereby maintaining current account balances. Posting to the general ledger accounts occur periodically, thereby maintaining the debit/credit equality of the general ledger and agreement between the control account and the accounts receivable subsidiary ledger. Review Exhibit 7-9 for an example of the cash receipts journal and the process of posting to the ledgers.

Objective 5 - Use the purchases journal, the cash payments journal, and the accounts payable ledger.

The **purchases journal** is the third type of special journal. It is used to record all credit purchases. In other words, anytime the business acquires anything "on account" or "on credit", that transaction will be recorded in the purchases journal. Because businesses deal with a large number of vendors it is important to maintain current accounts payable balances for each. A current balance for each vendor is accomplished by setting up and maintaining an **accounts payable subsidiary ledger**. The posting procedure for it is identical to the one discussed above for customers. Study Exhibit 7-10 for an example of the purchases journal and the process of posting to the ledgers.

The fourth type of special journal is the **cash payments journal**. This journal contains all transactions that include a credit to the cash account (i.e., a cash payment). The posting procedures for the cash payments journal are identical to the posting procedure for the cash receipts journal. Study Exhibit 7-11 for an example of the cash payments journal and the process of posting to the ledgers.

As mentioned before, the general journal is not a special journal. Additionally, the use of special journals does not eliminate the necessity for a general journal. For example, adjusting and closing entries will still have to be recorded in the general journal. In addition, some unusual transactions that occur during the accounting period will have to be recorded in the general journal because they do not "fit" into one of the special journal formats.

For example, when a seller allows a reduction in a customer's account, it notifies the buyer of the reduction by completing a form called a **credit memorandum**, or simply a **credit memo**. The entry to record a credit memo is as follows:

Sales Returns and Allowances	XXX	
Accounts Receivable-ABD Co.		XXX

> Helpful Hint: This is called a credit memo because it is issued by the seller and it "credits" the customer's account receivable account for the amount of the return or allowance.

By a process of elimination, you can determine that this entry does not fit into one of the special journals. You can ask yourself the following questions:

1. *Does this entry reflect a credit sale?* No, therefore, you cannot use the sales journal.
2. *Does this entry represent a cash receipt?* No, therefore, you cannot use the cash receipts journal.
3. *Does this entry represent a purchase on account?* No, therefore, you cannot use the purchases journal.
4. *Does this entry represent a cash payment?* No, therefore, you cannot use the cash payments journal.

So, if the entry cannot be recorded in one of the special journals, then you must revert back to the general journal.

Now, what if the customer had been given a cash refund? Then going through the four questions above, you would have determined that cash had been paid out to the customer, therefore, this transaction would be recorded in the cash payments journal.

Another example of an entry that does not "fit" into a special journal is when a merchandiser returns inventory to the supplier. When a buyer is returning merchandise to the seller, the buyer notifies the seller of the return by issuing a **debit memorandum**, also called a **debit memo**. The buyer would record the debit memo as follows:

Accounts Payable-XYZ Co.	XXX	
Inventory (or Purchase Returns and Allowances)		XXX

> Helpful Hint: This is called a debit memo because it is issued by the buyer and it "debits" the buyer's accounts payable account for the amount of the return or allowance.

Again, if you go through the four questions above, you will determine that this entry does not fit any one of the special journals; therefore, it must be entered into the general journal.

TEST YOURSELF

All the self-testing materials in this chapter focus on information and procedures that your instructor is likely to test in quizzes and examinations.

I. Matching   *Match each numbered term with its lettered definition.*

_____ 1. Subsidiary ledger
_____ 2. Cash payments journal   _____ 10. Formula
_____ 3. Control account   _____ 11. Hardware
_____ 4. Spreadsheet   _____ 12. Menu
_____ 5. Cash receipts journal   _____ 13. Purchases journal
_____ 6. Sales journal   _____ 14. Software
_____ 7. Accounting information system _____ 15. General journal
_____ 8. Credit memo   _____ 16. General ledger
_____ 9. Cell   _____ 17. Debit memo

A. An account whose balance equals the sum of the balances in a group of related accounts in a subsidiary ledger
B. Book of accounts that provides supporting details on individual balances, the total of which appears in a general ledger account
C. A computer program which organizes information into columns and rows
D. The intersection of a particular column and row on a spreadsheet
E. A document issued by a seller for a reduction in a customer's account
F. A means of expressing relationships among various cells in a spreadsheet
G. Equipment that makes up a computer system
H. Set of programs, or instructions, that cause the computer to perform the work desired
I. A list of options in a computer program
J. Special journal used to account for all purchases of inventory, supplies, and other assets on account
K. Special journal used to account for cash disbursements made by check
L. Special journal used to account for cash collections
M. Special journal used to account for credit sales
N. The combination of personnel, records, and procedures that a business uses to meet its need for financial data
O. The journal used to report all transactions that do not fit one of the special journals
P. A document issued by a business when it returns merchandise to the seller
Q. Ledger of accounts that are reported in the financial statements

II. Multiple Choice   *Circle the best answer.*

1. The four main features of an effective accounting information system are:

   A. control, organize data, compatibility, and good cost/benefit relationship.
   B. flexibility, compatibility, collect data, and control.
   C. process data, organize data, collect data, and good cost/benefit relationship.
   D. control, flexibility, compatibility, good cost/benefit relationship.

2. Internal controls are designed to:

   A. only protect assets.
   B. only achieve maximum revenue.
   C. only ensure accurate accounting records.
   D. protect assets and ensure accurate accounting records.

3. Electronic linkages allowing different computers to share information are called:

   A. spreadsheets.
   B. software.
   C. networks.
   D. databases.

4. When designing a business's chart of accounts, generally account numbers are assigned as follows:

   A. asset account numbers begin with 3.
   B. liability account numbers begin with 5.
   C. capital account numbers begin with 1.
   D. revenue account numbers begin with 4.

5. A firm's payment to a supplier for merchandise inventory purchased on account is recorded in the:

   A. cash receipts journal.
   B. purchases journal.
   C. cash payments journal.
   D. sales journal.

6. Individual amounts owed by customers for credit sales are found in the:

   A. accounts receivable journal.
   B. accounts receivable subsidiary ledger.
   C. sales journal.
   D. general ledger.

7. Which of the following transactions is *not* recorded in the cash receipts journal?

   A. Adjusting prepaid rent
   B. Borrowing money from the bank
   C. Receipt of customer payments
   D. Sale of equipment for cash

8. A debit posted to Accounts Payable in the general ledger would come from the:

   A. cash payments journal.
   B. sales journal.
   C. purchases journal.
   D. cash receipts journal.

9. When using a formula on an electronic spreadsheet, the symbol for multiply is:

   A. x
   B. @
   C. /
   D. *

10. Which of the following is a control account?

   A. Prepaid Rent
   B. Salary Payable
   C. Capital
   D. Accounts Payable

III. Completion *Complete each of the following statements.*

1. The procedures that a business uses to protect its assets are called _____.
2. When special journals are used, cash sales are recorded in the _____.
3. A general ledger account with a subsidiary ledger attached to it is called a _____.
4. When goods are returned, the buyer issues a _____ while the seller acknowledges the return by issuing a _____.
5. _____ are software programs organized by columns and rows.
6. An effective accounting information system should include four features: _____, _____, _____, and _____.
7. The three components that form a computerized accounting system are: _____, _____, and _____.
8. The intersection of a row and column in a spreadsheet is called a _____.
9. A cash refund paid to a customer will be recorded in the _____.
10. In a computerized system, posting occurs continuously with _____.

IV. Daily Exercises

1. Indicate in which journal each of the following transactions would be recorded. Use *S* for the Sales Journal, *P* for the Purchases Journal, *CR* for the Cash Receipts Journal, *CP* for the Cash Payments Journal, and *J* for the General Journal.

   _____ a.   Purchases of merchandise on account
   _____ b.   Purchases of merchandise for cash
   _____ c.   Sale on account
   _____ d.   Sale of merchandise for cash
   _____ e.   Merchandise returned for credit on account
   _____ f.   Merchandise returned by customer for cash
   _____ g.   Payment of salaries
   _____ h.   Collection on customer's account
   _____ i.   Collection on customer's account where sales discount is taken by a customer
   _____ j.   Payment on account where purchase discount is taken
   _____ k.   Owner's withdrawal of cash
   _____ l.   Depreciation expense

2. Record the following transactions in the space provided. Assume a perpetual inventory system.

  a. Sold merchandise on account to Duncan Miller, $2,100, terms 2/10, n/30. The cost of the inventory was $1,025.
  b. Duncan Miller returned $600 from the sale. The cost of the returned goods was $280.
  c. Received payment from Duncan Miller for the amount due. Miller paid within the discount period.

Date	Accounts and Explanation	PR	Debit	Credit
	.			

3. For each of the three transactions in item 2., indicate which special journal, if any, the transaction would be recorded.

  a. _____
  b. _____
  c. _____

4. **V. Exercises**

1. Enter the following transactions in the purchases journal or the cash disbursements journal of Jarvis's Auto Repair & Supply below. (You may omit posting references and check numbers.)

7/2	Purchased tires on account from Acme, $3,000, terms 1/10, n/30
7/3	Purchased belts and hoses for cash, $425
7/5	Jarvis withdrew $1,200 for personal use
7/6	Purchased miscellaneous replacement parts on account from Steve's Wholesalers, $950, terms 2/15, n/60
7/7	Paid utility bill, $181
7/8	Purchased office equipment on account from Office Supply, Inc., $265, terms n/30
7/10	Paid for the July 2 purchase
7/13	Paid $2,000 to the bank on a loan
7/20	Purchased batteries from Acme on account, $892, terms 1/10, n/30
7/27	Paid Steve's Wholesalers the balance due

Purchases Journal

			CREDITS	DEBITS		
			Accounts		Other Accounts	
Date	Account Credited	Terms	Payable	Inventory	Title	Amount

Cash Disbursements Journal

		DEBITS		CREDITS	
		Other	Accounts		
Date	Account Debited	Accounts	Payable	Inventory	Cash

2. After Diamond Builders had completed all posting for the month of May, the sum of the balances in the Accounts Payable subsidiary ledger did not agree with the balance in the Accounts Payable control account in the general ledger. Assume the control account beginning balance is correct. Locate and correct the errors in the subsidiary ledger accounts and determine the correct balance for each subsidiary account.

Name: Ace Building Supply
Address: 321 Gumbranch Road

Date	Item	Post Ref.	Debit	Credit	Balance
5/1	Balance	√			1,225
5/3		P		650	1,875
5/19		CD	1,225		650
5/22		J	75		725

Name: Spades Equipment & Small Tool
Address: 229 Bishop Avenue

Date	Item	Post Ref.	Debit	Credit	Balance
5/1	Balance	√			2,450
5/20		P	950		1,500
5/26		CD		2,450	3,950

Name: Heartland Office Supply
Address: 2402 University Ave.

Date	Item	Post Ref.	Debit	Credit	Balance
5/1	Balance	√			890
5/6		CD	890		1,780
5/22		P		1,025	2,805
5/26		J		275	2,530

3. Refer to the correct solution for Exercise 2 above and construct the Accounts Payable control account as it would appear for the month of May assuming Diamond Builders has only the three suppliers listed above in the Accounts Payable ledger.

Accounts Payable

Date	Accounts	PR	Debit	Credit	Balance

4. Analyze each of the following and indicate when the error will come to the attention of the accountant.

    a. When adding the columns in the cash disbursements journal, the cash credit column was totaled at $16,439. The actual total was $16,339.

    _____

    _____

    _____

    b. The receipt of an $800 check from a customer in payment of the account was recorded and posted as $80.

    _____

    _____

    _____

    c. When posting from the Cash Receipts journal, a check for $410 from Allen Company was correctly recorded but posted to Alan Company in the subsidiary ledger.

    _____

    _____

    _____

    d. A credit sale of $980 to Sanders, Inc. was correctly recorded in the sales journal but was not posted to their account in the subsidiary ledger.

    _____

    _____

    _____

VI. Beyond the Numbers

In this chapter you were introduced to control accounts and subsidiary ledgers, specifically Accounts Receivable which controls the customers' ledger and Accounts Payable which controls the creditors' ledger. What other general ledger accounts might be suitable for subsidiary ledgers and how might the subsidiary ledger be organized?

General Ledger account	Subsidiary ledger organized by
_____	_____
_____	_____
_____	_____
_____	_____
_____	_____

VII. Demonstration Problems

Demonstration Problem #1

A spreadsheet for Jacques's Landscaping Supply follows. All column subtotals and totals are identified with the letters *m* through *z*. For each cell, present the formula so that the correct figure will automatically be printed as the spreadsheet is completed.

Jacque's Landscaping Supply
Work Sheet
For the Year Ended December 31, 20X9

	A	B	C	D	E	F	G	H	I
		Trial Balance		Adjustments		Income Statement		Balance Sheet	
1		Debit	Credit	Debit	Credit	Debit	Credit	Debit	Credit
2	Accounts								
3	Cash	17,250						17,250	
4	Accounts Receivable	19,100						19,100	
5	Inventory	42,000						42,000	
6	Supplies	2,650			1,800			850	
7	Prepaid Expense	8,000			3,500			4,500	
8	Equipment	91,400						91,400	
9	Accum. Dep.-Equip.		39,100		7,800				46,900
10	Accounts Payable		22,675						22,675
11	Salary Payable.				810				810
12	Interest Payable				225				225
13	Unearned Revenue		1,420	900					520
14	Note Payable		40,000						40,000
15	Jacques, Capital		56,700						56,700
16	Jacques, Withdrawals	20,000						20,000	
17	Sales Revenue		297,460		900		298,360		
18	Sales Discounts	7,800				7,800			
19	Sales Ret. & Allow.	6,210				6,210			
20	Cost of Goods Sold	148,310				148,310			
21	Salary Expense	51,500		810		52,310			
22	Rent Expense	18,000				18,000			
23	Depreciation Expense			7,800		7,800			
24	Utilities Expense	6,940				6,940			
25	Supplies Expense			1,800		1,800			
26	Interest Expense	3,775		225		4,000			
27	Advertising Expense	14,420		3,500		17,920			
28	Total	*m*	*n*	*o*	*p*	*q*	*t*	*v*	*x*
29						*r*			*y*
30						*s*	*u*	*w*	*z*

m._____
n._____
o._____
p._____
q._____
r._____
s._____

t._____
u._____
v._____
w._____
x._____
y._____
z._____

Demonstration Problem #2

During March, Konfection Corporation had these transactions:

3/2 Issued invoice No. 1079 to record credit sale to Gardner, Inc., $800. All credit sales are made on the company's standard terms of 1/10, n/30. Cost of the sale was $275.

3/5 Collected cash of $390 from Lee, Inc. in full payment of their account receivable.

3/6 Collected note receivable, $10,000 plus interest of $600.

3/8 Issued invoice No. 1080 for sale on account to Molina, Inc., $1,200. Cost of the sale was $550.

3/12 Received $792 cash from Gardner, Inc., in settlement of their account receivable, net of discount, from the sale arising on March 2.

3/18 Sold inventory on account to Saecho, Inc., issuing invoice No. 1081 for $2,000. Cost of the sale was $975.

3/25 Received $3,005 from Langston, Inc., in full settlement of its account receivable. (The discount period has expired.)

3/28 Issued invoice No. 1082 to Langston Inc. for sale of $950. Cost of the sale was $390.

3/29 Sold goods on credit to Saecho, Inc., issuing invoice No. 1083 for $630. Cost of the sale was $280.

3/30 Issued credit in the amount of $1,325 for inventory that Saecho, Inc. returned because it had spoiled during shipment. The goods were discarded.

Selected accounts from the general ledger of Konfection Corporation show the following balances at March 1:

Acct. No.	Account Title	Balance	Acct. No.	Account Title	Balance
12	Cash	$5,662	400	Sales Revenues	-
20	Accounts Receivable	10,110	410	Sales Discounts	-
25	Inventory	23,685	420	Sales Returns and Allowances	-
30	Supplies	872	501	Cost of Goods Sold	-
40	Note Receivable	10,000	601	Interest Revenue	-

Konfection accounts receivable subsidiary ledger includes the following accounts and balances at March 1:

Account Title	Balance
Langston, Inc.	$ 3,005
Gardner, Inc.	1,080
Saecho, Inc.	4,725
Molina, Inc.	910
Lee, Inc.	390
	$10,110

Required:

1. Open the general ledger and the accounts receivable subsidiary ledger accounts given, and insert their balances at March 1. Place a check mark (√) in the posting reference column for each March 1 balance.
2. Record the transactions on page 9 of a sales journal, page 18 of a cash receipts journal, and page 2 of a general journal as appropriate. Note: Record sales returns and allowances in the general journal.
3. Post to the general ledger and the accounts receivable subsidiary ledger. Use complete posting references, including the account number as given above. The sales journal and cash received from customers should be posted daily to the accounts receivable subsidiary ledger, as should any sales returns and allowances from the general journal. Other transactions should be posted at the end of the month.
4. Prove the accuracy of posting by showing that the total of the balances in the subsidiary ledger equals the general ledger balance in Accounts Receivable.

Requirements 1 and 3 (open ledgers; post to ledgers)

Accounts Receivable Subsidiary Ledger   **General Ledger**

Langston, Inc.

Date	Ref.	Debit	Credit	Balance

Cash 12

Date	Ref.	Debit	Credit	Balance

Gardner, Inc.

Date	Ref.	Debit	Credit	Balance

Accounts Receivable 20

Date	Ref.	Debit	Credit	Balance

Saecho, Inc.

Date	Ref.	Debit	Credit	Balance

Inventory 25

Date	Ref.	Debit	Credit	Balance

Molina, Inc.

Date	Ref.	Debit	Credit	Balance

Supplies 30

Date	Ref.	Debit	Credit	Balance

Lee, Inc.				
Date	Ref.	Debit	Credit	Balance

Notes Receivable				40
Date	Ref.	Debit	Credit	Balance

Sales Revenue				400
Date	Ref.	Debit	Credit	Balance

Sales Discount				410
Date	Ref.	Debit	Credit	Balance

Sales Returns and Allowances				420
Date	Ref.	Debit	Credit	Balance

Cost of Goods Sold 501				
Date	Ref.	Debit	Credit	Balance

Interest Revenue				601
Date	Ref.	Debit	Credit	Balance

Requirement 2

SALES JOURNAL

Date	Account Debited	Invoice No.	Post Ref.	Debit A/R Credit Sales	Debit CGS Credit Inventory

CASH RECEIPTS JOURNAL

Page 18

	DEBIT			CREDIT		
				Other Accounts		
Date	Cash	Sales Discount	Accounts Receivable	Account Title	Post Ref.	Amount

GENERAL JOURNAL

Page 2

Date	Accounts and Explanation	PR	Debit	Credit

Requirement 4

Schedule of Accounts Receivable

Customer	Balance

SOLUTIONS

I. Matching

1. B	4. C	7. N	10. F	13. J	16. Q
2. K	5. L	8. E	11. G	14. H	17. P
3. A	6. M	9. D	12. I	15. O	

II. Multiple Choice

1. D The four main features of an effective accounting information system are control, flexibility, compatibility, and a good cost/benefit relationship.

2. D Internal controls are the methods and procedures used to authorize transactions, safeguard assets, and ensure the accuracy of accounting.

3. C Networks are the linkages that permit information sharing.

4. D Generally, revenue account numbers begin with the number 4. Assets begin with the number 1, Liabilities with the number 2, Capital with the number 3, and Expenses with the number 5.

5. C All cash payments are recorded in the cash payments (disbursements) journal.

6. B Amounts owed to the business by its customers for merchandise sold on account are accounts receivable of the business. Details of customers' accounts receivable are maintained in the Accounts Receivable Subsidiary Ledger.

7. A The cash receipts journal is used to record all cash received by the business. Of the items listed, only "adjusting prepaid rent" does not involve the receipt of cash. Adjusting entries are recorded in the general journal.

8. A The normal posting sources for Accounts Payable in the general ledger are the cash disbursements journal for cash payments that reduce the Accounts Payable balance and the purchases journal for inventory purchases that increase the Accounts Payable balance. The entry from the cash disbursements journal would be a debit to Accounts Payable. (Note: a debit memo entry from the general journal might also be posted to Accounts Payable.)

9. D The symbol for multiply is *.

10. D A control account is a general ledger account with a balance equal to the sum of the balances of a group of related accounts in a subsidiary ledger. Of the accounts listed, only accounts payable has a related subsidiary ledger. Accounts receivable is another account that has a related subsidiary ledger.

III. Completion

1. internal controls (Internal controls are the methods and procedures used to authorize transactions, safeguard assets, and ensure the accuracy of accounting records.)
2. cash receipts journal
3. Control account
4. debit memo, credit memo
5. Spreadsheets
6. control, compatibility, flexibility, favorable cost/benefit relationship (order not important)
7. hardware, software, personnel (order not important)
8. cell
9. cash payments journal.
10. on-line processing

IV. Daily Exercises

1. a. P   g. CP
    b. CP   h. CR
    c. S   i. CR
    d. CR   j. CP
    e. J   k. CP
    f. CP   l. J

2.

a.	Accounts Receivable - Miller		2,100	
	Sales			2,100
	Cost of Goods Sold		1,025	
	Inventory			1,025
b.	Sales Returns and Allowances		600	
	Accounts Receivable - Miller			600
	Inventory		280	
	Cost of Goods Sold			280
c.	Cash		1,470	
	Sales Discounts		30	
	Accounts Receivable - Miller			1,500

3. a. Sales Journal. All sales on account will be recorded in the sales journal.
    b. General Journal. Sales returns and allowances are recorded in the general journal because they do not fit into any one of the four special journals.
    c. Cash Receipts Journal. When a business collects on account from its customers, the receipt of cash is recorded in the cash receipts journal.

V. Exercises

1.

Purchases Journal

Date	Account Credited	Terms	CREDITS Accounts Payable	DEBITS Inventory	DEBITS Other Accounts Title	DEBITS Other Accounts Amount
7/2	Acme	1/10,n/30	3,000	3,000		
7/6	Steve's Wholesalers	2/15,n/60	950	950		
7/8	Office Supply Co.	n/30	265		Equipment	265
7/20	Acme	1/10,n/30	892	892		

Cash Disbursements Journal

Date	Account Debited	DEBITS Other Accounts	DEBITS Accounts Payable	CREDITS Inventory	CREDITS Cash
7/3	Inventory	425			425
7/5	Withdrawals	1,200			1,200
7/7	Telephone exp.	181			181
7/10	Acme		3,000	30	2,970
7/13	Note Payable	2,000			2,000
7/27	Steve's Wholesalers		950		950

Note: The payment on 7/10 was within the discount period:
Amount of the discount = 1% x $3,000 = $30

2.

Name: Ace Business Supply					
Address: 321 Gumbranch Road					
Date	Item	Post Ref.	Debit	Credit	Balance
5/1	Balance	√			1,225
5/3		P		650	1,875
5/19		CD	1,225		650
5/22		J	75		~~725~~ 575

Name: Spades Equipment and Small Tool					
Address: 229 Bishop Avenue					
Date	Item	Post Ref.	Debit	Credit	Balance
5/1	Balance	√			2,450
5/20		P	~~950~~	950	~~1,500~~ 3,400
5/26		CD	2,450	~~2,450~~	~~3,950~~ 950

Name: Heartland Office Supply						
Address: 2402 University Ave.						
Date	Item	Post Ref.	Debit	Credit	Balance	
5/1	Balance	√			890	
5/6		CD	890		0	
5/22		P		1,025	1,025	
5/26		J	275	275	800	750

3.

Accounts Payable

Date	Accounts	PR	Debit	Credit	Balance
5/1	Balance	√			4,565
5/22		J	75		4,490
5/26		J	275		4,215
5/31		P		2,625	6,840
5/31		CD	4,565		2,275

4.

a. Before posting column totals from a special journal, the debit/credit equality of the totals should be verified. When this is done, the credit column totals will be $100 more than the debit column totals.

b. Since the transaction was recorded as $80, the trial balance will balance and there will be agreement between the control account and the subsidiary ledger. However, our records indicate the customer still owes us $720 ($800 less the $80 receipt). No doubt the customer will bring the error to our attention when we re-bill the customer for an amount they have already paid.

c. As in b) above, the trial balance will balance and the control account and subsidiary ledger will agree. However, Allen Company will be re-billed even though they paid the account. When this happens the customer will notify the company of the error.

d. This error should come to our attention when we attempt to reconcile the accounts receivable control account with the total of the individual balances in our receivables subsidiary ledger. The control account balance will be correct while the total of the accounts in the subsidiary ledger will be understated $980.

VI. Beyond the Numbers

There are a number of different accounts you could have listed as potential control accounts. The list that follows contains only some of the possibilities.

General Ledger account	Subsidiary ledger organized by
Merchandise Inventory	different types of inventory items
Prepaid Insurance	individual policies
Computer Equipment	specific types of hardware - computers, monitors, printers, etc.
Notes Receivable	individual payers
Salaries Payable	individual employee's salaries

A subsidiary ledger is set up when the amount of activity in the control account is large enough to warrant the additional detail provided by a subsidiary ledger. Doing so keeps the general ledger "cleaner" while still providing the detail (in the subsidiary ledger) when needed.

VII. Demonstration Problems

Demonstration Problem #1 Solved

m. =sum(B3..B27) {add cell b3 through b27}

n. =sum(C9..C17)
o. =sum(D13..D27)
p. =sum(E6..E17)
q. =sum(F18..F27)
r. =(G28-F28) {sales - total expenses}
s. =(F28+F29)

t. =G17 {assign this cell the same value as cell G17}
u. =G28
v. =sum(H3..H16)
w. =H28
x. =sum(I9..I15)
y. =(H28-I28)
z. =(I28+I29)

Demonstration Problem #2 Solved and Explained

Requirements 1 and 3

Accounts Receivable Subsidiary Ledger

Langston, Inc.

Date	Ref.	Debit	Credit	Balance
3/1	√			3,005
3/25	CR 18		3,005	0
3/28	S 9	950		950

Gardner, Inc.

Date	Ref.	Debit	Credit	Balance
3/1	√			1,080
3/2	S 9	800		1,880
3/14	CR 18		800	1,080

Saecho, Inc.

Date	Ref.	Debit	Credit	Balance
3/1	√			4,725
3/18	S 9	2,000		6,725
3/29	S 9	630		7,355
3/31	GJ 2		1,325	6,030

General Ledger

Cash   12

Date	Ref.	Debit	Credit	Balance
3/1	√			5,662
3/31	CR 18	14,787		20,449

Accounts Receivable   20

Date	Ref.	Debit	Credit	Balance
3/1	√			10,110
3/31	GJ 2		1,325	8,785
3/31	S 9	5,580		14,365
3/31	CR 18		4,195	10,170

Inventory   25

Date	Ref.	Debit	Credit	Balance
3/1	√			23,685
3/31	S 9		2,470	21,215

Molina, Inc.

Date	Ref.	Debit	Credit	Balance
3/1	√			910
3/8	S 9	1,200		2,110

Lee, Inc.

Date	Ref.	Debit	Credit	Balance
3/1	√			390
3/5	CR 18		390	0

Supplies   30

Date	Ref.	Debit	Credit	Balance
3/1	√			872

Notes Receivable   40

Date	Ref.	Debit	Credit	Balance
3/1	√			10,000
3/6	CR 18		10,000	0

Sales Revenue   400

Date	Ref.	Debit	Credit	Balance
3/1	√			0
3/31	S 9		5,580	5,580

Sales Discount   410

Date	Ref.	Debit	Credit	Balance
3/1	√			0
3/31	CR 18	8		8

Sales Returns and Allowances   420

Date	Ref.	Debit	Credit	Balance
3/1	√			0
3/31	GJ 2	1,325		1,325

Cost of Goods Sold   501

Date	Ref.	Debit	Credit	Balance
3/1	√			0
3/31	S 9	2,470		2,470

Interest Revenue   601

Date	Ref.	Debit	Credit	Balance
3/1	√			0
3/6	CR 18		600	600

Requirement 2

SALES JOURNAL

Page 9

Date	Account Debited	Invoice No.	Post Ref.	Debit A/R Credit Sales	Debit CGS Credit Inventory
3/2	Gardner, Inc.	1079	√	800	275
3/8	Molina, Inc.	1080	√	1,200	550
3/18	Saecho, Inc.	1081	√	2,000	975
3/28	Langston, Inc.	1082	√	950	390
3/29	Saecho, Inc.	1083	√	630	280
	.			5,580	2,470
				(20) (400)	(501) (25)

CASH RECEIPTS JOURNAL

Page 18

	DEBIT		CREDIT			
				Other Accounts		
Date	Cash	Sales Discount	Accounts Receivable	Account Title	Post Ref.	Amount
3/5	390		390	Lee, Inc.	√	
3/6	10,600			Note Rec.	40	10,000
				Interest Rev.	601	600
3/12	792	8	800	Gardner, Inc.	√	
3/25	3,005		3,005	Langston, Inc.	√	
	14,787	8	4,195			10,600
	(12)	(410)	(20)			(√)

14,795   14,795

GENERAL JOURNAL

Page 2

Date	Accounts and Explanation	PR	Debit	Credit
3/30	Sales Returns and Allowances	420	1,325	
	Accounts Receivable—Saecho, Inc.	20/√		1,325
	To record return of merchandise from Saecho, Inc. for goods spoiled during shipment. The goods were discarded.			

Requirement 4

Schedule of Accounts Receivable

Customer	Balance
Langston, Inc.	$ 950
Gardner, Inc.	1,080
Saecho, Inc.	6,030
Molina, Inc.	2,110

$10,170

Note: The $10,170 total of the accounts receivable subsidiary ledger agrees with the accounts receivable controlling account.

Explanations

As you have probably noticed in your studies to date, there are a large number of similar transactions that occur in each problem set. This is true in the real world for most businesses as well. By using specialized journals, it is possible to save a significant amount of time in both the recording and posting of like transactions. The most common special journals are:

Special Journal	Used to Record
Cash receipts journal	all collections of cash
Cash disbursements journal	all disbursements of cash
Sales journal	merchandise sales on account
Purchases journal	all purchases on account

Actually using these specialized journals is a relatively straightforward task requiring little more than careful entry and systematic posting of the data into the appropriate subsidiary ledger account.

Chapter 8—Internal Control and Cash

CHAPTER OVERVIEW

In Chapter 7, you learned about an accounting information system. This chapter follows that discussion by introducing you to internal control and the processes a business follows to control the organization's assets. Because cash is the most liquid asset, this chapter applies internal control concepts to cash. However, internal control applies to all assets—topics covered in the next three chapters. The learning objectives for this chapter are to

1. Define internal control.
2. Tell how to achieve good internal control.
3. Prepare a bank reconciliation and related journal entries.
4. Apply internal controls to cash receipts.
5. Apply internal controls to cash payments.
6. Make ethical judgments in business.

CHAPTER REVIEW

Objective 1 - Define internal control.

Internal control is the organizational plan and all the related measures that an entity adopts to accomplish four objectives:

1. Safeguard assets
2. Encourage employees to follow company policy.
3. Promote operational efficiency
4. Ensure accurate, reliable accounting records.

A Federal law, the **Foreign Corrupt Practice Act**, passed in 1977, requires companies under SEC jurisdiction to maintain a system of internal control. In addition, the **Sarbanes-Oxley Act of 2002** requires managers to give careful attention to internal control in their companies.

Objective 2 – Tell how to achieve internal control.

An effective system of internal control has the following components:

1. **Competent, reliable, and ethical personnel**. Paying competitive salaries, training people thoroughly, and providing adequate supervision help to promote competence.
2. **Assignment of responsibilities**. All duties to be performed must be identified, and responsibility for the performance of those duties must be assigned to appropriate people.
3. **Separation of duties**. Separation of duties limits fraud and promotes the accuracy of the accounting records. Separation of duties has two parts:
   a) separation of operations from accounting
   b) separation of the custody of assets from accounting

4. **Internal and external audits.** Auditors evaluate the system of internal control to estimate the reliability of the accounting systems. Auditors also help to spot areas where improvements in internal control can be made. **Internal auditors** are employees of the company. **External auditors** are employed by public accounting firms and are hired by a business to audit its books.

5. **Documents and records.** Business documents and records are designed according to each company's needs and provide the details of business transactions. Source documents include sales invoices and purchase orders, and records include special journals and the general ledger. Good internal control requires documents to be prenumbered. A gap in the numbered sequence will call attention to a missing document.

6. **Electronic devices, computer controls and other controls.** Additional controls include electronic sensors for inventory, fireproof vaults to safeguard cash, point-of-sale terminals used to track revenues and cash, fidelity bonds to protect the business from employee theft, mandatory vacations and job rotation for employees and electronic data processing auditors for computer systems.

In order to remain competitive in today's business world, many businesses must buy and sell goods over the Internet, referred to as **e-Commerce.** Businesses that participate in e-Commerce must take security measures to protect their customers and encourage them to buy online. Some of the risks of e-Commerce are:
1. Stolen credit cards.
2. Computer viruses and Trojan horses
3. Impersonation of companies

Businesses use **encryption** of data and **firewalls** to secure e-Commerce data.

The limitations of an internal control system are determined by the opportunities available for collusion and the resources that management devotes to the system. Collusion between two or more people working together to defraud the firm may go undetected by the system of internal control. Internal control must be designed and judged in light of the costs and the benefits.

Because cash is the most liquid asset, and is relatively easy to conceal, steal, and move, a business must provide specific controls for cash. For accounting purposes, when we refer to cash, it includes currency, coins, checks, money orders, and money held in bank accounts. The bank account provides internal control over cash. Banks safeguard cash and provide detailed records of transactions.

Documents used to control bank accounts include:

- signature cards
- deposit tickets
- checks
- bank statements
- bank reconciliation

Banks send monthly statements to customers. The bank statement shows the beginning balance in the account, all transactions recorded during the month, and the ending balance. The bank also returns canceled checks with the statement.

Electronic Fund Transfer (EFT) is a system that relies on electronic impulses to account for cash transactions. EFT systems reduce the cost of processing cash transactions by reducing the documentary evidence of transactions. The monthly bank statement lists EFT deposits and EFT payments.

Monthly **bank reconciliations** are necessary because of timing differences between when cash transactions are recorded by the business and when the bank records those transactions. For example, if you mail a check to a supplier on the last day of the month, you will record the payment in the business records on that day. However, the check will not clear your bank until the supplier has received it and deposited it in his bank, sometime in the following month.

Objective 3 - Prepare a bank reconciliation and related journal entries.

The general format for a bank reconciliation is:

Balance per Bank		**Balance per Books**
Cash balance, last day of month		Cash balance, last day of month (from balance of general ledger)
+ Deposits in transit		
- Outstanding checks		+ Bank collections
± Correction of bank errors (if any)		+ Interest paid on deposits
		- Service charge
		± Correction of book errors (if any)
Adjusted bank balance	=	Adjusted book balance

Adjustments to the bank balance <u>never</u> require the preparation of journal entries because they represent items that have already been recorded in the accounting records of the business, but they have not been recorded by the bank as of the date on the statement. Adjustments to the bank balance include the following items:

1. **Deposits in transit** have been recorded by the company, but have not been recorded by the bank. There is often a time lag of a day or two until the deposit is sent to the bank and posted by the bank.
2. **Outstanding checks** are checks issued by the company and recorded in the company's books, but the checks have not yet been paid (recorded) by the bank. There is a time lag of several days until the checks are cashed or deposited by the payee and sent to the maker's bank to be paid.
3. **Corrections of bank errors** are the responsibility of the bank. The bank should be notified, and the corrections should appear on the next statement.

Adjustments to the books <u>always</u> require the preparation of journal entries because they represent items that have been recorded by the bank, but they have not been recorded in the accounting records of the business. It is only by making a journal entry that these transactions are recorded in the books of the business.

Adjustments to the book balance include the following items:

1. The bank collects money on behalf of depositors. Examples are a lock-box system where customers pay directly to the bank account. A bank may also collect on a note receivable for the depositor. The bank will notify the depositor of these collections on the bank statement. The journal entry for the collection of a note receivable and the related interest is:

Cash	XXX	
Note Receivable		XX
Interest Revenue		X

2. Interest Revenue is sometimes paid to the depositor on the checking account. The journal entry to record the interest is:

Cash	XX	
Interest Revenue		XX

3. Service charges are the bank's fees for processing transactions. The journal entry for a service charge is:

Miscellaneous Expense	X	
Cash		X

4. Nonsufficient funds (NSF) checks are customer checks that have been returned by the customer's bank because the customer's account did not have sufficient funds in the account to cover the amount of the check. Checks may also be returned if the maker's account has closed, the date is stale, the signature is not authorized, the check has been altered, or the check form is improper. The amount of returned checks is subtracted from the book balance and the following journal entry is made:

Accounts Receivable-Customer A	XX	
Cash		XX

5. The cost of printing checks is handled like a service charge. The journal entry is:

Miscellaneous Expense	XX	
Cash		XX

6. Errors on the books must be handled on a case-by-case basis. If checks are recorded on the books for the wrong amount, then a correcting journal entry must be prepared to correct the original entry.

Study Exhibit 8-6 carefully. Be sure you understand the components of a bank reconciliation and the journal entries needed to correct the Cash account balance.

When reported on the balance sheet, most companies list "Cash and equivalents"—this includes cash and other items similar enough to be included with cash (such as petty cash, short-term time deposits, and certificates of deposit).

Objective 4 - Apply internal controls to cash receipts.

The objective of internal control over cash receipts is to ensure that all cash is deposited in the bank. Companies receive cash over the counter and through the mail. Each source of cash calls for its own set of controls.

A cash register is a good device for management to control cash received in a store. Positioning the machine so that customers see the amounts rung up discourages cashiers from overcharging customers and pocketing the excess over actual prices. Issuing receipts requires cashiers to record the sale. Comparing actual receipts to cash register tapes maintained by the machine discourages theft.

For payments received from customers by mail, separation of duties among different people promotes good internal control. The mailroom clerk should open all mail and record incoming payments. The mailroom clerk should deliver checks to the cashier for deposit, and send remittance advices to the accounting department for posting. Comparison of mailroom totals, cashier totals, and accounting totals should be made daily.

Where large numbers of cash transactions occur, there is often a small difference between actual cash received and cash recorded. An account entitled **Cash Short and Over** is used to account for such differences. The account is used as a balancing account for the journal entry and is debited for cash shortages and credited for cash overages. An example of the journal entry to record an overage is:

Cash (from cash drawer)	20,010	
Cash Short and Over (plug)		10
Sales (from cash register tape)		20,000

A debit balance in Cash Short and Over appears on the income statement as a miscellaneous expense; a credit balance in Cash Short and Over appears as Other Revenue. A large debit or credit balance in the account (representing shortage or overage) should be investigated promptly.

Objective 5 - Apply internal controls to cash payments.

Internal controls over cash payments are as important as controls over cash receipts. Companies make most payments by check. They also may make smaller payments from a petty cash fund. However, before a check can be issued, additional control procedures have occurred. Before a check is written to pay for a purchase, the payment packet should include: approved purchase orders, receiving reports verifying that goods received conform to the purchase order, an invoice which agrees with both the purchase order and receiving report. When all of these documents agree, then a check can be issued for payment. (See Exhibit 8-9 and 8-10 in your text.) Additionally, many companies require two signatures before a check can be sent.

Businesses keep a **petty cash** account to have cash on hand for minor expenses that do not warrant the time required to write a check. Such minor expenses may include taxi fares, local delivery costs, and small amounts of office supplies.

Suppose a petty cash fund of $200 is established. The cash is placed under the control of a custodian and the following entry is made:

Petty Cash	200	
Cash		200

This same entry is also used to increase the amount in the fund, say from $200 to $300:

Petty Cash	100	
Cash		100

Cash from the fund is disbursed using petty cash tickets, which document each disbursement. Cash on hand plus the total of the petty cash tickets should always equal the fund balance. This is referred to as an **imprest fund**. If the fund comes up short, debit Cash Short and Over. If the fund comes up over, credit Cash Short and Over.

The petty cash fund must be periodically replenished, particularly on the balance sheet date. A check is drawn for the amount of the replenishment. An entry is made as follows:

Various accounts listed on petty cash tickets	XX	
Cash		XX

Note: Once the fund is established, no entry is made to the Petty Cash account except to change the total amount in the fund. The expenses on the petty cash tickets are recorded in the journal when the fund is replenished.

Objective 6 - Make ethical judgments in business.

Most businesses have codes of ethics to which their employees are expected to conform. In addition, the accounting profession has the AICPA Code of Professional Conduct and the Standards of Ethical Conduct for Management Accountants. In many situations, the ethical course of action is clear. However, when this is not the case, the following steps may prove helpful:

1. Determine the facts
2. Identify the ethical issues
3. Specify the alternatives
4. Identify the people involved
5. Assess the possible consequences
6. Make the decision

Review the decision guidelines at the end of Chapter 8.

TEST YOURSELF

All the self-testing materials in this chapter focus on information and procedures that your instructor is likely to test in quizzes and examinations.

I. Matching   *Match each numbered term with its lettered definition.*

_____ 1. External auditors
_____ 2. Firewall
_____ 3. Bank statement
_____ 4. Separation of duties
_____ 5. Electronic fund transfer
_____ 6. Nonsufficient funds check
_____ 7. Outstanding check
_____ 8. Service charge

_____ 9. Collusion
_____ 10. Bank collection
_____ 11. Bank reconciliation
_____ 12. Deposit in transit
_____ 13. Imprest system
_____ 14. Internal control
_____ 15. Petty cash

A. A deposit recorded by the company but not by the bank
B. A check for which the payer's bank account has insufficient money to pay the check
C. A check issued by a company and recorded on it's books but not yet paid by the bank
D. A document prepared by the bank that shows the beginning and ending balances in a depositor's account and lists the month's transactions that affect the account
E. A fund containing a small amount of cash that is used to pay minor expenditures
F. A component of internal control where management divides responsibility between two or more people
G. Where two or more people work together as a team to defraud a company
H. A system that accounts for cash transactions by electronic impulses rather than paper documents
I. A method of accounting for petty cash by which the balance in the Petty Cash account is compared to the sum of cash on hand plus petty cash disbursement tickets
J. Bank's fee for processing a depositor's transactions
K. Collection of money by the bank on behalf of a depositor
L. Employed by public accounting firms; hired to audit a client's books
M. A control device used to prevent access to a network by non-members
N. Process of explaining the difference between a depositor's accounting records and the bank's records related to a depositor's bank account
O. The organizational plan and all related measures adopted by an entity to safeguard assets, ensure accurate and reliable accounting records, promote operational efficiency, and encourage adherence to company policies

II. Multiple Choice *Circle the best answer.*

1. Jason Laramy handles cash receipts and has the authority to write off accounts receivable. This violates separation of:

    A. custody of assets from accounting.
    B. operations from accounting.
    C. duties within the accounting function.
    D. authorization of transactions from custody of related assets.

2. Felipe Toledo from the purchasing department also oversees the annual inventory of the company's warehouse. This violates separation of:

    A. custody of assets from accounting.
    B. operations from accounting.
    C. duties within the accounting function.
    D. authorization of transactions from custody of related assets.

3. When preparing a bank reconciliation, which of the following items do *not* require a journal entry?

    A. Interest collected on notes receivable
    B. Outstanding checks
    C. EFT payment of note payable
    D. Bank service charge

4. The journal entry to record an NSF check returned by the bank is:

    A. debit Cash, credit Accounts Receivable.
    B. debit Accounts Payable, credit Cash.
    C. debit Accounts Receivable, credit Cash.
    D. debit Miscellaneous Expense, credit Cash.

5. Which of the following is *not* an internal control procedure for cash receipts?

    A. Comparing actual cash in the cash register to the totals on the cash register tape
    B. The cash drawer on the cash register only opens when the clerk enters an amount on the keypad.
    C. Paying bills by check
    D. Enabling customers to see amounts entered on cash receipts

6. A debit balance in Cash Short and Over is reported on the income statement as:

    A. Other Revenue
    B. Cost of Goods Sold
    C. General Expenses
    D. Miscellaneous Expenses

7. Which of the following documents is prepared first?

    A. Invoice
    B. Receiving report
    C. Purchase order
    D. Check

8. Which of the following documents is prepared last?

    A. Invoice
    B. Receiving report
    C. Purchase order
    D. Check

9. Which of the following would *not* be paid out using a petty cash fund?

   A. Postage
   B. Computer equipment
   C. Gasoline for delivery truck
   D. Pencils from local office supply

10. Which of the following is *not* an internal control for cash?

    A. Fidelity bonds
    B. Point-of-sale terminal
    C. Electronic sensors
    D. Fireproof vault

III. Completion *Complete each of the following statements.*

1. _____ is prepared by the depositor to explain the difference between the cash balance on the books and the cash balance shown by the bank.

2. Under the Foreign Corrupt Practices Act, _____ is (are) responsible for maintaining adequate internal controls.

3. _____ auditors are regular employees of a business; _____ auditors are independent of the business.

4. In a good internal control system, has the following objectives:
   a.) _____
   b.) _____
   c.) _____
   d.) _____

5. The documents used to control a bank account are:
   a.) _____
   b.) _____
   c.) _____
   d.) _____
   e.) _____

6. When setting up a petty cash fund, the first step is to _____.

7. Separation of duties includes _____ and
   _____.

8. When preparing the bank reconciliation, outstanding checks are _____ from the
   _____.

9. _____ insure a company against theft by an employee.

10. _____ is a temporary account used to reconcile discrepancies that result from cash transactions.

IV. Daily Exercises

1. Indicate how each of the following items is treated in a bank reconciliation. Use *AB* for additions to the bank balance; *AC* for additions to the company's book balance; *DB* for deductions from the bank balance; and *DC* for deductions from the firm's book balance.

   _____ a. A deposit for $175 was not recorded in the books
   _____ b. A check for $45 was entered in the books as $54
   _____ c. Bank collection of a note receivable plus accrued interest
   _____ d. Bank service charges
   _____ e. A deposit was credited by the bank to the firm's account in error
   _____ f. Deposits in transit
   _____ g. Interest earned on checking account
   _____ h. Outstanding checks
   _____ i. NSF checks
   _____ j. EFT payment of utility bill
   _____ k. Charge for check reorder

2. Examine your answers in Daily Exercise #1 and indicate which reconciling items will require a journal entry.

3. A small heating and air conditioning company maintains a $300 imprest petty cash fund. At the end of the month, there were receipts for miscellaneous expenditures totaling $275 and $20 in coins and currency. In the space below, record the entry to replenish the fund. Was the petty cash fund short or over, or was it in balance?

Date	Accounts and Explanation	PR	Debit	Credit

4. There are four circumstances where the account Petty Cash is used in a journal entry. What are they?

   a. _____
   b. _____
   c. _____
   d. _____

IV. Exercises

1. Lee's bank statement gave an ending balance of $815.00. Reconciling items include: deposit in transit, $260.00; service charge, $12.00; outstanding checks, $198.00; and interest earned on her checking account, $2.00. What is the adjusted bank balance after the bank reconciliation is prepared?

2. Using the information in Exercise 1 above, what was the unadjusted ending balance in Lee's checking account?

3. During the month of November, Philip's Photo Co., had the following transactions in its Petty Cash fund.

   11/1   Established Petty Cash fund, $275
   11/6   Paid postage, $35
   11/8   Paid freight charges, $15
   11/11 Purchased office supplies, $40
   11/22 Paid miscellaneous expenses, $66
   11/30 Replenished the Petty Cash fund ($167 was in the fund)

   Prepare the journal entries required by each of the above transactions.

Date	Accounts and Explanation	PR	Debit	Credit

VI. Beyond the Numbers

At the Fat Lady Sings Opera House, you notice that there is a box office at the entrance where the cashier receives cash from customers. Once the customers pay, the cashier presses a button and a machine ejects serially numbered tickets that are given to the customers. To enter the opera house, a customer must present his or her ticket to the door attendant. The attendant tears the ticket in half and returns the stub to the customer. The other half of the ticket is dropped into a locked box.

1. What internal controls are present in this scenario?
2. What should management do to make these controls more effective?
3. How can these controls be rendered ineffective?

_____
_____
_____
_____
_____
_____
_____
_____
_____
_____

VII. Demonstration problems

Demonstration Problem #1

The following petty cash transactions occurred in Oct:

10/1	Management decided to establish a petty cash fund. A check for $300 was written and cashed with the proceeds given to Betty Jones, who was designated custodian of the fund.
10/1	James Silverman, the owner of the business immediately took $25 for lunch money.
10/4	$15.95 was disbursed to reimburse an employee for an air-express package paid for with personal funds.
10/6	COD freight charges on Supplies were paid, $25.00.
10/9	$37 was spent on postage stamps while the postage meter was being repaired.
10/11	The owner "borrowed" another $30 from the fund.
10/12	COD freight charges on merchandise were paid, $45.
10/13	Because the fund was running low on cash, Ms. Jones requested a check to replenish the fund. As there was $122.05 on hand, Ms. Jones requested a check for $177.95. However, her supervisor authorized a check for $277.95 so sufficient funds would be on hand and only require monthly replenishment.
10/16	The monthly charge for the office newspaper was paid, $22.50
10/19	COD charges on merchandise were paid, $43.
10/20	The owner took $100 from the fund.
10/22	Ms. Jones took $25 from the fund to purchase coffee and supplies for the office coffee room.
10/25	The owner's spouse arrived by taxi. The fare of $22 plus a $5 tip was paid from the petty cash fund.
10/26	$75 was paid from the fund to have the front windows washed.

| 10/28 | A coworker did not have lunch money. Ms. Jones gave the coworker $20 from the fund and took a post-dated check for that amount. |
| 10/31 | The company decided to replenish the fund on the last working day each month. There was $84.50 left in the fund. |

Required:

1. Record the appropriate transactions in the General Journal.
2. Post any entries to the Petty Cash account.

Requirement 1(General Journal entries)

Date	Accounts and Explanation	PR	Debit	Credit

Requirement 2 (Post entries to Petty Cash Fund)

Petty Cash Fund

Demonstration Problem #2

Selected columns of the cash receipts journal and the check register of Shell Co. appear as follows on March 31, 20X9:

Cash Receipts Journal (Posting reference is CR)			Check Register (Posting reference is CD)	
Date	Cash Debit		Check No.	Cash Credit
Mar. 3	$ 175		716	$ 322
7	710		717	2,244
12	428		718	544
14	880		719	576
24	3,715		720	509
28	1,525		721	501
31	428		722	817
			723	282
			724	1,074
Total	$ 7,861		Total	$ 6,869

The cash account of Shell Co. shows the following information on March 31, 20X9:

Cash

Date	Item	PR	Debit	Credit	Balance
Mar. 1	Balance				$ 6,753
31		CR 1	7,861		14,614
31		CD 2		6,869	7,745

Shell Co. received the following bank statement on March 31, 20X9:

Bank Statement for Shell Co.

Beginning balance		$ 6,852
Deposits and other credits:		
Mar 4	175	
8	710	
11	1,308	BC
13	428	
15	880	
25	3,715	
31	13	INT
	7,229	
	$14,081	

Checks and other debits:

Mar. 3	$ 572	
7	322	
11	2,244	
12	544	
15	576	
20	135	NSF
24	509	
30	817	
31	22	SC
	5,741	
Ending balance:	$8,340	

Legend:

BC = Bank Collection	NSF = Nonsufficient Funds Check
SC = Service Charge	INT = Interest Earned

Additional data for the bank reconciliation:

1. The $1,308 bank collection on Mar. 11 includes $108 interest revenue. The balance was attributable to the collection of a note receivable.
2. The correct amount of Check Number 716 is $223, a payment on account. The Shell Co. bookkeeper mistakenly recorded the check in the check register as $322.
3. The NSF check was received from Fred's Motor Co.
4. The bank statement includes a $572 deduction for a check drawn by Morton Co. The bank has been notified of its error.
5. The service charge consists of two charges: $12 for the monthly account charge and $10 for the NSF check.

Required:

1. Prepare the bank reconciliation of Shell Co. on March 31, 20X9.
2. Record the entries based on the bank reconciliation. Omit explanations.

Requirement 1 (Bank reconciliation)

Shell Co.
Bank Reconciliation
March 31, 20X9

Requirement 2 (Entries based on bank reconciliation)

Date	Accounts and Explanation	PR	Debit	Credit

SOLUTIONS

I. Matching

1. L	4. F	7. C	10. K	13. I
2. M	5. H	8. J	11. N	14. O
3. D	6. B	9. G	12. A	15. E

II. Multiple Choice

1.   A   Handling cash receipts and having authority to write off accounts receivable puts the person in a position to illegitimately write off an account on which payment has been received and pocket the cash. This is a violation of separation of custody of assets from accounting. Laramy has custody of the cash receipts and as well as accounting duties related to that cash.

2.   B   When one person has a role in the daily operations of the business, such as purchasing, and has authority to oversee the annual inventory count, this violates the separation of operations from accounting. Too much control might allow someone from the purchasing department to manipulate purchase records and remove goods from the warehouse without being detected.

3.   B   Outstanding checks are cash payments that have been recorded in the cash payments journal of the business but have not yet been recorded (or cleared) by the bank. The other items listed are items that will be reflected in the banks records, but have not yet been recorded on the books of the business.

4.   C   An NSF check represents a previously recorded cash receipt that has no substance and, accordingly, must be reversed; reduce cash (credit) and reestablish the receivable (debit).

5.   C   Paying bills by check is an internal control procedure for cash disbursements, not cash receipts. The other items listed are internal control procedures for cash receipts.

6.   D   A debit balance means a cash shortage exists. It is reported as a miscellaneous expense.

7.   A   The purchasing process starts when the purchaser sends a purchase order to the supplier.

8.   D   The check is prepared last.

9.   B   A petty cash fund is used to pay for minor expenditures. Computer equipment would not be considered a minor expenditure, and would not be purchased using a petty cash fund.

10.   C   Electronic sensors attempt to control inventory, not cash.

III. Completion

1. A bank reconciliation
2. management (Companies under SEC jurisdiction are required to maintain an appropriate system of internal control. This requirement is a responsibility of the management of the company.)
3. Internal; external (Internal auditors report directly to the company's president or audit committee of the board of directors. External auditors audit the entity as a whole and usually report to the stockholders.)
4. a.) Safeguard assets; b.) encourage employees to follow company policy; c.) promote operational efficiency; d.) ensure accurate, reliable accounting records. (Order does not matter.)
5. a.) Signature card; b.) deposit ticket; c.) check; d.) bank statement; e.) bank reconciliation (Order does not matter.)
6. open the fund. (A petty cash fund is opened when a check is issued to Petty Cash by debiting the Petty Cash account and crediting the Cash in Bank.)
7. separation of operations from accounting; separation of custody of assets from accounting
8. subtracted; balance per bank.
9. fidelity bonds
10. Cash Short and Over

IV. Daily Exercises

1. a) AC   e) DB   i) DC
    b) AC   f) AB   j) DC
    c) AC   g) AC   k) DC
    d) DC   h) DB

2. From #1 above, items a, b, c, d, g, i, j and k will all require a journal entry.
3.

Miscellaneous Expense	275	
Cash Short and Over	5	
Cash		280

   The fund was short by $5.00.
4. The Petty Cash account is part of a journal entry when
    a. the fund is established
    b. the size of the fund is increased
    c. the size of the fund is decreased
    d. to close the fund

V. Exercises

1.

Balance per bank statement (unadjusted)	$815.00
Add:	
Deposit in transit	260.00
	1,075.00
Deduct:	
Outstanding checks	198.00
Adjusted bank balance	877.00

2. This requires you to work backwards. Start by setting up what is known and then solve for the unknown balance. Remember that the adjusted balance in the checkbook will equal the adjusted bank balance on the bank reconciliation.

Balance per checkbook (unadjusted)	?
Add:	
Interest earned	2.00
	?
Deduct:	
Service charge	12.00
Adjusted book balance *(same as adjusted bank balance from #1.)*	877.00

Unadjusted Book balance + 2.00 - 12.00 = 877.00
Unadjusted Book balance = $887.00

3.

Date	Accounts and Explanation	PR	Debit	Credit
11/1	Petty Cash		275	
	Cash in Bank			275
11/30	Miscellaneous Expense		16	
	Postage Expense		35	
	Delivery Expense		15	
	Supplies (an asset)		40	
	Cash Short and Over		2	
	Cash in Bank			108

Note: You make an entry to record the various expenses only when the Petty Cash fund is replenished at the end of the month.

VI. Beyond the Numbers

1. Notice that there is separation of duties—one person issues the ticket and collects the money, and the other person oversees the admission to the opera house. Thus, a ticket is necessary to gain entrance.

   The tickets are serially numbered. Management can determine the amount of cash that should be in the drawer by multiplying the price of each ticket by the number of tickets issued.

2. To make the controls effective, management should 1) record the serial number of the first and last ticket sold on each cashier's shift, 2) maintain control over the unsold tickets, and 3) count the cash at the beginning and end of each shift. Also, management can compare the number of customers in the audience with the number of tickets taken at the door.

3. The controls are ineffective if there is collusion by the cashier and the door attendant. The door attendant may choose to keep the entire ticket instead of tearing it in half. The ticket is then given to

the cashier to be sold again. The cashier can then pocket the cash received for the "used" tickets. Remember, internal controls are ineffective if collusion exists.

VII. Demonstration Problems

Demonstration Problem #1

Requirement 1

Only three journal entries were required for this problem! Remember, the purpose of a petty cash fund is to make small disbursements while avoiding the time and cost of writing checks. Therefore, entries are only recorded when a fund is established, when the fund balance is changed, and when the fund is replenished.

10/1	Petty Cash	300.00	
	Cash in Bank		300.00
10/13	Silverman, Withdrawals	55.00	
	Postage Expense ($15.95 + $37.00)	52.95	
	Supplies	25.00	
	Inventory	45.00	
	Petty Cash	100.00	
	Cash in Bank		277.95

Amounts taken by the owner are charged to the owner's Withdrawals account. Freight charges on merchandise are debited to the Inventory account. Remember, freight charges on assets are debited to the asset account, not to an expense account. The receipts plus remaining cash did reconcile to the beginning balance of $300.00, so there was no Cash Short and Over. Since the supervisor authorized the fund to be replenished with $277.95 rather than the amount needed of $177.95, the additional $100.00 represents an increase to the petty cash fund balance.

10/31	Inventory	43.00	
	Silverman, Withdrawals	127.00	
	Accounts Receivable	20.00	
	Miscellaneous Expense ($22.50 + $25.00 + $75.00)	122.50	
	Cash Short and Over	3.00	
	Cash		315.50

The newspaper, coffee money, and window washing were all charged to Miscellaneous Expense, although they could be debited to separate accounts. The post-dated check is charged to Accounts Receivable because it represents an amount the employee owes the business. Allowing an employee to "borrow" from the petty cash fund violates effective internal control procedures and should be stopped immediately. If permitted to continue, the petty cash fund will contain nothing but a stack of post-dated checks! Finally, the receipts plus the remaining cash did not reconcile to the petty cash fund balance of $400.00, so Cash Short and Over was debited for a shortage of $3.00.

Requirement 2

Petty Cash Fund

10/1	300		
10/13	100		
Bal.	400		

Assuming the company is correct in its estimates that a $400 balance is sufficient for the petty cash fund, the general ledger account, Petty Cash Fund, will remain as presented above, with the $400 balance undisturbed.

Demonstration Problem #2

Requirement 1

Shell Co.
Bank Reconciliation
March 31, 20X9

BANK:		
Balance 3/31		$ 8,340
Add:		
Deposit in transit of 3/28		1,525
Deposit in transit of 3/31		428
Correction of bank error		572
		10,865
Less:		
Outstanding checks		
Check # 721	501	
Check # 723	282	
Check # 724	1,074	1,857
Adjusted bank balance 3/31		$ 9,008
BOOKS:		
Balance 3/31		$ 7,745
Add:		
Bank collection of note receivable,		
including interest of $108		1,308
Interest earned on bank balance		13
Error - Check #716		99
		9,165
Less:		
Bank Service charge		12
NSF check ($135 + service charge $10)		145
Adjusted book balance 3/31		$ 9,008

Explanation: bank reconciliation

1. A bank reconciliation prepared on a timely basis provides good internal control over a company's cash accounts. Comparing the cash balance in the general ledger with the cash balance maintained by the bank makes errors easy to detect.

2. The month-end balance shown in the general ledger rarely agrees with the month-end balance shown on the bank statement. The difference generally occurs for one of two reasons:

   1. Timing differences: These occur because of the time lag that occurs when one record keeper records a transaction before the other. Typical timing differences include:

      - Deposits in transit (the bank has yet to record)
      - Outstanding checks (the bank has yet to record)
      - Bank service charges (the company has yet to record)
      - Notes collected by the bank (the company has yet to record)
      - Interest earned on account (the company has yet to record)
      - NSF checks (the company has yet to record)

   2. Errors: An error must result in an adjustment by the record keeping party that made the error. If the company makes the error, a general journal entry is made. The correcting entry will include an increase or decrease to the Cash account. Note that if the bank has made the error, the proper procedure is to notify the bank promptly. Since the company's records are accurate, no journal entry is needed.

Requirement 2

Date	Accounts and Explanation	PR	Debit	Credit
a.	Cash		1,308	
	Note Receivable			1,200
	Interest Revenue			108
	Note Receivable collected by the bank.			
b.	Cash		13	
	Interest Revenue			13
	Interest earned on bank balance.			
c.	Miscellaneous Expense		12	
	Cash			12
	Bank service charge.			
d.	Accounts Receivable – Fred's Motors		145	
	Cash			145
	NSF check returned by bank plus service charge.			
e.	Cash		99	
	Accounts Payable			99
	To correct error in recording Check #716			

Explanations: Journal Entries

Entries (a) and (b) are necessary to record the increase in the cash account attributable to 1) the collection of interest and principal on the note receivable, and 2) interest earned on the account paid by the depository bank. These are timing differences that occur because of the time lag between the recording of an item on the bank's books and the books of the company. The bank has already recorded these items in its records (as evidenced by the bank statement), and the company must do so when it learns of the transaction(s).

Entries (c) and (d), which are similar to entries (a) and (b) reduce cash on the company's books. The bank has already recorded these timing differences. Entry (c) reduces cash for the account service charges for the monthly period and brings the account up to date. The entry for the NSF check is necessary to establish an account receivable for Fred's Motor Co. They had paid the company with a check that was deposited in the cash account. Because the check was returned unpaid for nonsufficient funds, the company must pursue collection of the debt and record on its books that $145 is still owed. Notice that the original amount of the check was $135, but now Fred's Motor Co. owes for the amount of the original check plus the $10 that the bank charged Shell Co. for the NSF Check.

Entry (e) represents the correction of an error. Check #716 was recorded in the cash disbursements journal as a reduction to Cash of $322 instead of $223. This error resulted in $99 too much being deducted from the company's checking account. To correct the error, $99 must be added back to the account.

Note: No entry is required for the bank error. Once notified, the bank needs to correct their books.

CHAPTER OVERVIEW

In Chapter 8 you learned about the importance of internal control, with the specific application of internal control procedures to cash and other highly liquid current assets. Chapter 9 extends the discussion to include other current assets, specifically receivables—both accounts and notes. The learning objectives for this chapter are to

1. Design internal controls for receivables.
2. Use the allowance method of accounting for uncollectibles by the percent-of-sales and the aging-of-accounts methods.
3. Use the direct write-off method to account for uncollectibles.
4. Account for notes receivable.
5. Report receivables on the balance sheet.
6. Use the acid-test ratio and days' sales in receivables to evaluate a company.

CHAPTER REVIEW

Receivables arise when goods or services are sold on credit. The basic types of receivables are:

- **Accounts receivable** are amounts that customers owe a business for purchases made on credit. Accounts receivable are collectible according to a firm's normal terms of sale, such as net 30 days. Accounts receivable are current assets and are sometimes called **trade receivables**.

- **Notes receivable** occur when customers sign formal agreements to pay for their purchases. These agreements are called **promissory notes**, and usually extend for periods of 60 days or longer. The portion of notes receivable scheduled to be collected within a year is classified as a current asset; any remaining amount is classified as a long-term asset.

- **Other receivables** may exist that include miscellaneous items such as loans to employees.

Helpful hint: Review Exhibit 9-1 in your text for the correct statement placement of these receivables.

Objective 1 - Design internal controls for receivables.

The main issues in controlling and managing the collection of receivables are:

1. Extending credit only to creditworthy customers
2. Separating cash-handling, credit, and accounting duties
3. Pursuing collection from customers to maximize cash flow

The main issues in accounting for receivables are:

1. Reporting receivables at the net realizable value (the amount we expect to collect)
2. Reporting the expense associated with uncollectible accounts

Helpful Hint: See the Decision Guidelines on page 313

It is imperative that cash handling and cash accounting duties be separated; otherwise, too many opportunities exist for employees to steal cash from the company. This is true in both the receivables department and the credit department.

Extending credit to customers involves the risk that some customers will not pay their obligations. The Uncollectible Account Expense account (also called Doubtful Account Expense or Bad Debt Expense) allows a company to recognize the cost the business incurs when it is unable to collect from some credit customers. This expense is a cost of doing business, and therefore, should be measured, recorded, and reported. There are two methods used by accountants to account for uncollectible accounts:

- The **allowance method** is the preferred way to account for Uncollectible Account Expense because it does a better job of matching the expense with the revenue earned. This method records collection losses in the same accounting period as the sale occurs and is based on estimates, rather than waiting to see which specific customers the company will not collect from.
- The **direct write-off method** records collection losses at the time the account becomes uncollectible. This method does not do a good job of matching the expense with the revenue earned because the revenue could be earned in one accounting period and the account could be written-off in a subsequent accounting period.

The **Allowance for Uncollectible Accounts** account is a contra asset account to Accounts Receivable that reports the estimate of the portion of the accounts receivable that the business **does not** expect to collect. Remember, contra accounts are subtracted from a related account. Examples from earlier chapters are Accumulated Depreciation (which is subtracted from a related plant asset) and Sales Discounts (which is subtracted from Sales Revenue). On the balance sheet, Accounts Receivable would appear as follows:

Accounts Receivable	XXX
- Allowance for Uncollectible Accounts	(XX)
= Net Accounts Receivable	XXX

The *net accounts receivable* also referred to as the *net realizable value* of the receivables reports the portion of the accounts receivable that the business **does** expect to collect.

Objective 2 - Use the allowance method to account for uncollectibles by the percent-of-sales and aging-of-accounts methods.

As previously mentioned, using the allowance method requires an estimate of uncollectible accounts. The journal entry to recognize uncollectible account expense is an adjusting entry that is recorded at the end of the accounting period with all the other adjusting entries that have been discussed. There are two allowance methods to account for uncollectible accounts:

1. The **percent-of- sales method** estimates the uncollectible accounts expense as a percentage of net credit sales, using the company's past experience to set the percentage. This method is called the *income statement approach* because the basis of the estimate, net credit sales, comes from the income statement. The amount of the journal entry is equal to net credit sales multiplied by the estimated percent uncollectible, and is recorded as:

Uncollectible Account Expense	XXX	
Allowance for Uncollectible Accounts		XXX

    Notice that the journal entry credits Allowance for Uncollectible Accounts not Accounts Receivable. This is because at the time the adjusting entry is made, the company does not know which specific customer will not pay. Remember that Accounts Receivable has a subsidiary ledger that consists of all the individual customer accounts. If a journal entry credits Accounts Receivable, then it must also credit a specific customer's account. The company cannot do this until it knows specifically who will not pay. The Allowance for Uncollectible Accounts account allows the accountant to reduce the total accounts receivables by the amount the company does not expect to collect before it knows who actually will not pay; thus, the account allows the company to report net accounts receivable.

2. **Aging-of- accounts** involves grouping accounts receivable according to the length of time they have been outstanding. This method is called the *balance sheet approach* because the basis of the estimate, accounts receivable, comes from the balance sheet. Accounts are usually grouped into 30-day increments, such as 1-30, 31-60, 61-90, and over 90 days. This is called aging the accounts. Each age has a different estimated percent uncollectible. This should make sense to you since the longer an account remains outstanding, the less likely it becomes that the company will collect the amount owed. The amount uncollectible for each age group is equal to the total receivables in that age group multiplied by the estimated percent uncollectible for that group. Then the amounts uncollectible for each age group are added together to get the total amount of estimated uncollectible accounts receivable. Review Exhibit 9-2 in your text.

    Remember that the Allowance for Uncollectible Accounts account reports the portion of the total accounts receivable that the company does not expect to collect. Therefore, the amount of the adjusting entry to recognize Uncollectible Account Expense will be the amount needed to bring the Allowance account to the total estimated uncollectible accounts receivable calculated using the aging-of-accounts method. Therefore, if the existing balance in the Allowance for Uncollectible Accounts is a credit, the amount of the journal entry will be less than the total estimated uncollectible accounts receivable. If the existing balance in the Allowance for Uncollectible Accounts is a debit, the amount of the journal entry will be greater than the total estimated uncollectible accounts receivable.
    The expense is recorded as:

| Uncollectible Account Expense | XX | |
| Allowance for Uncollectible Accounts | | XX |

Notice that the accounts for the adjusting entry using each method are the same. It is the amounts of the entry that differ as a result of using the two methods.

Study Tip: When using an estimate based on sales, adjust *for* the estimated amount; when using an estimate based on accounts receivable, adjust *to* the estimated amount. See Exhibit 9-3 in your text.

When using the allowance method, when a specific accounts receivable is determined to be uncollectible and is written off, the journal entry will be as follows:

| Allowance for Uncollectible Accounts | XX | |
| Accounts Receivable-Customer A | | XX |

Note that this entry does not affect an expense account because the estimated expense has already been recorded. The Allowance account will show the estimated uncollectible account expense and the actual write-off of accounts receivable as follows:

Allowance for Uncollectible Accounts

	Beg. Bal
Actual Write-off of	**Estimated Uncollectible**
Accounts Receivable	**Account Expense** (occurs
(occurs throughout the	at the end of the
accounting period)	accounting period)
	End. Bal

Occasionally, a business will collect an account receivable that has previously been written off. When this occurs, and the company uses the allowance method, two journal entries are required.

| Accounts Receivable-Customer A | XX | |
| Allowance for Uncollectible Accounts | | XX |

| Cash | XX | |
| Accounts Receivable-Customer A | | XX |

The first entry reestablishes the customer's receivable account for the amount the customer has indicated will be paid. Basically, it reverses the original write-off entry. The customer could be paying the full amount owed or some amount less than what is owed. You would not reestablish the customer's account receivable for more than what you expect to collect from that customer. The second entry records the cash received from the customer. It is important to use two entries in order to keep accurate payment information on each customer.

Objective 3 - Use the direct write-off method to account for uncollectibles.

Using the **direct write-off method**, the company writes off an account receivable directly to an expense account when the account is deemed uncollectible. In other words, the allowance account is not used.

The journal entry for a direct write-off is:

Uncollectible Account Expense	XX	
Accounts Receivable		XX

The direct write-off method is easy to use. Its major drawback is that the uncollectible account expense is not matched with the revenues to which it relates because the expense is usually recorded long after the corresponding revenue is recorded.

Should a customer's account carry a credit balances (usually the result of overpayments or returns following payments), the credit balance represent an obligation of the business to pay the customer and should be reported on the balance sheet as liabilities (rather than "netted" against the debit balances in Accounts Receivable).

Credit Card and Bankcard Sales

In the retail industry, credit card and bankcard usage has become universal which has shifted the risk of collection from the retail company to the credit card company. Credit cards and bankcards not only enable merchants to reduce the risk of uncollectible accounts receivable but also eliminate the need for accounts receivable subsidiary ledgers.

When a customer presents a credit card as payment for a purchase, a sales slip is prepared. The merchant keeps one copy, the customer keeps one copy, and one copy is forwarded to the credit card company. The credit card company charges the merchant a fee for processing the charge sale. This fee is usually a percent-of-sales, and ranges up to 5%. The merchant records:

Accounts Receivable - Credit Card Co.	XX	
Sales Revenue		XX

When the credit card company receives the charge slips, it processes them, bills its cardholders, and reimburses the merchant. The merchant records this entry:

Cash	XX	
Credit Card Discount Expense	XX	
Accounts Receivable - Credit Card Co.		XX

Bankcard sales (VISA, MasterCard) are treated differently from the credit card sales illustrated above. When a customer uses a bankcard, the transaction is immediately recorded at both the bank and the merchant. Therefore, the transaction is similar to a cash sale because the business receives its cash at the point of sale. A bankcard sale would be recorded as follows:

Cash	XX	
Bankcard Discount Expense	XX	
Sales Revenue		XX

Objective 4 - Account for notes receivable.

Notes receivable are more formal than accounts receivable. Usually, the maker (debtor) will sign a promissory note as evidence of the debt and must pay the principal amount plus interest to the payee (creditor) on the maturity date. The maturity value is the sum of the principal amount plus the interest.

Review Exhibit 9-4 in your text to be certain you are familiar with the following terms:

Promissory note	Interest period (note period or note term)
Maker	Maturity date (due date)
Payee	Maturity value
Principal amount	Interest rate
Interest	

The formula for computing interest is:

$$\text{Principal} \times \text{Interest Rate} \times \text{Time} = \text{Interest Amount}$$

It is important to study the examples in the text. You must be able to compute interest based on years, months, and days.

Generally notes arise from three events, as follows:

Sold goods and received a promissory note:

1)	Notes Receivable	XX	
	Sales		XX

Receipt of a note from a customer in payment of the account:

2)	Notes Receivable	XX	
	Accounts Receivable		XX

Loaned money and received a promissory note:

3)	Notes Receivable	XX	
	Cash		XX

Interest revenue is earned as time passes, and not just when cash is collected. If the interest period of the note extends beyond the current accounting period, then part of the interest revenue is earned in the current accounting period and part is earned in the next accounting period.

Interest must be accrued (you were introduced to accrued revenue in Chapter 3) for the amount that has been earned in the current period but not yet collected. The adjusting entry to record accrued interest is:

```
Interest Receivable                    XX
    Interest Revenue                        XX
```

On the maturity date, the payee will record collection of the note with this entry:

```
Cash (principal + interest)            XX
    Notes Receivable (principal only)           XX
    Interest Receivable (accrued in previous period) XX
    Interest Revenue (accrued in the current period) XX
```

This entry records: 1) the amount of cash received; 2) the collection of the note; 3) the collection of the interest receivable from the prior accounting period; and 4) the collection of the remaining interest revenue earned in the current accounting period.

If the maker of the note does not pay at maturity, the maker has **dishonored** (defaulted on) the note. The note agreement is no longer in force, but the payee (creditor) still has a claim against the maker (debtor). The payee usually transfers the claim from Notes Receivable to Accounts Receivable and records the interest revenue earned:

```
Accounts Receivable                    XX
    Notes Receivable                        XX
    Interest Revenue                        XX
```

Objective 5 - Report receivables on the balance sheet.

Firms report the value of accounts receivable on the balance sheet in various ways:

1. As a net value:

    Accounts Receivable (net of allowance for doubtful accounts) $XXX

2. With an explanatory note:

    Accounts Receivable (note X) $XXX

3. With detail in the body of the balance sheet:

```
Accounts Receivable                              $XXX
    Less:  Allowance for Uncollectible Accounts       XX        $XXX
```

Objective 6 - Use the acid-test ratio and the days' sales in receivables to evaluate a company.

The **acid-test (quick) ratio** measures the ability of a business to pay all of its current liabilities if they become due immediately.

Acid-test Ratio = $\dfrac{\text{Cash + Short-term investment + Net current receivables}}{\text{Current Liabilities}}$

> **Study Tip:** Remember that inventory, supplies, and prepaid expenses are not used to compute the acid-test ratio.

Days' sales in receivables (also called the collection period) measures the average number of days it takes the company to collect its receivable accounts.

One day's sales = $\dfrac{\text{Net Credit Sales (or Total Revenues)}}{365}$

Days' sales in receivables $= \dfrac{\text{Average Net Accounts Receivable*}}{\text{One day's sales}}$

*Average Net Accounts Receivable $= \dfrac{\text{Beginning Receivables + Ending Receivables}}{2}$

The days' sales in receivables, or collection period, should be compared to the company's credit terms in order to evaluate how the company is doing. If a company has credit terms of net 30, then they should have a collection period of approximately 30 days. If a company offers a discount, for example 2/10, n/30, then the collection period should be shorter than 30 days.

Chapter Appendix: Discounting a Note Receivable

A note receivable is a negotiable instrument. Frequently, a business will sell a note receivable to a bank when it needs the cash prior to the maturity date of the note. Selling a note receivable before its maturity date is called discounting a note receivable. The seller receives less than the maturity value (that is, gives up some of the interest revenue) in exchange for receiving cash. The discounted value, called the proceeds, is the amount the seller (business) receives from the purchaser (bank).

Proceeds are computed as:

Principal amount of the note
+ Interest (Principal × Rate × Time) (entire length of note)
= Maturity Value
- Discount (Maturity value × Discount Rate × Time) (time bank holds note)
= Proceeds

243

The business records the following entry when selling a note receivable:

Cash	XX (Proceeds)	
Notes Receivable		XX (Face Value of Note)
Interest Revenue		XX (difference if Proceeds > Face Value)

Sometimes the proceeds are less than the principal amount. In this situation, the entry is:

Cash	XX(Proceeds)	
Interest Expense	XX(difference if Proceeds < Face Value)	
Notes Receivable		XX(Face Value of Note)

Review Exhibit 9A-1 in your text.

TEST YOURSELF

All the self-testing materials in this chapter focus on information and procedures that your instructor is likely to test in quizzes and examinations.

I. Matching   *Match each numbered term with its lettered definition.*

_____ 1. Aging-of-accounts
_____ 2. Allowance for Uncollectible Accounts
_____ 3. Days' sales in receivables
_____ 4. Direct write-off method
_____ 5. Discounting a notes receivable
_____ 6. Interest
_____ 7. Maturity date
_____ 8. Payee
_____ 9. Promissory note
_____ 10. Uncollectible Account Expense

_____ 11. Allowance method
_____ 12. Creditor
_____ 13. Debtor
_____ 14. Dishonor a note
_____ 15. Interest period
_____ 16. Maker of a note
_____ 17. Maturity value
_____ 18. Principal amount
_____ 19. Receivable
_____ 20. Interest rate

A. Measures how long it takes a business to collect its average accounts receivable.
B. The party to a credit transaction who obtains a receivable
C. The party to a credit transaction who makes a purchase and credits a payable
D. Failure of the maker of a note to pay at maturity
E. A method of accounting for bad debts in which the company records uncollectible account expense and credits the customer's account receivable when the credit department decides that a customer's account receivable is uncollectible
F. Selling a note receivable before its maturity
G. Revenue to the payee for loaning out the principal, and expense to the maker for borrowing the principal
H. The person who signs a note and promises to pay the amount required by the note agreement
I. The date on which the final payment of a note is due
J. The entity who receives promised future payment on a note
K. The amount loaned out or borrowed
L. A written promise to pay a specified amount of money on a particular future date
M. A monetary claim against a business or an individual which results from selling goods or rendering services on credit
N. A way to estimate bad debts by analyzing individual accounts receivable according to the length of time they have been due
O. A contra asset account related to accounts receivable
P. A method of recording collection losses based on estimates made prior to determining that specific accounts are uncollectible
Q. The percentage rate multiplied by the principal amount to compute the amount of interest on a note
R. The time during which interest is computed
S. The sum of the principal and interest due at the maturity of a note
T. Cost of extending credit that arises from the failure to collect from credit customers

II. Multiple Choice   *Circle the best answer.*

1. Using the allowance method, writing off a specific account receivable will:

   A. increase net income.
   B. decrease net income.

   C. not affect net income.
   D. affect net income in an undetermined manner.

2. Uncollectible Account Expense is:

   A. a component of Cost of Goods Sold.
   B. an operating expense.

   C. a reduction to Sales.
   D. an Other Expense.

3. Which of the following will result if the adjusting entry for Uncollectible Account Expense is not recorded at the end of the year?

   A. Expenses will be overstated.
   B. Net Income will be understated.

   C. Liabilities will be understated.
   D. Assets will be overstated.

4. Net Realizable Value is equal to:

   A. Accounts Receivable - Allowance for Uncollectible Accounts
   B. Accounts Receivable + Allowance for Uncollectible Accounts
   C. Accounts Receivable - Uncollectible Account Expense
   D. Accounts Receivable + Uncollectible Account Expense

5. Accounts Receivable has a debit balance of $22,500 and the Allowance for Uncollectible Account has a credit balance of $1,500. A specific account of $200 is written off. What is the amount of net receivables after the write-off?

   A. $22,300
   B. $21,300

   C. $21,000
   D. $20,800

6. Allowance for Uncollectible Accounts is:

   A. an expense account.
   B. a contra liability account.

   C. a contra asset account.
   D. a liability account.

7. A 2-year note receivable reported on the balance sheet is classified as a:

   A. current asset.
   B. long-term asset.

   C. long-term liability.
   D. both A. and B.

8. Interest is equal to:

   A. Principal × Rate
   B. Principal ÷ Rate ÷ Time

   C. Principal × Rate ÷ Time
   D. Principal × Rate × Time

9. Using the direct write-off method, writing off a specific account receivable will:

   A. increase net income.
   B. decrease net income.
   C. not affect net income.
   D. affect net income in an undetermined manner.

10. Which of the following does not describe a business's cost of extending credit to customers who do *not* pay?

    A. Bad Debt Expense
    B. Uncollectible Account Expense
    C. Account Receivable Expense
    D. Doubtful Account Expense

III. Completion   *Complete each of the following statements.*

1. The direct write-off method of accounting for bad debt violates the _____ principle.
2. The method of estimating bad debts that focuses on the balance sheet is the _____ method.
3. Net accounts receivable refers to the portion of the total accounts receivable the business _____ expect to collect.
4. The method of estimating bad debts that focuses on the income statement is the _____ method.
5. The two allowances methods are: a.) _____ and b.) _____
6. Under the allowance method, the amount of uncollectible account expense is determined by using _____.
7. The _____ measures the ability of a business to pay all its current liabilities if they become due immediately.
8. The days' sales in receivables is also referred to as the _____.
9. On a promissory note, the person signing the note is called the _____ and the entity to which the promise of payment is being made is called the _____.
10A. The discount period refers to the length of time _____.

IV. Daily Exercises

1. Creative Solutions uses the Allowance method to account for bad debts. Indicate the effect that each of the following transactions will have on gross Accounts Receivable, the Allowance for Bad Debt, net Accounts Receivable, and Bad Debt Expense. Use "+" for increases; "—" for decreases; and "0" for no effect.

	Gross Accounts Receivable	Allowance for Bad Debt	Net Accounts Receivable	Bad Debt Expense
An account receivable is written off	_____	_____	_____	_____
An account receivable is reinstated	_____	_____	_____	_____
A customer pays his account receivable	_____	_____	_____	_____
2.0% of $1,000,000 in sales is estimated to be uncollectible	_____	_____	_____	_____
1.75% of $135,000 in accounts receivable is estimated to be uncollectible (the balance in the allowance account is a credit of $800)	_____	_____	_____	_____

2. Compute the missing amounts. Use a 360-day year and round to the nearest dollar.

	Principal	Interest rate	Time	Interest	Maturity Value
A.	$ 3,000	11%	6 months	_____	_____
B.	$10,000	8%	60 days	_____	_____
C.	_____	4%	90 days	_____	$9,045
D.	$ 14,000	_____	3 months	$315	_____

248

3. From the following list, present the current asset section of the balance sheet:

Accounts Receivable		$ 78,500
Allowance for Uncollectible Accounts		8,560
Cash		168,250
Inventory		325,400
Short-term Investments		35,600
Notes Receivable (60-days)		20,000
Notes Receivable (2-year)		45,000
Prepaid Expense		19,685

4. From the items in Daily Exercise #3, list those that would be used in calculating the acid-test ratio.

5. Carson Co. uses an allowance method in accounting for bad debts. Three months ago, it wrote off a $2,500 receivable from customer Jefferson. In today's mail, Carson receives a check from Jefferson for the entire amount along with a note apologizing for the delay in paying the delinquent invoice. Record the entry for the check from Jefferson.

Date	Accounts and Explanation	PR	Debit	Credit

6. Using the information in daily exercise #5, assume Carson Co. uses the direct write-off method for bad debts. Record the entry for the $2,500 payment.

Date	Accounts and Explanation	PR	Debit	Credit

V. Exercises

1. Santa Fe Market has a $210,000 balance in Accounts Receivable on December 31, 20X6. The Allowance for Uncollectible Accounts has a $700 credit balance. Credit sales totaled $650,000 for the year.

   a. If Santa Fe Market uses the percent-of-sales method and estimates that 1.5% of credit sales may be uncollectible, what is the Uncollectible Account Expense for 20X6?

   b. What is the ending balance in the Allowance for Uncollectible Accounts after adjustments?

   c. Would your answers to a. and b. be different if the Allowance for Uncollectible Accounts had a $700 debit balance? Explain your answer.

2. Assume the same account balances in Exercise #1 for Santa Fe Market:

   a. If Santa Fe Market uses the aging-of-accounts method and has determined that $11,000 of Accounts Receivable is uncollectible, what is the Uncollectible Account Expense for 20X6?

   b. What is the ending balance in the Allowance for Uncollectible Accounts after adjustments?

   c. Would your answers to a. and b. be different if the Allowance for Uncollectible Accounts had a $700 debit balance?

3. A $20,000, 120-day, 10% note is discounted at the bank at 12%, 15 days before maturity. What is the appropriate journal entry? Round to the nearest dollar.

Date	Accounts and Explanation	PR	Debit	Credit

4. From the following information, calculate the following ratios for 20X9: (Assume all sales are on credit.)
   a. Acid-test ratio
   b. Days' sales in receivables

	20X9	20X8
Cash	28,000	30,000
Short-term investments	155,000	143,000
Accounts receivable	282,000	135,000
Allowance for Uncollectible Accounts	9,400	9,000
Inventory	961,500	945,000
Prepaid expenses	48,760	53,920
Other current assets	26,410	21,485
Current liabilities	310,650	297,630
Sales	3,828,630	3,525,430
Sales discounts	19,775	20,360
Sales returns and allowances	86,125	84,650

5. Minatare Manufacturing Company sells truck beds. Assume the company uses a periodic inventory system. The company engaged in the following transactions involving promissory notes:

Jan   10   Sold beds to Glynn Company for $30,000, terms n/30.
      20   Accepted a 90-day, 12-percent note in settlement of the account from Glynn.
      ?   On the maturity date (must determine), received payment in full for note and interest from Glynn.
May   5   Sold beds to Mannesto Company for $20,000, terms n/10.
      15   Received $4,000 cash and a 60-day, 13-percent note for $16,000 in settlement of the Mannesto account.
      ?   When asked to pay on the maturity date, Mannesto dishonored the note.
Aug   2   Wrote off the Mannesto account as uncollectible after receiving news that the company declared bankruptcy. Minatare uses the allowance method for accounting for uncollectible accounts.
      5   Received a 90-day, 11-percent note for $15,000 from Sinostos Company in settlement of an account receivable.
      ?   When asked to pay, Sinostos dishonored the note.
Nov   9   Received payment in full from Sinostos.
      15   Received payment in full from Mannesto Corporation.

Prepare the necessary journal entries to record the above transactions. A "?" in the date column indicates that the maturity date of each note needs to be determined. Round to the nearest dollar.

Date	Accounts and Explanation	PR	Debit	Credit

VI. Beyond the Numbers

Review the information given in Exercise 3, but assume the interest rate and discount rate in the note was reversed. Therefore, assume the note carried a 12% interest rate while the bank was offering a 10% discount. At what point during the term of the note should the business discount the note? Support your answer.

_____
_____
_____
_____
_____
_____
_____
_____
_____
_____
_____
_____
_____

VII. Demonstration Problems

Demonstration Problem #1

Henderson, Inc. manufactures machine parts. The company's year-end trial balance for 20X9 reported the following:

	Debit	Credit
Accounts Receivable	3,125,200	
Allowance for Uncollectible Accounts		62,050

Assume that net credit sales for 20X9 amounted to $39,750,000 and Allowance for Uncollectible Accounts has not yet been adjusted for 20X9. Use the allowance method.

Required:

1. At the end of 20X9, the following accounts receivable were deemed uncollectible:

Shen Inc.	$ 8,520
Brown Corporation	4,125
Gonzalez Products	6,050
APL Co.	12,940
Total	$31,635

Prepare the 20X9 journal entry necessary to write off the above accounts.

2. Assume that the company uses the percent-of-sales method to estimate Uncollectible Account Expense. After analyzing industry averages and prior years' activity, management has determined that Uncollectible Account Expense for 20X9 should be 0.75% of net credit sales. Prepare the journal entry to record and adjust the Allowance for Uncollectible Accounts account.

3. Show the balance sheet presentation for Accounts Receivable after the adjustment in #2 has been posted.

4. Assume that the company uses the aging-of-accounts method. The aging schedule prepared by the company's credit manager indicated that an Allowance of $235,000 for uncollectible accounts is appropriate. Prepare the appropriate journal entry.

5. Show the balance sheet presentation for Accounts Receivable after the adjustment in #4 has been posted.

6. Calculate the days' sales in receivables assuming the adjustment in #4 above and beginning net receivables were $2,742,107.

Requirement 1 (Write-off of uncollectible accounts)

Date	Accounts and Explanation	PR	Debit	Credit

Requirement 2 (Adjustment to record Uncollectible Account Expense using the percent-of-sales method)

Date	Accounts and Explanation	PR	Debit	Credit

Requirement 3 (Balance sheet presentation)

Requirement 4 (Adjustment to record Uncollectible Account Expense using the aging-of-accounts method)

Date	Accounts and Explanation	PR	Debit	Credit

Requirement 5 (Balance sheet presentation)

Requirement 6 (Days' sales in receivables)

Demonstration Problem #2

Jacqueline's Boutique Designs is an exclusive, clothing designer. The accounting period of Jacqueline's ends December 31. Assume the company uses a perpetual inventory system. During 20X1 and 20X2, the business engaged in the following transactions:

20X1

Jun 1	Loaned $20,000 to Leather Clothiers, a supplier. Received a one-year 9% note.
Jun 10	Sold $11,000 in merchandise on account to Laurel Fashions, terms n/45. The cost of the sale was $6,750.
Jul 25	Received a 90-day, 10% note from Laurel Fashions in payment of their account.
Oct 23	Laurel Fashions paid the interest due on his note and replaced the old note with a new 120-day note at 12% interest.
Nov 1	Loaned $12,000 to KPT International, a supplier. Received a 120-day, 12% note.
Dec 21	Discounted the KPT note at the bank at 8%.

20X2

Feb 20	Laurel Fashions dishonored their note.
Jun 1	The bank notified Jacqueline's Boutique their note from Leather Clothiers was paid in full.
Sep 1	After numerous attempts to collect the Laurel Fashions account were unsuccessful, the account was written off. (Jacqueline's uses the allowance method).
Nov 1	Laurel Fashions sent Jacqueline's a check for $7,500 in partial settlement of the account previously owed. Laurel gave no indication that they would be able to pay the balance owed.

Required:
1. Prepare the necessary journal entries to record the 20X1 transactions on the books of Jacqueline's Boutique.
2. Make any adjusting entries needed on December 31, 20X1.
3. Record the 20X2 entries.

Requirement 1 (20X1 entries)

GENERAL JOURNAL

Date	Accounts and Explanation	PR	Debit	Credit

Date	Accounts and Explanation	PR	Debit	Credit

Requirement 2 (December 31, 20X1 adjusting entries)

GENERAL JOURNAL

Date	Accounts and Explanation	PR	Debit	Credit

Requirement 3 (20X2 entries)

GENERAL JOURNAL

Date	Accounts and Explanation	PR	Debit	Credit

SOLUTIONS

I. Matching

1. N	5. F	9. L	13. C	17. S
2. O	6. G	10. T	14. D	18. K
3. A	7. I	11. P	15. R	19. M
4. E	8. J	12. B	16. H	20. Q

II. Multiple Choice

1.   C   Writing off a specific account receivable using the allowance method takes the form of:

      Allowance for Uncollectible Accounts   XX
         Accounts Receivable   XX
      Both accounts involved are balance sheet accounts; accordingly, net income is not affected.

2.   B   Uncollectible Account Expense is estimated and recorded as an adjusting entry. It is a function of the operations of the business and is an operating expense.

3.   D   Failing to record the Uncollectible Accounts Expense also means that no increase in the Allowance for Uncollectible Accounts (contra accounts receivable) was recorded. Accordingly, expenses are understated and assets are overstated.

4.   A   Net realizable value or net accounts receivable is the result of netting the Accounts Receivable balance against its contra account, Allowance for Uncollectible Accounts. Net realizable value represents the portion of the total Accounts Receivable the company does expect to collect.

5.   C   When Accounts Receivable and the Allowance are both reduced by $200, Net Accounts Receivable will be unchanged.
      [$22,500 - $1,500 = ($22,500 - $200) - ($1,500 - $200)]

6.   C   Allowance for Uncollectible Accounts is a companion account to Accounts Receivable and has a normal credit balance while Accounts Receivable has a normal debit balance. A contra account has two distinguishing characteristics: 1) it always has a companion account, and 2) its normal balance is opposite that of the companion account.

7.   D   A note receivable is an asset. However, a two-year note receivable has a current and long-term portion. The portion of the receivable that will be converted to cash within the current accounting period is a current asset, while the portion of the receivable that will be collected in the following accounting period is a long-term asset.

8.   D   Interest is a function of the principal, the interest rate, and the term of the loan.

9.   B   Writing off an account using the direct write-off method will increase expenses that will have the effect of decreasing net income.

10. C   Of the items listed, all except "Accounts Receivable Expense" are acceptable account titles (descriptions) for the business's cost of extending credit to customers who do not pay.

III. Completion

1. matching (The direct write-off fails to match the business's cost of extending credit to customers who do not pay with the revenue generating the expense.)
2. aging-of-accounts (Aging the accounts focuses on estimating the appropriate balance in the contra account receivable account, Allowance for Uncollectible Accounts.)
3. does. (When the accounts receivable represent a significant portion of a company's current assets, the company must report the net accounts receivable, or the portion of the total accounts receivable that the company does expect to collect. The company does this by using an Allowance for Uncollectible Accounts account that holds the portion of the total accounts receivable the company *does not* expect to collect.
4. percent-of-sales (The percent-of-sales method focuses on calculating the appropriate cost to match against sales in the current period as Uncollectible Accounts Expense.)
5. percent-of-sales and aging-of-accounts
6. estimates (The estimated percent uncollectible is based on the company's past experience.)
7. acid-test (quick) ratio
8. collection period
9. maker, payee
10. from date the note is discounted to the maturity date

IV. Daily Exercises

1.	Gross Accounts Receivable	Allowance for Bad Debt	Net Accounts Receivable	Bad Debt Expense
An account receivable is written off	-	-	0	0
An account receivable is reinstated	+	+	0	0
A customer pays his account receivable	-	0	-	0
1.5% of $900,000 in sales is estimated to be uncollectible	0	+	-	+
3% of $80,000 in accounts receivable is estimated to be uncollectible (the balance in the allowance account is a credit of $200)	0	+	-	+

2.

   A. Interest = $3,000 × .11 × 6/12 = $165
       Maturity value = $3,000 + $165 = $3,165

   B. Interest = $10,000 × .08 × 60/360 = $133
       Maturity value = $10,000 + $133 = $10,133

   C. Maturity value = principal + interest
       Interest = principal × rate × time
       $9,045 = P + (P × .04 × 90/360)
       P = $8,955
       Interest = $90

   D. Interest = principal × rate × time
       $315 = $14,000 × R × 3/12
       R = 9%
       Maturity value = principal + interest
       Maturity value = $14,000 + $320 = $14,320

3.

Cash		$ 168,250
Short-Term Investments		35,600
Accounts Receivable	$ 78,500	
Less: Allowance for uncollectible accounts	8,560	69,940
Notes Receivable		20,000
Inventory		325,400
Prepaid Expenses		19,685
		$ 638,875

4. The acid-test ratio only uses those current assets that can be converted into cash quickly; therefore, the following would be included: Cash, Short-Term Investments, Accounts Receivable (net), and Notes Receivable.

    For most businesses, Inventory is not considered a quick asset and prepaid expenses are never included.

5. When a previously written off receivable is collected, two entries are required. One entry re-instates the receivable, while the second entry records the collection.

Accounts Receivable-Jefferson.	2,500	
Allowance for Uncollectible Accounts		2,500
To re-instate the Jefferson account		
Cash	2,500	
Accounts Receivable - Jefferson		2,500
To record collection of the Jefferson account		

6.

Accounts Receivable - Jefferson	2,500	
Bad Debt Expense		2,500
Cash	2,500	
Accounts Receivable - Jefferson		2,500

V. Exercises

1.
   a. Uncollectible Account Expense = .015 × $650,000 = $9,750
   b. Ending balance in Allowance for Uncollectible Accounts = $700 + $9,750 = $10,450
   c. The amount of Uncollectible Account Expense would be the same. However, the balance in the Allowance for Uncollectible Accounts would be different ($9,750 - 700 = $9,050).

2.
   a. The current balance in the Allowance account is $700 credit and the desired balance in the Allowance account is $11,000 credit. The Uncollectible Account Expense will be $11,000 - $700 = $10,300.
   b. The ending balance will be $11,000.
   c. The Allowance account would require a credit of $11,700 to bring the balance to a credit of $11,000; the corresponding debit is to the Uncollectible Account Expense. The ending balance in the Allowance account will be the same, $11,000.

3.

Cash	20,564	
Interest Revenue		564
Note Receivable		20,000

Maturity value = $20,000 + ($20,000 × .10 × 120/360) = $20,667

Discount = $20,667 × .12 × 15/360 = $103

Proceeds = $20,667 - $103 = $20,564

4. a.

$$\text{Acid-test ratio} = \frac{\$28,000 + \$155,000 + \$282,000 - \$9,400}{\$310,650} = 1.47$$

b.

$$\text{Days' sales in receivables} = \frac{(\$272,600 + \$126,000) \div 2}{\$3,722,370 \div 360} = 19.54 \text{ days}$$

5.

Date	Accounts and Explanation	PR	Debit	Credit
20X6				
Jan 10	Account Receivable-Glynn Co.		30,000	
	Sales Revenue			30,000
20	Notes Receivable-Glynn Co.		30,000	
	Accounts Receivable-Glynn Co.			30,000
Apr 20	Cash (maturity value)		30,900	
	Notes Receivable-Glynn Co. (principal)			30,000
	Interest Revenue ($30,000 x .12 x 90/360)			900
May 5	Accounts Receivable-Mannesto Co.		20,000	
	Sales Revenue			20,000
15	Cash		4,000	
	Notes Receivable-Mannesto Co.		16,000	
	Accounts Receivable-Mannesto Co.			20,000
July 14	Accounts Receivable-Mannesto Co. (maturity value)		16,347	
	Notes Receivable-Mannesto Co. (principal)			16,000
	Interest Revenue ($16,000 x .13 x 60/360)			347
Aug 2	Allowance for Uncollectible Accounts		16,347	
	Accounts Receivable-Mannesto Co.			16,347
5	Notes Receivable-Sinostos Co.		15,000	
	Accounts Receivable-Sinostos Co.			15,000
Nov 3	Accounts Receivable-Sinostos Co. (maturity value)		15,413	
	Notes Receivable-Sinostos Co. (principal)			15,000
	Interest Revenue ($15,000 x .11 x 90/360)			413
9	Cash		15,413	
	Accounts Receivable-Sinostos Co.			15,413
15	Accounts Receivable-Mannesto Co.		16,347	
	Allowance for Uncollectible Accounts			16,347
15	Cash		16,347	
	Accounts Receivable-Mannesto Co.			16,347

VI. Beyond the Numbers

The business should discount the note (sell it to the bank) as soon as possible, preferably upon receiving the note. Why? Assuming the note is discounted upon receipt, the entries would be:

Exercise 3

Cash	20,107	
Interest Revenue		107
Note Receivable		20,000

(Maturity value is $20,800; the discount is $693 = $20,800 \times 10\% \times 120/360$; proceeds are $20,800 - $693 = 20,107$)

If you examine this entry carefully, you will see that the interest has been earned without the holder (the business) keeping the note for even one day. This will only occur where the discount rate is less than the interest rate on the note.

VII. Demonstration Problems

Demonstration Problem #1

Requirement 1 (Write-off of uncollectible accounts)

Date	Accounts and Explanation	PR	Debit	Credit
20X9				
Dec 31	Allowance for Uncollectible Accounts		31,635	
	Accounts Receivable - Shen, Inc.			8,520
	Accounts Receivable - Brown Corporation			4,125
	Accounts Receivable – Gonzalez Products			6,050
	Accounts Receivable - APL Co.			12,940
	To write off uncollectible accounts.			

Requirement 2 (Adjustment to record Uncollectible Account Expense using the percentage-of-sales method)

Uncollectible Account Expense	298,125	
Allowance for Uncollectible Accounts		298,125

Net credit sales of 20X9 were $39,750,000. Uncollectible Account Expense for 20X9 is therefore $298,125 (39,750,000 × 0.75% = 298,125). An examination of the activity to date in the Uncollectible Account Expense and Allowance for Uncollectible Accounts reveals the effect of the entries made in Requirements 1 and 2.

Uncollectible Account Expense		Allowance for Uncollectible Accounts		Accounts Receivable	
(2) 298,125		(1) 31,635	Bal. 62,050	Bal. 3,125,200	(1) 31,635
Bal. 298,125			(2) 298,125	Bal. 3,093,565	
			Bal. 328,540		

Note that the Allowance account started at $62,050. In requirement 1, it was reduced by $31,635 when the uncollectible accounts were written off against the Allowance account. Note that prior to the 20X9, adjustment, the Allowance was down to $30,415 ($62,050 - $31,635 = $30,415). The Allowance was then adjusted upward to $328,540 in Entry 2, when the company recorded 20X9 Uncollectible Account Expense of $298,125.

Requirement 3 (Balance Sheet representation)

Accounts Receivable	3,093,565	
Less: Allowance for Uncollectible Accounts	328,540	2,765,025

Requirement 4 (Adjustment to record Uncollectible Account Expense using the aging-of-accounts)

Uncollectible Account Expense	204,585	
Allowance for Uncollectible Accounts		204,585

When the aging-of-accounts method is used, the adjustment brings Allowance for Uncollectible Accounts to the balance indicated by the aging schedule. Before adjustment, the balance in the allowance account was $30,415. The facts reveal that the desired balance in the allowance account should be set at $235,000. The difference between the unadjusted balance and the desired balance ($235,000 - $30,415 = $204,585) represents the amount of the adjustment and the amount of expense.

Study Tip: When using the percent-of-sales method, adjust for the estimate. When using accounts receivable as a basis for the estimate, adjust to the estimate (i.e., the estimate should be the balance in the allowance account after the adjusting entry is posted).

Requirement 5 (Balance Sheet representation)

Accounts Receivable	3,093,565	
Less: Allowance for Uncollectible Accounts	235,000	2,858,565

Requirement 6 (Days' Sales in receivable)

Sales in receivables = Average net Accounts Receivable ÷ One day's sales
One day's sales = Net sales ÷ 365 = $39,750,000 ÷ 365 = $108,904 (rounded)
Average net Accounts Receivable = ($2,742,107 + $2,858,565) ÷ 2 = $2,800,336
Days' sales in receivables = $2,800,336 ÷ $108,904 = 25.7 days

Demonstration Problem #2 Solved and Explained

Requirement 1 (20X1 entries)

20X1

June 1	Notes Receivable - Leather Clothiers	20,000	
	Cash		20,000

This entry is necessary to record the loan transaction with the debtor Leather Clothiers. A note receivable account is debited indicating that the debtor has signed a written promise to pay Jacqueline's $20,000 plus interest, due in one year.

Jun 10	Accounts Receivable-Laurel Fashions	11,000	
	Sales Revenue		11,000
10	Cost of Goods Sold	6,750	
	Inventory		6,750

These two entries are necessary to record the sale of inventory to Laurel Fashions.

July 25	Notes Receivable-Laurel Fashions	11,000	
	Accounts Receivable-Laurel Fashions		11,000

When a customer does not pay their account within the terms of the sale, they may be asked to sign a promissory note and convert their account receivable to a note receivable.

Oct 23	Cash	275	
	Notes Receivable-Laurel Fashions	11,000	
	Interest Revenue		275
	Notes Receivable-Laurel Fashions		11,000

This entry records the interest only payment made by Laurel. October 23 is the maturity date of the original note, and since Laurel did not repay the principal, another note is issued, but at a higher interest rate of 12%. The journal entry could have omitted the debit and credit to the Notes Receivable-Laurel account; however, you would have to make sure that you establish the issue date of the new note of October 23 in order to correctly accrue the interest at December 31.

| Nov. 1 | Note Receivable - KPT International | 12,000 | |
| | Cash | | 12,000 |

This entry records the three-month loan to KPT International. Because the interest on the note is actually paid at maturity, and the note was held during two accounting periods, an adjusting entry will be necessary on December 31 to record one month of accrued interest.

Dec 21	Cash	12,286	
	Interest Revenue		286
	Notes Receivable-KPT International		12,000

When a note receivable is discounted, the bank charges a discount. The discount is calculated by the bank based on the maturity value of the note, the bank's discount rate, and the length of time the bank holds the note until maturity. The maturity value is the amount the bank ultimately expects to receive when the note is collected. The $12,480 maturity value of the KPT International note includes the principal of the note ($12,000) plus the interest required to be paid by the debtor (in this case, $480). The interest expense or interest revenue arising from the discounting transaction is derived by simply netting the proceeds actually received from the bank with the principal (or "face" amount) of the note. The proceeds will be the maturity value minus the bank's discount.

COMPUTATIONS:

Principal	$12,000
Plus: Interest ($12,000 × .12 × 120/360)	480
Maturity value	12,480
Less: Discount ($12,480 × .08 × 70/360)	194
Proceeds	12,286

Proceeds	$ 12,286
Less: Principal of note	12,000
Interest Revenue	286

Requirement 2 (December 31, 20X1 adjusting entries)

| Dec. 31 | Interest Receivable | 1,303 | |
| | Interest Revenue | | 1,303 |

This entry records the interest earned on the note owed by Leather Clothiers from June 1 through December 31 and the note owed by Laurel Fashions from October 23. Interest is earned on the Leather Clothiers note at $1,050 or ($20,000 × .09 × 7/12). Interest earned on the Laurel note is $253 or ($11,000 x .12 x 69/360). $1,050 + $253 = $1,303.

Requirement 3 (20X2 entries)

```
20X2
Feb 20    Accounts Receivable-Laurel Fashions        11,440
               Note Receivable-Laurel Fashions                  11,000
               Interest Receivable                                  253
               Interest Revenue                                     187
```

This entry is required to record the dishonored note by Laurel Fashions. The maturity value of the note reverts to an Account Receivable and the Note Receivable-Laurel Fashions account is credited to show that the note no longer exists. The credit to Interest Receivable accounts for the accrued interest recorded on December 31. And, the Interest Revenue represent the interest accrued from January 1, 20X2 through February 10, 20X2, the maturity date of the note.

```
Jun. 1    Cash                                       21,800
               Interest Receivable                               1,050
               Interest Revenue                                    750
               Notes Receivable-Leather Clothiers               20,000
```

This entry is required to record the note paid in full by Leather Clothiers. The credit to Interest Receivable accounts for the accrued interest on this note from December 31. And, the Interest Revenue represent the interest accrued from January 1, 20X2 through June 1, 20X2 the maturity date of the note.

```
Sept. 1   Allowance for Uncollectible Accounts       11,440
               Accounts Receivable – Laurel Fashions            11,440
```

Under the allowance method, the balance in the accounts receivable is written off against the allowance account.

```
Nov 1   Accounts Receivable – Laurel Fashions         7,500
               Allowance for Uncollectible Accounts              7,500

     1  Cash                                           7,500
               Accounts Receivable – Laurel Fashions             7,500
```

These two entries are required to record the receipt of payment from Laurel Fashions after the account has been written off. The first entry reestablished the Account Receivable and the second entry records the collection of cash. Notice that the Account Receivable is not reestablished for the total amount originally owed by Laurel. This is because Laurel has only sent a check for $7,500 and has not indicated they have any intention to pay the remaining amount. Jacqueline's would be overstating the Accounts Receivable by reestablishing the original amount owed since it is not an amount they can expect to collect.

Chapter 10—Plant Assets and Intangibles

CHAPTER OVERVIEW

We have discussed how companies maintain control over three very important current assets: cash, receivables, and inventories. In this chapter, we continue the discussion with specific applications to non-current assets, also called long-lived, or long-term assets. Long-term assets include things such as equipment, buildings, natural resources, and intangible assets; all of which are used to support the operations of the business. The learning objectives for the chapter are to

1. Measure the cost of a plant asset.
2. Account for depreciation.
3. Select the best depreciation method for tax purposes.
4. Account for the disposal of a plant asset.
5. Account for natural resources.
6. Account for intangible assets.

CHAPTER REVIEW

Objective 1 - Measure the cost of a plant asset.

Business assets are classified as current or long-term assets. Current assets are considered to be useful for one year or less. Long-term assets are expected to be useful longer than a year. Plant assets (also called fixed assets) are long-term assets that a business uses in operations such as land, buildings, equipment, automobiles and airplanes. Plant assets are tangible; that is, they have physical form.

Typically, we think in terms of the cost of something being equal to the purchase price. For example, when you go to purchase a jacket, what is the total cost of the jacket? You would pay the price indicated on the price tag, plus sales tax, if any, plus any shipping and handling if you placed the order online. Thus, the total cost of the jacket would be more than the amount marked on the price tag. Thus, for accounting purposes, we recognize the total cost of a plant asset as the purchase price plus all other amounts paid to acquire the asset and make it ready for its intended use.

- The **cost of land** includes the purchase price, brokerage commission, survey fees, legal fees, any related taxes including back property taxes, costs to grade or clear the land, and costs to demolish or remove any unwanted buildings or structures. The cost of land is not depreciated, as land does not decrease in usefulness over time. **Land improvements**, such as roads, paving, fencing, driveways, parking lots, and lawn sprinkler systems, are not included in the cost of land because the usefulness of the land improvement decreases over time. Improvements to land should be recorded in a separate asset account and depreciated over the land improvement's estimated useful life.

- The **cost of a building** includes the purchase price, brokerage commission, taxes, and any expenditure to repair or renovate the building to make it ready for its intended use.

- The **cost of machinery and equipment** includes the purchase price less any discounts, plus transportation charges, transportation insurance, sales and related taxes, commissions, and installation and training costs. It is important to recognize that the only costs that become part of the acquisition cost of the asset are those costs incurred before the asset is used. Any routine expenditure that is incurred after the asset is used is recorded as an expense.

- The cost of **furniture and fixtures** includes the purchase price less any discounts, plus all other costs incurred to get the asset ready to use. Furniture and fixtures include desks, chairs, file cabinets, and display racks used in the business.

Sometimes a company purchases several assets for one single amount (also known as a **group purchase** or a **basket purchase**). When this type of transaction occurs, the total cost of the basket purchase must be divided between each individual asset purchased using the relative-sales-value method. To use the **relative-sales-value method**, it is necessary to:

1. Determine the market value of each asset by appraisal of the assets.
2. Add the individual asset market values together to obtain the total market value of all assets that have been acquired.
3. Calculate a ratio of the market value of each individual asset to the total market value of all assets (item 1 divided by item 2).
4. Multiply the ratio for each asset (from item 3) by the total purchase price paid for the assets. The resulting amounts will be considered the cost of each of the assets in the basket purchase.

When a company spends money on a plant asset, it must decide between two categories of expenditures:

- **Capital expenditures** are expenditures that significantly affect the asset by 1) increasing the asset's productive capacity, 2) increasing the asset's efficiency, or 3) extending the asset's useful life. Capital expenditures are **capitalized,** meaning they are debited to an asset account:

Asset	XX	
Cash (or Accounts/Notes Payable)		XX

- **Revenue expenditures** are routine in nature and maintain the existing condition of an asset or restore an asset to good working order. Revenue expenditures are debited to an expense account:

Expense Account	XX	
Cash (or Accounts Payable)		XX

The majority of expenditures related to plant assets are repairs to the assets. **Major or extraordinary repairs** are capital expenditures, while **ordinary repairs** are revenue expenditures. Review Exhibit 10-3 in your text.

Objective 2 - Account for depreciation.

Depreciation is the process of allocating a plant asset's cost to expense over the useful life of the asset. Depreciation refers to the portion of the cost of an asset that is recognized as expense, or matched, to the same accounting period as the revenue that is generated by the use of the asset. Remember, the contra-asset account, Accumulated Depreciation, is used to record the total amount of a plant asset's cost that has been recorded as depreciation expense.

Depreciation can be caused by normal wear and tear that results from using an asset on a regular basis. For example, an automobile has a limited number of miles that it can be driven before it wears out and is no longer useful to the business. Depreciation also results from obsolescence. An asset becomes obsolete when another asset can do the same job more efficiently. Computers, software and electronic equipment may become obsolete before the asset physically wears out. Thus, an asset's useful life to the business may be shorter than its actual physical life.

It is important to be clear on what depreciation is *not*:
- *Depreciation is not a process of valuation.* In an accounting context, depreciation does not refer to the market value of assets, nor is the amount of depreciation expense recognized based on the market value of assets. Depreciation is nothing more than systematically shifting a portion of the cost of the asset off the balance sheet and onto the income statement as depreciation expense.
- *Depreciation does not mean that the business sets aside cash to replace an asset when it is used up.* A company may use some type of reserve fund or cash fund to set aside money to replace an asset when it is used up. Depreciation has nothing to do with establishing any type of cash fund for the future replacement of an asset.

The adjusting journal entry to record depreciation is:

Depreciation Expense	XX	
Accumulated Depreciation		XX

To measure the amount (XX) of depreciation to recognize, it is necessary to first identify three elements about an asset:
1. **The plant asset's cost** (discussed in Objective 1)
2. **Estimated useful life** is the length of service a business expects from the plant asset. Useful life may be expressed as a length of time, units of output, or other measures. For example, a computer may be expected to be useful for four years, while a copier might be expected to make one million copies over its useful life. Note that the useful life of an asset is an *estimate* of the usefulness of an asset and is not necessarily related to the physical life. For example, an asset such as a computer may become obsolete long before it physically deteriorates.
3. **Estimated residual value** is the expected cash value of an asset at the end of its useful life. It is also called scrap or salvage value.

Then, the accountant must select an appropriate depreciation method for the asset. There are three major methods that exist for computing the amount (XX) of depreciation expense to recognize each accounting period:

1. The **straight-line (SL) depreciation method** allocates the depreciable cost of a plant asset to depreciation expense in equal amounts over the life of the asset. The **depreciable cost** of an asset is its cost minus residual value. Depreciable cost refers to the portion of the total cost of the asset that will be recognized as depreciation expense over the asset's estimated useful life.

The formula to determine the amount of depreciation expense to record using the straight-line method of depreciation is:

$$\text{Depreciation expense} = \frac{\text{cost - residual value (depreciable cost)}}{\text{estimated useful life in years}}$$

The straight-line depreciation rate can be determined by the following formula:

SL rate (%) = 1 ÷ Useful life in years

For example, if you have an asset that is estimated to have a five-year useful life. Then the SL rate would be (1 ÷ 5) = 20%. This means that the company will depreciate 20% of the asset's depreciable cost each year.

Recall that the adjusting entry to record depreciation expense is:

Depreciation Expense	XX	
Accumulated Depreciation		XX

As accumulated depreciation increases each year, the remaining **book value of the asset** (cost - accumulated depreciation) declines. The book value of an asset refers to the portion of the cost of the asset that **has not** been depreciated. The final book value of an asset will be equal to its residual value.

Helpful Hint: See Exhibit 10-6 for an example of straight-line depreciation.

2. The **units-of-production (UOP) depreciation method** allocates the depreciable cost of an asset to depreciation expense based on the number of units of output that the asset is expected to produce. When using the UOP method of computing depreciation expense, you must first calculate the UOP depreciation per unit of output before you can calculate the amount of depreciation expense. The UOP depreciation per unit of output is calculated as follows:

$$\text{UOP depreciation per unit of output (or the depreciable cost per unit)} = \frac{\text{cost - residual value (depreciable cost)}}{\text{useful life in units}}$$

Once you have calculated the UOP depreciation per unit of output, the amount of depreciation expense for the period can be determined by multiplying it by the units of output for the period:

Depreciation Expense = UOP depreciation per unit of output × units of output in the period

Helpful Hint: See Exhibit 10-7 for an example of units-of-production depreciation.

While the straight-line method could be used for any plant asset, the UOP method is not appropriate for all assets. Rather, it is used for assets where the life is a function of use rather than time. (For example, the basis of depreciating an airplane might be more appropriately measured using flight hours rather than years. Similarly, an automobile's useful life might be more appropriately measure using miles.)

Study Tip: Of the three methods discussed in this section, UOP is the only one that ignores time in the formula. Also, SL and UOP both require that the depreciable cost of the asset be determined first, and then divided by the appropriate depreciation base, either years or units.

---

3. The **double-declining-balance (DDB) method** is an accelerated depreciation method. **Accelerated depreciation** simply means that a larger portion of an asset's cost is allocated to depreciation expense in the early years of an asset's life, and a smaller portion is allocated to depreciation expense toward the end of the asset's useful life. DDB is different from SL and UOP, in that the residual value is ignored when determining the amount of depreciation expense to recognize for the accounting period.

To compute double-declining-balance depreciation, use the following steps:
   a. Compute the straight-line depreciation rate per year:

   SL rate (%) = 1 ÷ Useful life in years

   b. Multiply the straight-line depreciation rate per year by 2 (double it) to obtain the double-declining-balance rate:

   DDB rate (%) = (1 ÷ Useful life in years) × 2

   c. To determine the amount of depreciation expense to recognize each period, multiply the asset's book value at the beginning of the year (remember that book value equals cost minus accumulated depreciation) by the DDB rate. Book value will decrease each period; therefore depreciation expense will decrease each period. Note that the residual value of the asset is ignored until the book value of the asset approaches the asset's residual value.

   Depreciation Expense = DDB rate × book value

   d. When the book value of the asset approaches the asset's residual value in the final year, adjust the year's depreciation expense so that the remaining book value of the asset is equal to the residual value.

   Final year's depreciation expense = Book value - Residual value

   Depreciation is no longer recorded after the book value of the asset is reduced to the residual value, even if the asset is still in use.

Helpful Hint: See Exhibit 10-8 for an example of double-declining-balance depreciation.

Objective 3 - Select the best depreciation method for tax purposes.

Although depreciation expense is a noncash expense, the amount of depreciation expense recorded affects the amount of income tax a business pays. A higher amount of depreciation expense will reduce taxable income, and therefore income tax payments. Using an accelerated depreciation method will increase depreciation expense in the early years of an asset's life. This will decrease taxable income and income taxes, but only initially. The cash available to the business increases because tax payments are reduced.

For federal income tax purposes, the IRS has in place a **Modified Accelerated Cost Recovery System (MACRS**, pronounced "makers"). MACRS ignores both residual value and estimated useful life, and simply assigns assets to one of eight life classes, most of which (but not all) are based on double-declining balance. See Exhibit 10-11 in your text for an example of the MACRS schedule.

If a plant asset is held for only part of the year, partial year depreciation is computed by multiplying the full year's depreciation by the fraction of the year that the asset is held.

If a company finds that a change is warranted in the estimate of a plant asset's useful life, using the straight-line depreciation method, it computes revised annual depreciation expense this way:

$$\frac{\text{Book value - Residual value}}{\text{Remaining life}}$$

If an asset becomes fully depreciated (i.e., book value = residual value) but remains in use, both the asset and contra asset account should remain in the ledger until the business disposes of the asset.

Objective 4 - Account for the disposal of a plant asset.

With the possible exception of land, eventually a plant asset will no longer serve the needs of the business. The business will generally dispose of the asset by junking it, selling it, or exchanging it. The simplest accounting entry occurs when a company junks an asset. If the asset is fully depreciated with no residual value, the entry to record its disposal is:

Accumulated Depreciation—Asset	XX	
Asset		XX

If the asset is not fully depreciated or has a residual value, a loss is recorded for the remaining book value:

Accumulated Depreciation—Asset	X	
Loss on Disposal of Asset	X	
Asset		XX

These entries have the effect of removing the asset from the books. Notice that the company gives up the old asset, and does not receive anything back at the time of disposal.

When an asset is sold, the company gives up the old asset and receives cash at the time of the disposal. Use the following steps to properly remove the asset from the accounting records:

Step 1: Update depreciation for the partial year of service. Depreciation is recorded from the beginning of the accounting period to the date of the sale:

Depreciation Expense	XX	
Accumulated Depreciation—Asset		XX

Step 2: Compute the remaining book value:

Book Value = Cost - Accumulated Depreciation

Step 3: Record the journal entry to remove the asset from the books.

If cash received is greater than the remaining book value, a gain is recorded:

Cash	XX	
Accumulated Depreciation—Asset	XX	
Asset		XX
Gain on Sale of Asset		XX

If cash received is less than the remaining book value, a loss is recorded:

Cash	XX	
Loss on Sale of Asset	XX	
Accumulated Depreciation—Asset	XX	
Asset		XX

Gains and losses will appear on the income statement. Gains will increase income and losses will decrease income.

When plant assets are exchanged or traded in, the company gives up the old asset and receives a new asset at the time of the disposal. Therefore, the balance for the old asset must be removed from the books and the replacement asset must be recorded. Use the following steps to record an exchange.

Step 1: Update depreciation for the partial year of service. Depreciation is recorded from the beginning of the accounting period to the date of the exchange:

      Depreciation Expense   XX
          Accumulated Depreciation—Asset   XX

Step 2: Compute the remaining book value of the old asset:

      Book Value = Cost - Accumulated Depreciation

Step 3: Record the journal entry to remove the asset from the books.

      Asset (new)   XX
      Accumulated Depreciation—Asset (old)   XX
          Asset (old)   XX
          Cash   XX

[handwritten annotation:] Selling Price - Book Value / Gain or Loss (Cr.) (Dr.)

The debit to Accumulated Depreciation-Asset (old) and the credit to Asset (old) remove the old asset from the books just as we have seen before when an asset was junked or sold. The credit to cash represents how much cash had to be paid at the time the old asset was traded in on a new similar asset. The amount that becomes the cost basis of the new asset is equal to the book value of the old asset plus any cash paid at the time of the exchange. This is the most common type of exchange transaction. Notice that no gain or loss is recognized at the time of the exchange.

Objective 5 - Account for natural resources.

Depletion expense is that portion of the cost of **natural resources** used up in a particular period and is computed using the units-of-production formula. The appropriate entry is:

      Depletion Expense   XX
          Accumulated Depletion   XX

Objective 6 - Account for intangible assets.

Intangible assets are assets that have no physical substance, yet they still support the operations of the business. They include patents, copyrights, trademarks, brand names, franchises, leaseholds, and goodwill. The acquisition cost of an intangible asset is recorded as:

      Intangible Asset   XX
          Cash   XX

The cost of intangible assets is expensed through **amortization** over the asset's estimated useful life using the straight-line method. Amortization is recorded as:

      Amortization Expense   XX
          Intangible Asset   XX

The term amortization is to intangible assets what depreciation is to tangible assets. However, there are some differences. Note that the book value of the intangible asset is reduced directly. There is no

Accumulated Amortization account. Additionally, the residual value of most intangible assets is zero. Finally, the useful life of many amortizable assets is much shorter than the legal life of such assets—for example; copyrights have a legal life of 50 years beyond the author's life, but will be amortized for accounting purposes over a much shorter period of time.

One important type of intangible asset is **goodwill**. Goodwill is recorded only when another company is acquired and the price paid for the company is greater than the market value of the net assets. To determine if goodwill exists, subtract the market value of the acquired company's net assets (assets – liabilities) from the price paid for the acquired company. If Price Paid > Market Value of Net Assets, then the acquiring company would record goodwill. If Price Paid < Market Value of Net Assets, then no goodwill exists.

Goodwill is not amortized. To account for goodwill, each year a company will evaluate the current market value of any goodwill it may have acquired. If the value of the goodwill has increased, then there is nothing to record. If the value of goodwill has decreased, then the company will record a loss to write-down the goodwill on the balance sheet and recognize the loss on the income statement

According to GAAP, research and development (R&D) costs must be recorded as expenses when incurred.

C 10-2

TEST YOURSELF

All the self-testing materials in this chapter focus on information and procedures that your instructor is likely to test in quizzes and examinations.

I. Matching   *Match each numbered term with its lettered definition.*

_____ 1. Accelerated depreciation
_____ 2. Extraordinary repairs
_____ 3. Double-declining-balance
_____ 4. Relative-sales-value method
_____ 5. Straight-line depreciation
_____ 6. Units-of-production
_____ 7. Amortization
_____ 8. Copyright

_____ 9. Depletion
_____ 10. Goodwill
_____ 11. Intangible asset
_____ 12. Revenue expenditure
_____ 13. Patent
_____ 14. MACRS
_____ 15. Capitalize

A. The exclusive right to reproduce and sell a book, musical composition, film, or other work of art
B. A method of depreciation for federal income tax purposes
C. The portion of a natural resource's cost that is allocated to expense in a particular period
D. An accelerated method of depreciation that computes annual depreciation by multiplying the asset's decreasing book value by a constant percentage, which is two times the straight-line rate
E. Repair work that generates a capital expenditure
F. Excess of the cost of an acquired company over the sum of the market value of its net assets
G. An asset with no physical form
H. Costs incurred to maintain an asset
I. A grant from the federal government giving the holder the exclusive right to produce and sell an invention
J. An allocation technique for identifying the cost of each asset purchased in a group for a single amount
K. A depreciation method that writes off a relatively large amount of an asset's cost at the beginning of its useful life
L. An allocation of cost to expense that applies to intangible assets
M. Depreciation method in which an equal amount of depreciation expense is assigned to each year (or period) of asset use
N. A depreciation method in which a fixed amount of depreciation is assigned to each unit of output produced by the plant asset
O. To include a related cost as part of an asset's cost

II. Multiple Choice *Circle the best answer.*

1. All of the following are intangible assets except:

   A. patent.
   B. trademark.

   C. furniture and fixtures.
   D. goodwill.

2. Which of the following long-lived assets is *not* depreciated?

   A. Delivery truck
   B. Computer

   C. Copy machine
   D. Coal mine

3. The cost of equipment includes all of the following except:

   A. sales tax.
   B. repairs that occur one year after installation.

   C. freight charges.
   D. installation costs.

4. If depreciation expense for an asset is the same amount every year, the depreciation method is:

   A. double-declining-balance.
   B. MACRS.

   C. straight-line.
   D. units-of-production.

5. The depreciation method that ignores time is:

   A. double-declining-balance.
   B. MACRS.

   C. straight-line.
   D. units-of-production.

6. You are computing depreciation for the first year of an asset's life. Which depreciation method ignores residual value?

   A. Double-declining-balance
   B. MACRS

   C. Straight-line
   D. Units-of-production

7. Depletion is computed using which of the following depreciation methods?

   A. Double-declining-balance
   B. MACRS

   C. Straight-line
   D. Units-of-production

8. The depreciable cost of an asset equals:

   A. cost – total depreciation
   B. cost - accumulated depreciation.
   C. cost - residual value.
   D. cost - the current year's depreciation expense.

9. The cost of repairing a gear on a machine would probably be classified as:

   A. capital expenditure.
   B. extraordinary repair expense.
   C. intangible asset.
   D. revenue expenditure.

10. Which of the following costs should be capitalized?

   A. Gas and oil for a delivery van
   C. Research and development costs for new products
   B. Repainting the interior of the sales floor
   D. Replacing the engine in the delivery truck

III. Completion   *Complete each of the following.*

1. The general rule for measuring the cost of an asset is

   _____

   _____.

2. Depreciation is defined as

   _____.

3. The Accumulated Depreciation account reports _____

   _____.

4. Goodwill results when the _____ of the acquired company is
   _____ than the _____.

5. When two or more assets are purchased in a group, the total cost of the assets is allocated to
   individual assets by the _____ method.

6. To calculate depreciation, you must know the following four items: 1)_____,
   2)_____, 3)_____, and 4)_____.

7. Depreciation is an example of the _____ principle.

8. _____ relates to natural resources, while _____ relates
   to intangible assets.

9. _____ is used to depreciate assets for federal tax purposes.

10. The most widely used depreciation method for financial statements is _____.

11. Costs related to plant assets can be classified as either _____ expenditures
    or _____ expenditures.

IV. Daily Exercises

1. On August 1, 20X5, Frank Brumby, owner of New Yorker Deli, purchased a new commercial-sized grill and oven for the business from International Epicurean Supply. The new equipment carried an invoice price of $10,250 plus a 7.5% sales tax. In addition, the purchaser was responsible for $481 of freight charges. The terms of the sale was 2/15, n/30. Upon receipt of the new equipment, Brumby paid $1,075 to have the oven installed and connected. To finance this purchase, Brumby borrowed $11,000 from the bank for 90 days at 10% interest, which allowed him to pay the invoice on August 9.

For each item related to the purchase of the equipment, indicate the amount of each cost component and classify each as either revenue or capital expenditures.

Cost	Amount	Classification
a) Purchase price of equipment	_____	_____
b) Sales tax	_____	_____
c) Freight	_____	_____
d) Purchase discount, if any	_____	_____
e) Installation	_____	_____
f) Interest on loan	_____	_____

2. Based on your answers from #1, calculate the fully capitalized cost of the new equipment.

3. Review the information in Daily Exercise #1 above, and calculate depreciation for 20X5, using both the straight-line and the double-declining balance methods. The equipment is estimated to have a six-year life with a $750 residual value.

4. On January 2, 20X8, Peterson Petroleum purchased a producing oil field for $95,000,000. Peterson estimated the oil field contained approximately 100,000,000 barrels of crude oil. When all the oil had been extracted, the property would be abandoned. By the end of the year, Peterson had extracted 7,625,000 barrels of oil. Calculate the depletion expense for the year and record the necessary adjusting entry.

5. Review the facts in question #4 above, and assume the property was purchased on July 31, 20X8. How would the answer change given the later purchase date?

V. Exercises

1. A company buys Machines A, B, and C for $260,000. The market values of the machines are $80,000, $150,000, and $75,000, respectively. What cost will be allocated to each machine?

2. Scenic Equipment Co. purchased a machine for $72,000 on January 4, 20X4. Scenic expects the machine to produce 30,000 units over five years and then expects to sell the machine for $3,000. Scenic produced 4,000 units the first year and 8,000 units the second year. Compute the depreciation expense for 20X4 and 20X5. Round your answer to the nearest dollar.

	20X4	20X5
Straight-line	_____	_____
Units-of-production	_____	_____
Double-declining-balance	_____	_____

4. On January 8, 20X1, Noland Company purchased used equipment for $15,200. Noland expected the equipment to remain in service for four years. The equipment was depreciated on a straight-line basis with $1,200 salvage value. On April 30, 20X3, Noland sold the equipment for $3,600. Record the following transactions:

   a. The purchase of the equipment
   b. Depreciation expense for 20X1 and 20X2
   c. Depreciation expense through April 30, 20X3
   d. The sale of the equipment.

Date	Account and Explanation	PR	Debit	Credit

5. On July 1, 20X4, Nan Company purchased Tucket Company for $3,200,000 cash and a $1,700,000 promissory note. The market value of Tucket's assets was $5,350,000, and Tucket had liabilities of $1,975,000.

   a. Compute the cost of the goodwill purchased by Nan Company.

   b. Record the purchase by Nan Company.

Date	Account and Explanation	PR	Debit	Credit

   c. Record the value of the goodwill on 12/31/X4, assuming the estimated market value on that date is $1,268,000.

Date	Account and Explanation	PR	Debit	Credit

VI. Beyond the Numbers

Evaluate the following statement: "I do not see any problems in paying for next year's budgeted capital expenditures. We have estimated we will need approximately $110,000 for new equipment and we have more than three times that amount in our depreciation reserves (accumulated depreciation) at the moment."

_____

_____

_____

_____

VII. Demonstration Problems

Demonstration Problem #1

On January 1, 20X1, Clawster, Inc. purchased three pieces of equipment. Details of the cost, economic life, residual value, and method of depreciation are shown below:

Equipment	Cost	Useful Life	Residual Value	Depreciation Method
A	$ 42,000	7 yrs	$7,000	straight-line
B	37,000	50,000 units	1,000	units-of-production
C	20,000	5 yrs	2,000	double-declining-balance

Required:

1. Prepare a schedule computing the depreciation expense for each piece of equipment over its useful life.
2. Prepare the journal entry to record the disposal of Equipment A. Assume that it is fully depreciated and is scrapped.
3. Prepare the journal entry to record the sale of Equipment B for $1,000. Assume that it has been depreciated over its useful life.

Requirement 1 (Schedule of depreciation)

	A	B	C
Asset cost	_____	_____	_____
Less: Residual value	_____	_____	_____
Depreciable cost	_____	_____	_____

Equipment A
Schedule of Depreciation Expense
(Straight-Line Method)

Year	Depreciable Cost per Year	Depreciable Rate	Depreciation Expense
20X1			
20X2			
20X3			
20X4			
20X5			
20X6			
20X7			

Equipment B
Schedule of Depreciation Expense
(Units-of-production)

Year	Depreciable Cost per unit	Units Produced	Depreciation Expense
20X1		11,520	
20X2		8,650	
20X3		21,000	
20X4		8,830	

Equipment C
Schedule of Depreciation Expense
(Double-Declining-Balance)

Year	Book Value × Rate	Depreciation Expense	Book Value
20X1			
20X2			
20X3			
20X4			
20X5			

Requirement 2 (Journal entry—Equipment A)

Date	Account and Explanation	PR	Debit	Credit

Requirement 3 (Journal entry—Equipment B)

Date	Account and Explanation	PR	Debit	Credit

Demonstration Problem #2

Requirement 1

On April 5, 20X2, Mandy Manufacturing Company purchased a machine for $30,000 cash. Its estimated useful life was 10 years with no salvage value. Additional expenses were made for transportation, $1,500; and installation costs, $1,900. On January 2, 20X8 repairs costing $12,000 were paid in cash, increasing the efficiency of the machine and extending its useful life to four years beyond the original estimate. On December 1, 20X9, some worn-out parts were replaced for $400 cash. The company closes its books on December 31 and uses the straight-line depreciation method.

Required:

Present journal entries to record the following:
1. the purchase of the machine
2. payment of transportation and installation costs
3. depreciation for 20X2
4. the repair on January 2, 20X8
5. depreciation for 20X8
6. the repair on December 1, 20X9
7. depreciation for 20X9

Date	Account and Explanation	PR	Debit	Credit

SOLUTIONS

I. Matching

1. K	5. M	9. C	13. I
2. E	6. N	10. F	14. B
3. D	7. L	11. G	15. O
4. J	8. A	12. H	

II. Multiple Choice

1.   C   Furniture and fixtures is a tangible asset.

2.   D   A coal mine is a natural resource and as such is depleted, not depreciated.

3.   B   The cost of equipment includes all amounts paid to acquire the asset and to ready it for its intended use. Repairs to equipment indicate that it is in use and therefore should not be included as part of the equipment's cost. Repairs that occur after installation will be expensed in the period in which they are incurred.

4.   C   Straight-line depreciation is the only method of depreciation that results in the same amount of depreciation every year. The other methods, double-declining-balance and units-of-production, will result in differing amounts of depreciation each year.

5.   D   Units-of-production depreciation is based on the number of units produced by the depreciable asset. Straight-line and double-declining balance use time as a component of the depreciation expense calculation.

6.   A   Double-declining balance ignores residual value in the depreciation calculation. To determine depreciation expense using double-declining balance (DDB), multiply the DDB rate by the book value at the beginning of the period, except in the last year. In the last year, subtract residual value from book value to determine the depreciation expense for that year.

7.   D   Both depletion and units-of-production follow the same general formula: (cost – residual value) ÷ useful life in units.

8.   C   Item B equals the asset's book value. Items A & D have no significance.

9.   D   Repairing a gear on a machine would be considered a routine repair. Revenue expenditures maintain an asset in its existing condition or restore the asset to good working order. Capital expenditures are those that increase capacity or efficiency of the asset or extend its useful life.

10.   D   Replacing the engine in the delivery truck would be considered an extraordinary or major repair and would be capitalized, or added to the cost of the asset. The other costs are revenue expenditures and should be debited to expense accounts.

III. Completion

1. to sum all the costs incurred to bring the asset to its intended purpose (or use), net of all discounts.

2. a systematic allocation of an asset's cost to expense (Depreciation shifts a portion of the cost of an asset off the balance sheet and onto the income statement to support the matching principle. Depreciation is not a method of asset valuation.)

3. the portion of the cost of the asset that has been depreciated. (The cost of the asset is determined at the point of acquisition. Then the cost is expensed according to the appropriate depreciation method. The debit to Depreciation Expense is balanced by a credit to Accumulated Depreciation.)

4. purchase price, greater, the market value of the net assets. (Goodwill is recorded only when another company is acquired and the price paid for the company is greater than the market value of the assets.)
5. relative-sales-value (The need to depreciate each asset separately makes it necessary to allocate the purchase price by some reasonable manner.)
6. cost; estimated useful life; estimated residual value; depreciation method (Order is not important.)
7. matching (Matching means to identify and measure all expenses incurred during the period and to match them against the revenue earned during that period.)
8. depletion; amortization
9. MACRS
10. straight-line
11. capital; revenue (Order not important.)

IV. Daily Exercises
1.

	Cost	Amount	Classification
a)	Purchase price of equipment	$ 10,250	Capital expenditure
b)	Sales tax	753	Capital expenditure
c)	Freight	481	Capital expenditure
d)	Purchase discount, if any	(205)	Capital expenditure
e)	Installation	1,075	Capital expenditure
f)	Interest on loan	275	Revenue expenditure

Study Tip: The discount is in parentheses because it represents a reduction in the cost of the equipment. The interest on the loan does not qualify as a capital expenditure.

---

2. $12,354
    Given the answers in part 1, the calculation is $10,250 + 753 + 481 - 205 + 1,075. The accounts would appear as follows:

Grill/Oven		Interest Expense	
10,250	205	275	
753			
481			
1,075			
Bal. 12,354			

3. Straight-Line = (Cost - Residual Value) ÷ Life
    = ($12,354 - $750) ÷ 6 years
    = $1,934 per year (rounded)
    $1,934 × 5/12 for partial year = $806 (rounded)

    Double-Declining Balance = Book Value × Rate
    Rate = 1/6 × 2 = 2/6 = 33.3%
    $12,354 × .333 × 5/12 for partial year = $1,714 (rounded)

Study Tip: For assets placed in service during the year, depreciation is calculated for a partial year.

---

4. For natural resources, the most appropriate method is units of production.

   UOP =   (Cost - Residual Value) ÷ Estimated Total Production
        = $95,000,000 ÷ 100,000,000 barrels
        = $0.95 per barrel
   $0.95 x 7,625,000 barrels = $7,243,750

12/31/X8	Depletion Expense	7,243,750	
	Accumulated Depletion		7,243,750

5. Assuming a later purchase date, the answer would be the same. Why? Units-of-production ignores time in the formula; only actual production is relevant.

V. Exercises

1. Machine A = [$80,000 / ($80,000 + $150,000 + $75,000)] × $260,000] = $67,600
   Machine B = [$150,000 / ($80,000 + $150,000 + $75,000)] × $260,000] = $127,400
   Machine C = [$75,000 / ($80,000 + $150,000 + $75,000)] × $260,000] = $65,000
   (Proof: $67,600 + $127,400 + $65,000 = $260,000)

2.

	20X4	20X5
Straight-line	13,800	13,800
Units-of-production	9,200	18,400
Double-declining-balance	28,800	17,280

   Straight-line = ($72,000 - $3,000) / 5 years = $13,800

   Units-of-production = (72,000 - 3,000) / 30,000 units = $2.30 per unit
       20X4 = $4,000 × $2.30= $9,200
       20X5 = $8,000 × $2.30= $18,400

   Double-declining-balance:
       DDB rate = (1 / 5) × 2 = .40
       20X4 = .40 × $72,000 = $28,800
       Book value = $72,000 - $28,800 = $43,200
       20X5 = .40 × $43,200 = $17,280

3.

   Annual depreciation = ($15,200 - $1,200) / 4 = $3,500
   Accumulated depreciation 1/1/X1 = 2 years x $3,500 per year = $7,000

1/8/X1	Equipment		15,200	
	Cash			15,200
	Purchase equipment			

12/31/X1	Depreciation Expense		3,500	
	Accumulated Depreciation			3,500
12/31/X2	Depreciation Expense		3,500	
	Accumulated Depreciation			3,500
4/30/X3	Depreciation Expense		1,167	
	Accumulated Depreciation			1,167
	Dep. for 4 months in 20X3 (4/12 × 3,500) = 1,167			
4/30/X3	Cash		3,600	
	Accumulated Depreciation		8,167	
	Loss on Sale of Asset		3,433	
	Equipment			15,200
	Loss = (Cost - Accumulated Depreciation) + Cash			
	= Book Value + Cash			
Because cash received ($3,600) is less than book value ($15,200 - $8,167 = $7,033), there is a loss of $3,433 ($7,033- $3,600) on the sale.				

4.

A.

Purchase price for Tucket		$4,900,000
Market value of Tucket	5,350,000	
Less: Tucket's liabilities	1,975,000	
Market value of Tucket's net assets		3,375,000
Goodwill		1,525,000

B.

Date	Account and Explanation	PR	Debit	Credit
7/1	Assets		5,350,000	
	Goodwill		1,525,000	
	Liabilities			1,975,000
	Cash			3,200,000
	Note Payable			1,700,000

C.

Date	Account and Explanation	PR	Debit	Credit
12/31	Loss on Goodwill		257,000	
	Goodwill			257,000
	Write-down of goodwill ($1,525,000-$1,268,000)			

VI. Beyond the Numbers

The person making the statement is confused about depreciation reserves (i.e., accumulated depreciation). There is no cash involved in accounting for depreciation; therefore, the balance in accumulated depreciation does not represent any money available for future use. The balance in accumulated depreciation represents the amount of the related assets' cost that has been recognized as an expense because of the assets' loss of usefulness to the business.

VII. Demonstration Problems

Demonstration Problem #1 Solved and Explained

	A	B	C
Asset cost	$42,000	$37,000	$20,000
Less: Residual value	7,000	1,000	2,000
Depreciable cost	$35,000	$36,000	$18,000

Study Tip: Under the double-declining-balance method, the residual value is not considered until the book value approaches residual value.

Equipment A
Schedule of Depreciation Expense
(Straight-Line Method)

Year	Depreciable Cost	Depreciable Rate	Depreciation Expense
20X1	$ 35,000	1/7	$ 5,000
20X2	35,000	1/7	5,000
20X3	35,000	1/7	5,000
20X4	35,000	1/7	5,000
20X5	35,000	1/7	5,000
20X6	35,000	1/7	5,000
20X7	35,000	1/7	5,000
		Total	$35,000

The book value of the equipment after 20X7 is $7,000 (cost - accumulated depreciation = $42,000 - $35,000 = $7,000).

Equipment B
Schedule of Depreciation Expense
(Units-of-Production)

Year	Depreciable Cost per unit	Units Produced	Depreciation Expense
20X1	$ .72	11,520	$ 8,294
20X2	$ .72	8,650	6,228
20X3	$ .72	21,000	15,120
20X4	$ .72	8,830	6,358
Total		50,000	$36,000

*The depreciable cost per unit = ($36,000 / 50,000 units = $0.72).
The book value after 20X4 is $1,000 ($37,000 - $36,000 = $1,000).

Study Tip: The depreciable cost is not affected by the method used. The method simply determines how the depreciable cost will be spread over the asset's life.

Equipment C
Schedule of Depreciation Expense
(Double-Declining-Balance)

Year	Book Value × Rate	Depreciation Expense	Book Value
20X1	.40 × 20,000	8,000	$12,000
20X2	.40 × 12,000	4,800	7,200
20X3	.40 × 7,000	2,880	4,320
20X4	.40 × 4,200	1728	2,592
20X5	(2,592 – 2,000)	592	2,000

The straight-line depreciation rate for an asset with useful life of five years is 1/5 per year, or 20%. Double the straight-line rate is 2/5, or 40%. This rate does not change from 20X1 through 20X5.

Study Tip: The most frequent error made by students in applying double-declining-balance deals with the residual value. Unlike units-of-production, with DDB, the residual value is not taken into account until the final year of the asset's life.

Depreciation expense for Equipment C in the fifth year is not $1,037 ($2,592 × .40) because in the fifth year depreciation expense is the previous year's book value less the residual value ($2,592 - $2,000 = $592).

Requirement 2 (Journal entry—Equipment A)

Date	Account and Explanation	PR	Debit	Credit
	Accumulated Depreciation—A		35,000	
	Loss on Disposal of Equipment		7,000	
	Equipment A			42,000

When fully depreciated assets cannot be sold or exchanged, an entry removing them from the books is necessary upon disposal. The entry credits the asset account and debits its related Accumulated Depreciation account. If the fully depreciated asset has no residual value, no loss on the disposal occurs. In most cases, however, it will be necessary to record a debit to a Loss on Disposal account to write off the book value of a junked asset. When an asset is fully depreciated, the book value of the asset will equal the residual value. There can never be a gain on the junking or scrapping of an asset.

Requirement 3 (Journal entry—Equipment B)

Date	Account and Explanation	PR	Debit	Credit
	Cash		1,000	
	Accumulated depreciation—B		36,000	
	Equipment B			37,000

A gain is recorded when an asset is sold for a price greater than its book value. A loss is recorded when the sale price is less than book value. In this case, Equipment B and its related Accumulated

Depreciation account are removed from the books in a manner similar to Equipment A. The book value of the asset is $1,000. As this equals the selling price, no gain or loss results.

Demonstration Problem #2 Solved and Explained

Date	Account and Explanation	PR	Debit	Credit
1.	Machine		30,000	
	Cash			30,000
2.	Machine		1,500	
	Cash			1,500
	Transportation cost.			
	Machine		1,900	
	Cash			1,900
	Installation cost.			

Both the transportation and installation costs are debited to the Machine account because they are necessary costs incurred to place the asset in service. Therefore, the total cost basis for the machine is $33,400, not $30,000.

3.	Depreciation Expense—Machine		2,505	
	Accumulated Depreciation			2,505

($33,400 (see above) / 10 = 3,340 × 9/12 = $2,505)

Since the asset was acquired and placed in service early in April, the first year's depreciation is 9/12 of the company's financial period. Thereafter, annual depreciation is $3,340.

4.	Machine		12,000	
	Cash (or Accounts Payable)			12,000

This is clearly a capital expenditure because the machine will last past its original life estimate. Therefore, the cost should be reflected in an asset account, not in an expense account.

5.	Depreciation Expense—Machine		3,175	
	Accumulated Depreciation			3,175

Accumulated depreciation through 12/31/X7 is $19,205. For 20X2, depreciation is $2,505; 20X3 to 20X7 is equal to $3,340 per year × 5 = $16,700. $2,505 + $16,700 = $19,205.

Therefore, on 1/2/X8 book value is $14,195 ($33,400 - $19,205). The $12,000 debit in entry (4) increases book value to $26,195, and now life is four years more than the original life estimate. As of 1/2/X8, the machine is 5 years, 9 months old. The revised life estimate is now 14 years. Therefore, as of 1/2/X8, the asset has 8 years, 3 months of life left (14 years - 5 years, 9 months). To calculate the new depreciation amount, divide book value ($26,195) by remaining life (8.25 years) or $3,175 per year (rounded).

6.	Repair Expense		400	
	Cash			400

This is clearly a revenue expenditure—one necessary to maintain the asset.

7.	Depreciation Expense—Machine		3,175	
	Accumulated Depreciation			3,175

See explanation for #5 above.

Chapter 11—Current Liabilities and Payroll

CHAPTER OVERVIEW

Chapter 11 continues to focus on the components of the balance sheet, but now we are going to switch to the other side of the accounting equation and examine liabilities, specifically current liabilities and payroll. Long-term liabilities are examined in Chapter 15. The learning objectives for this chapter are to

1. Account for current liabilities of known amount.
2. Account for current liabilities that must be estimated.
3. Compute payroll amounts.
4. Record basic payroll transactions.
5. Use a payroll system.
6. Report current liabilities on the balance sheet.

CHAPTER REVIEW

Liabilities are things that the business owes to others. A company may have the obligation to transfer assets (for example, to make cash payments for purchases on account) or to provide services or goods in the future (for example, to earn unearned revenue). Current liabilities are: (1) due within one year or within the company's operating cycle if it is longer than one year and (2) will be satisfied with current assets.

Objective 1 - Account for current liabilities of known amount.

Current liabilities include liabilities of a known amount and liabilities that are estimated.

Current liabilities of a known amount are:

- **Accounts payable**: amounts owed to suppliers for goods or services purchased on account.
- **Short-term notes payable:** notes due within one year. Companies issue notes payable to borrow cash, to purchase inventory, or to purchase plant assets. Interest expense and interest payable must be accrued at the end of the accounting period.

Suppose a company acquires a plant asset and issues a note payable. The entry is:

Plant Asset	XX	
Notes Payable, Short-Term		XX

Accrued interest expense and interest payable are recorded at the end of the accounting period with this entry:

Interest Expense	XX	
Interest Payable		XX

When the note is paid off at maturity, the entry is:

Notes Payable, Short-Term (principal)	XX
Interest Payable(from adjusting entry at end of previous period)	XX
Interest Expense (to record interest expense for current period)	XX
Cash (maturity value of note = principal + interest)	XX

- A business collects sales tax from customers and then forwards the money to the state at regular intervals. Sales tax is not an expense to the business because it does not represent money that the business must pay out of its own resources, but rather represents money collected from customers that is subsequently sent to the state.

To record the collection of sales tax:

Cash	XX	
Sales Revenue		XX
Sales Tax Payable		X

To record the payment of sales tax to the state:

Sales Tax Payable	X	
Cash		X

- Some long-term liabilities, such as notes, bonds, or mortgages are paid in installments. The principal of the debt is classified as either current or long-term. The current maturities of long-term debt is the portion of the total debt that is payable within one year. It is reported in the current liabilities section of the balance sheet because it will be paid with current assets. The remainder is reported in the long-term liabilities section of the balance sheet.

- Accrued expenses are expenses that have not yet been paid and therefore represent a liability to the business. Accrued expenses are current liabilities. Examples of accrued expenses include interest payable and payroll items. Deferred revenues, or unearned revenues, occur when a company receives cash from customers before earning the revenue. As goods are delivered or services are rendered, revenue is recorded. Unearned revenue is recorded as:

Cash	XX	
Unearned Revenue		XX

As the unearned revenue is earned, it is recorded as:

Unearned Revenue	XX	
Revenue		XX

Objective 2 - Account for current liabilities that must be estimated.

When a business knows that a liability exists, but does not know the exact amount, the amount must be estimated. A product warranty is an example of a liability that must be estimated. When a product warranty is offered, the warranty serves as an enticement to the customer to purchase from one company over another that sells the same product, but that may not offer a product warranty. Therefore, the existence of the warranty assists in generating the revenue. However, at the time the product is sold, the company has no way of knowing exactly which products will come back for replacement or service under the warranty. Therefore, the company must make an estimate regarding the amount of warranty expense to recognize for the period of the sale in an effort to adhere to the matching principle. Remember, the matching principle requires that expenses be matched with revenues. By analyzing past experience or past performance within the industry, a company can reasonably estimate the amount of warranty expense that will be incurred as a result of defective products.

Estimated Warranty Payable is a current liability, and is recorded as an adjusting entry at the end of the accounting period as:

Warranty Expense	XX	
Estimated Warranty Payable		XX

When a product is repaired within the warranty period, the entry will be recorded as:

Estimated Warranty Payable	X	
Cash		X

It is important to notice that when a repair or replacement occurs within the warranty period, the Estimated Warranty Payable (rather than Warranty Expense) is debited.

A **contingent liability** is a potential liability that depends on a future event that may occur as the result of a past transaction. Contingent liabilities may be difficult to estimate, as in lawsuits, where the courts determine the amounts. The disclosure principle requires companies to keep outsiders informed of relevant information about the company.

Contingent liabilities are divided into three categories:

Probability of loss:	How to report the contingency:
• *Remote*	Ignore. Do not report or disclose in the financial statements.
• *Reasonable possible*	Describe the situation in an explanatory note to the financial statements.
• *Probable and the loss can be estimated*	Record an expense (or loss) and an actual liability based on estimated amounts.

Accounting for both current liabilities and contingent liabilities can pose ethical challenges for the business. Because some current liabilities must be estimated (which means the related expense is also estimated), owners and managers may attempt to manipulate the amount of the estimate in an attempt to manipulate the amount of reported net income. In addition, someone may choose to overlook, or underestimate, the amount of a contingent liability. External auditors are particularly concerned with unreported liabilities and want to ensure that the financial statements are accurate.

Review the Decision Guidelines following the contingent liability discussion in your text.

Objective 3 - Compute payroll amounts.

Gross pay is the total amount of salary or wages an employee earns before taxes and deductions. Net pay, or "take-home pay" is the amount of the payroll check the employee receives. Deductions withheld from employees' pay fall into two categories:
- *Required deductions*, such as federal or state income taxes and Social Security tax (FICA).
- *Optional deductions*, such as union dues, insurance premiums, charitable contributions and any other amounts withheld at the employee's request.

The amount of state or federal income tax withheld is determined by the amount earned, the number of withholding allowances claimed by the employee and the employee's marital status. This information is supplied to the business when the employee completes a W-4 form (see Exhibit 11-4 in your text).

FICA taxes are subdivided into two parts:
1. Old age, survivors' and disability insurance (OASDI). The amount of OASDI is determined by multiplying 6.2% (.062) by the employee's total earnings up to a maximum amount of $87,000 in 2003. Any earnings over $87,000 are not subject to OASDI.
2. Medicare tax (health insurance). The amount of Medicare paid by every employee is 1.45% (.0145) of the employee's total earnings. There is no earnings limit for the Medicare tax.

The amounts withheld from gross pay are liabilities that occur in the course of compensating employees. These amounts are collected in the same manner as sales tax, and submitted to the respective entity for payment.

In addition to taxes withheld from employees' earnings, the employer is responsible for payment of the employer's share of FICA taxes, state and federal unemployment taxes. These amounts are expenses to the employer, not payroll deductions. Employers pay FICA tax equal to the amount withheld from employees.

Objective 4 - Record basic payroll transactions.

The following example shows how payroll entries are made:

Suppose that when you graduate, you get a job that pays $3,000 per month, and you are paid monthly. Assume also that your employer pays $200 per month for your health insurance and $100 per month for your pension. Your pay stub reports the following:

Gross pay	$3,000
FICA (assuming an 8% rate)	240
Income Taxes (given)	450
Net Pay	$2,310

Your employer's entry to record salary expense is:

Salary Expense (gross pay)	3,000	
Employee Income Tax Payable		450
FICA Tax Payable		240
Salary Payable to Employee (net pay)		2,310

Your employer would record payroll tax expense as:

Payroll Tax Expense	426	
FICA Tax Payable (a matching amount)		240
State Unemployment Tax Payable		162
(3,000 x 5.4%)		
Federal Unemployment Tax Payable		24
(3,000 x .8%)		

Finally, your employer would record fringe benefits expense:

Health Insurance Expense	200	
Pension Expense	100	
Employee Benefit Payable		300

Objective 5 - Use a payroll system.

A **payroll system** includes these components:

1. **A payroll register**
2. **A payroll bank account**
3. **Payroll checks**
4. **An earnings record for each employee**

1. The payroll register lists individual earnings and deductions for employees as well as totals. Computerized systems may also compute employer payroll tax expense such as FICA taxes and federal and state unemployment taxes. The payroll register is the source document for recording the payroll. (See Exhibit 11-7.)
2. The company deposits money in the payroll bank account exactly to cover net pay.

3. Most companies issue payroll checks which list gross pay, deductions, and net pay. Using the example in the previous section, the entry your employer makes when your check is distributed to you is:

Salary Payable	2,310	
Cash (Payroll account)		2,310

Assume that you are the only employee of your company. Then payroll taxes are remitted to the government, and the entry is:

Employee Income Tax Payable	450	
FICA Tax Payable	480	
State Unemployment Tax Payable	162	
Federal Unemployment Tax Payable	24	
Cash (Regular account)		1,116

Note: The FICA Tax Payable amount ($480) includes both the amount withheld from your paycheck ($240) and the amount recorded by your employer as payroll tax expense ($240).

When your employer remits the payments for your health insurance and pension, the entry is:

Employee Benefit Payable	300	
Cash (Regular account)		300

4. Employers maintain earnings records (see Exhibit 11-10), which are used in preparing payroll tax returns (Form 941—see Exhibit 11-9) and tax statements (W-2 forms) for employees.

When employees are eligible to receive post-retirement benefits (usually medical insurance), companies are required by FASB to accrue the expense each period. These benefits are another example of accrued liabilities.

Internal Control and Payroll

Special controls for payroll accounting are necessary because of the large number of transactions and the number of different parties involved. These controls are designed to maintain an efficient system while, at the same time, safeguarding payroll disbursements. Efficiency is achieved when separate bank accounts are maintained for payroll checks, while payroll disbursements are safeguarded through the separation of duties related to personnel (hiring and firing) and payroll (check distribution, time cards, employee identification cards, etc.)

Objective 6 - Report current liabilities on the balance sheet.

At the end of the fiscal year, liabilities are reported on the balance sheet. The year-end payroll liability is the amount of payroll expense still unpaid. Study Exhibits 11-12 and the Decision Guidelines in your text to review how current liabilities are reported on the balance sheet and the categories of current liabilities.

TEST YOURSELF

All the self-testing materials in this chapter focus on information and procedures that your instructor is likely to test in quizzes and examinations.

I. Matching *Match each numbered term with its lettered definition.*

_____ 1. 941
_____ 2. Unearned revenue
_____ 3. FICA tax
_____ 4. W-2
_____ 5. Gross pay
_____ 6. Net pay
_____ 7. W-4
_____ 8. Contingent liabilities

_____ 9. Accrued liability
_____ 10. Short-term note payable
_____ 11. Unemployment compensation tax
_____ 12. Withheld income tax
_____ 13. Postretirement benefits
_____ 14. Warranty Payable
_____ 15. Employee benefits

A. A liability which may arise in the future
B. Represents amounts that are owed but have not yet been paid
C. Benefits which an employee will receive after retirement
D. The form submitted to the federal government reconciling the employer's liability for withheld income and FICA taxes
E. A form submitted by each employee indicating the employee's marital status and number of withholding allowances claimed
F. Represents cash received before the good has been delivered or service provided.
G. Employee compensation that the employee does not receive immediately in cash, such as health and life insurance and retirement pay
H. A form summarizing each employee's annual gross wages and deductions
I. Income taxes that are deducted from employees' gross pay and remitted to the government
J. The amount of employee compensation that the employee actually takes home
K. A common form of financing due within one year.
L. An example of an estimated liability
M. Payroll tax paid by employers to the government, for the purpose of paying benefits to people who are out of work
N. Social Security tax which is withheld from employees' pay and matched by the employer
O. The total amount of salary, wages, commissions, or any other employee compensation before taxes and other deductions are taken out

II. Multiple Choice   *Circle the best answer.*

1. Which of the following is *not* a current liability?

   A. Warranty Payable
   B. Benefits Expense
   C. Unearned Revenue
   D. Contingent liability

2. Interest on a short-term note payable is recorded:

   A. at the maturity date.
   B. at the end of the accounting period.
   C. in monthly payments.
   D. both A. and B.

3. Which of the following is probably a contingent liability?

   A. Interest payable
   B. Notes payable
   C. Estimated Warranty Payable
   D. Accounts payable

4. The major expense of most service organizations is:

   A. Payroll Expense.
   B. Interest Expense.
   C. Cost of Goods Sold.
   D. Rent Expense.

5. A contingent liability is recorded when:

   A. a loss is probable but cannot be estimated.
   B. a loss is possible.
   C. a loss is probable and can reasonably be estimated.
   D. a loss can be reasonably estimated.

6. Which of the following has a maximum amount an employee must pay in a year?

   A. Federal income tax
   B. Medicare tax
   C. State income tax
   D. Social Security (OASDI) tax

7. Which of the following is *not* a component of a payroll system?

   A. Payroll checks
   B. Payroll register
   C. Payroll petty cash fund
   D. Earnings records

8. Which of the following is *not* a control for safeguarding cash in a payroll system?

   A. Separating hiring duties from the paycheck disbursement duties
   B. Requiring employees to wear identification badges
   C. Maintaining two payroll bank accounts
   D. Having employees punch a time clock

9. Which of the following is *not* required to calculate federal withholding tax?

   A. marital status
   B. withholding allowances
   C. social security number
   D. amount of gross pay

305

10. Which of the following payroll items only are paid by the employer?

   A. FICA taxes
   B. State and Federal Unemployment taxes
   C. Health and life insurance premiums
   D. Retirement savings plans

III. Completion   *Complete each of the following statements.*

1. Estimating the warranty expense for the period of sale is an example of applying the _____ principle.
2. Current Maturities of Long-Term debt is a(n) _____ account.
3. Providing information related to a contingent liability is an example of adhering to the _____ principle.
4. To calculate the amount to withhold for income taxes, the following information is required: _____, _____, _____, and _____.
5. The W-2 is completed by the _____ and reports the _____.
6. The W-4 is completed by the _____ and indicates the _____.
7. Withheld federal income taxes and FICA taxes are reported to the government on form _____, which is submitted _____.
8. FICA is an acronym for the _____.
9. The account title Payroll Tax Expense reflects which specific payroll taxes? _____ _____.
10. For a contingent liability to be recorded, FASB requires that the liability be both _____ and _____.

IV. Daily Exercises

1. Indicate whether each of the following is paid by the employee (deducted from his gross pay), or recorded as payroll tax expense by the employer.

	Deducted from employee's gross pay	Payroll tax expense
Charitable contributions		
Social Security (OASDI) tax		
Federal income tax		
Unemployment tax		
Union dues		
Medicare tax		

2. During the month of April, Bill's Surf Shop sold 10 surfboards costing $500 each. All sales are subject to a 6 percent sales tax. Bill's Surf Shop collected cash for 3 of the surfboards, and the remaining sales were on account. Assume a periodic inventory system.

   a.) For the month of April, prepare the journal entry to record the sale and related liabilities for the month.

   b.) Sales tax must be remitted by the 15th of the following month. Prepare the journal entry to record the remittance of the sales tax.

Date	Accounts and Explanation	PR	Debit	Credit

3. Record the following transactions:

   a. On December 1, a used truck is purchased for $12,000, and a six-month, 12% note payable is issued.

Date	Accounts and Explanation	PR	Debit	Credit

   b. Adjust for interest as of December 31, the close of the fiscal year.

Date	Accounts and Explanation	PR	Debit	Credit

   c. The payment of the note on June 1.

Date	Accounts and Explanation	PR	Debit	Credit

4. If a company has net sales of $4,200,000, and past experience indicates estimated warranty expense to be 2.5% of net sales, record the adjusting entry for the warranty liability. Assume a customer returns an item for repair covered by the warranty the following month, and it costs the company $95 to repair the item. Prepare the journal entry to record the repair.

Date	Accounts and Explanation	PR	Debit	Credit

V. Exercises

1. Fairbanks Corporation, whose fiscal year ends June 30, 20X8 completed the following transactions involving notes payable. Record the journal entries for each of the following transactions for 20X8:

   May 21   Purchased a new piece of equipment by issuing a 60-day, 14 percent note payable for $36,000.
   June 30   Made the end-of-year adjusting entry to accrue interest expense on the note.
   July 20   Paid off the note plus interest on the equipment.

GENERAL JOURNAL

Date	Accounts and Explanation	PR	Debit	Credit

2. Richard Simons earns $10.00 per hour with time and a half for more than 40 hours per week. During the second week of the new year, he worked 48 hours. Richard's payroll deductions include federal income tax at 15%, state income tax at 6%, Social Security (OASDI) tax at 6%, Medicare at 1.5%, and a contribution to United Giving of $15.00 per week. Make the journal entry that records Richard's gross and net pay for the week.

GENERAL JOURNAL

Date	Accounts and Explanation	PR	Debit	Credit

VI. Beyond the Numbers

Review the information in Exercises 1 above and, record the transactions as they would appear on the books of the payee (the bank) for the life of the note.

GENERAL JOURNAL

Date	Accounts and Explanation	PR	Debit	Credit

VII. Demonstration Problems

Demonstration Problem #1

Green Stems, Inc. is a small flower shop that employs three people. Glen Green is the floral designer and Rose Petals and Janice Flowers are part-time employees. Prior to the current pay period, Glen has earned $85,800, Rose has earned $6,800, and Janice has earned $5,400. For the month of December, 20X9, Glen's gross salary was $7,800. Rose worked 55 hours, 40 of them at her regular wage of $10.00 per hour, and the remaining 15 hours at time and a half for overtime. Janice worked 35 hours, all at her regular rate of $10.00 per hour.

Assume the following additional facts:

FICA tax 8% (.08) on a base of $87,000
Federal unemployment rate = .8% (.008) on a base of $7,000
State unemployment rate = 5.4% (.054) on a base of $7,000

Individual income tax withholding:

	Federal	State
Glen Green	$1,725.00	$315.00
Rose Petals	90.00	28.00
Janice Flowers	26.00	12.00

Voluntary monthly withholding:

Glen Green	$20 (United Way)
Rose Petals	$10 (U.S. Savings Bonds)

Employee benefits:
The company contributes to a pension plan an amount equal to 6% of gross income.
The company also pays 80% of the health insurance premiums for Glen Green. The company's portion of the total health insurance premiums is $350.

Required:

1. Compute the gross and net pay of each employee for the month of December.
2. Record the following payroll entries that Green Stems, Inc. would make for:
   a. Expense for employee salary and wages, including overtime pay
   b. Employer payroll taxes
   c. Expense for employee benefits
   d. Payment of cash to employees
   e. Payment of all payroll taxes
   f. Payment for employee benefits and voluntary withholdings
3. What was the total payroll expense incurred by Green Stems, Inc. for the month of December? How much cash did the business actually disburse for its payroll?

Requirement 1

Explanation	Green	Petals	Flowers	Totals
Gross Pay:				
Deductions:				
Net Pay:				

Requirement 2

GENERAL JOURNAL

Date	Accounts and Explanation	PR	Debit	Credit

Requirement 3

<u>Total December Payroll Expense</u>

_____   _____
_____   _____
_____   _____
_____   _____
_____   _____
                                     ===============

<u>Total Cash Disbursed in December</u>

_____
_____
_____
===============================

Demonstration Problem #2

The following events occurred in December Vega Del Toro Corporation:

1. On December 1, borrowed $15,000 from the bank, signing a six-month note at 9% interest.
2. During December a competitor filed a lawsuit against the company alleging violation of antitrust regulations. If the company loses the suit, it is estimated damages will exceed $1 million. The probability of loss is remote.
3. The December payroll totaled $45,000, which will be paid on January 10. (Ignore payroll deductions and the employer's payroll tax expense.)
4. Sales on credit for the month amounted to 700 units at $200 each, subject to a retail sales tax of 7.5% due January 15. Each unit carries a 90-day warranty requiring the company to repair or replace the unit if it becomes defective during the warranty period. The estimated cost to the company to honor the warranty is $45, and past experience has shown that approximately 3% of the units will be returned during the warranty period.

Required:

1. Record the external transactions and, where appropriate, the required adjusting entries at December 31.
2. Based on your entries in Requirement 1, present the current liability section of the balance sheet at December 31.

Requirement 1 (Journal entries)

Date	Accounts and Explanation	PR	Debit	Credit

Date	Accounts and Explanation	PR	Debit	Credit

Requirement 2 (Current liability section of balance sheet)

SOLUTIONS

I. Matching

1. D	5. O	9. B	13. C
2. F	6. J	10. K	14. L
3. N	7. E	11. M	15. G
4. H	8. A	12. I	

II. Multiple Choice

1.   B   Of the items listed, all are liabilities that are due within one year except for benefits expense, which is an expense to the company. (Some of the liabilities could be long-term. For example, a 3 year warranty or lawsuit going to court in 2 years.)

2.   D   Interest on a note payable is recorded at the end of the accounting period if the term of the note extends beyond the current accounting period and at the maturity date of the note.

3.   C   A contingent liability is a potential liability that depends on a future event arising out of a past transaction. Of the items listed, all except "estimated warranty payable" are actual liabilities of a known amount.

4.   A   Recall that Cost of Goods Sold is the largest expense for a merchandising business. The efforts of employees are a significant part of doing business in service companies and, accordingly, Payroll is often the major expense.

5.   C   The FASB says to record an actual liability when 1) it is probable that the business has suffered a loss, and 2) its amount can be reasonable estimated.

6.   D   The Social Security tax has the OASDI component, which has an upper limit that is set by law.

7.   C   Of the items listed, all are components of a payroll except for the "payroll petty cash fund" which is a nonexistent item.

8.   C   Of the items listed, only C is not a control for safeguarding cash in a payroll system.

9.   C   Federal income taxes are based on gross earnings, marital status, and number of withholding allowances.

10.   B   Of the items listed, only Federal and State Unemployment taxes are expenses solely of the employer. Employee FICA taxes are matched by the employer. An employer may also participate in partial payment of health and life insurance premiums and retirement plans.

III. Completion

1. matching (Matching means to identify and measure all expenses incurred during the period and to "match" them against the revenue earned during that period.)
2. current liability (It represents the amount of the principal that is payable within one year.)
3. disclosure (providing relevant information to outsiders)

4. gross earnings, marital status, number of withholding allowances claimed, length of pay period
5. company; yearly gross wages and deductions
6. employee; number of withholding allowances claimed
7. 941; quarterly
8. Federal Insurance Contribution Act
9. FICA and federal and state unemployment taxes
10. probable; reasonably estimated

IV. Daily Exercises

1.

	Paid by employee	Paid by employer
Charitable contributions	X	
Social Security tax	X	X
Federal income tax	X	
Unemployment tax		X
Union dues	X	
Medicare tax	X	X

(You may also be aware of employers who match charitable contributions of their employees.)

2.

Date:		Description	Post. Ref.	Debit	Credit
	a.	Cash		1,590	
		Accounts Receivable		3,710	
		Sales			5,000
		Sales Tax Payable			300
	b.	Sales Tax Payable		300	
		Cash			300

3.

a. Truck	12,000	
Note Payable		12,000
b. Interest Expense	120	
Interest Payable		120
($12,000 x 12% x 1/12)		
c. Note Payable	12,000	
Interest Payable	120	
Interest Expense	600	
Cash		12,720

4.

317

Warranty Expense		105,000	
Estimated Warranty Payable			105,000
($4,200,000 x 2.5%)			
Estimated Warranty Payable		95	
Cash			95

V. Exercises

1.

GENERAL JOURNAL

Date	Accounts and Explanation	PR	Debit	Credit
20X8				
May 21	Equipment		36,000	
	Note Payable			36,000
Jun 30	Interest Expense		560	
	Interest Payable			560
	(36,000 x .14 x 40/360)			
Jul 20	Note Payable		36,000	
	Interest Payable		560	
	Interest Expense (36,000 x .14 x 20/360)		280	
	Cash			36,840

2.

GENERAL JOURNAL

Date	Accounts and Explanation	PR	Debit	Credit
	Wage Expense		520.00	
	Federal Income Tax Payable			78.00
	State Income Tax Payable			31.20
	FICA Tax Payable ($520 \times (0.06 + 0.015)$)			39.00
	United Way Payable			15.00
	Wage Payable			356.80
	Wage Expense = (40 hrs x $10) + (8 hrs x $10 x 1.5)			
	= 400 + 120 = 520			

VI. Beyond the Numbers

1.

Date	Accounts and Explanation	PR	Debit	Credit
May 21	Note Receivable		36,000	
	Cash			36,000
Jun 30	Interest Receivable		560	
	Interest Revenue			560
Jul 20	Cash		36,840	
	Note Receivable			36,000
	Interest Receivable			560
	Interest Revenue			280

Study Tip: If it is a Note Payable to the maker, then it must be a Note Receivable to the payee.

VII. Demonstration Problems

Demonstration Problem #1 Solved and Explained

Requirement 1

	Gross Pay	
Glen Green	$7,800	(Salary)
Rose Petals	625	(40 hrs x 10 + 15 overtime hrs x $15)
Janice Flowers	350	(35 hrs x $10 per hr.)
Total Gross Pay	$8,775	

Gross pay represents an employee's total earnings before any amounts (for taxes, contributions, and so on) are deducted from the employee's paycheck.

Explanation	Green	Petals	Flowers	Totals
Gross pay	7,800.00	625.00	350.00	8775.00
Deductions:				
Federal tax	(1,725.00)	(90.00)	(26.00)	(1,841.00)
State tax	(315.00)	(28.00)	(12.00)	(355.00)
Withheld FICA tax:				
Green ($1,200 x .08)	(96.00)			
Petals ($625 x .08)		(50.00)		
Flowers ($350 x .08)			(28.00)	(174.00)
Voluntary Contributions:				
United Way	(20.00)			(20.00)
U.S. Savings Bonds		(10.00)		(10.00)
Employee portion of Health Insurance	(87.50)			(87.50)
Net Pay:	5556.50	447.00	284.00	6287.50

Social Security taxes withheld from wages are subject to a base of $87,000. Wages earned below the base are taxed at 8%, amounts over the base rate are not subject to the tax. Since Petals and Flowers have cumulative earnings of $6,800 and $5,400, respectively, all of their December wages are subject to the 8% tax. Prior to December, Green's cumulative earnings totaled $85,800. As a result, only $1,200 ($87,000 - $85,800) of the $7,800 earned in December is subject to the Social Security tax. The remaining $6,600 earned by Green exceeds the base and is therefore not subject to the tax. There is no earnings limit to the Medicare tax.

Requirement 2

GENERAL JOURNAL

Date	Accounts and Explanation	PR	Debit	Credit
a.	Salary and Wages Expense		8,775.00	
	Employee Federal Income Tax Payable			1,841.00
	(1,725 + 90 + 26)			
	Employee State Income Tax Payable			355.00
	(315 + 28 + 12)			
	FICA Tax Payable			174.00
	(96 + 50 + 28)			
	United Giving Contribution Payable			20.00
	U.S. Savings Bonds Payable			10.00
	Employee Benefits Payable *			87.50
	Salary Payable to Employees			6,287.50

* Employee's portion of the health insurance premium is computed as follows:
1. $350.00 = .80x, where x = total health insurance premium
2. x = $437.50
3. $437.50 x .20 (Green's portion) = $87.50

b.	Payroll Tax Expense		208.10	
	FICA Tax Payable			174.00
	(96 + 50 + 28)			
	State Unemployment Tax Payable			29.70
	(200 + 350) x .054			
	Federal Unemployment Tax Payable			4.40
	(200 + 350) x .008			

The cost of payroll to an employer will often exceed the actual compensation earned by employees by a substantial amount. The employer must match the employee contribution to FICA tax, as well as pay both the federal and state unemployment taxes. In addition numerous employee benefits (often in the form of pension contributions and health and life insurance) can greatly increase the cost of payroll.

Note that in many cases, the company does not incur an expense for a tax or voluntary contribution, but rather acts merely as a collector for the federal or state government (or as a collector for another third party). The only taxes and other collections or payments that ultimately result in an expense to the business are those paid by the business, such as employer FICA tax (both Social Security and Medicare), federal and state unemployment tax, and pension contribution.

<u>Current Month's Compensation Subject to Tax</u>

	Green	Petals	Flowers
FICA			
$87,000 base - $85,800	1,200		
$87,000 base - $6,800		625	
$87,000 base - $5,400			350
State Unemployment Tax			
$7,000 - $85,800	none		
$7,000 - $6,800		200	
$7,000 - $5,400			350
Federal Unemployment Tax			
$7,000 - $85,800	none		
$7,000 - $6,800		200	
$7,000 - $5,400			350

Note that Petals earned compensation of $625, and only the amount of earnings below the $7,000 base is subject to the unemployment taxes. Since her earnings after being paid for December total $7,425, only her wages under the base ($7,000 - $6,800), or $200 are subject to the taxes.

GENERAL JOURNAL

Date	Accounts and Explanation	PR	Debit	Credit
c.	Pension Expense (7,800 + 625 + 350) x .06		526.50	
	Insurance Expense (employer's portion of insurance)		350.00	
	Employee Benefit Payable			876.50
d.	Salary Payable to Employees		6,287.50	
	Cash			6,287.50
e.	Employee Federal Income Tax Payable		1,841.00	
	Employee State Income Tax Payable		355.00	
	FICA Tax Payable (174.00 + 174.00)		348.00	
	State Unemployment Tax Payable		29.70	
	Federal Unemployment Tax Payable		4.40	
	Cash			2,578.10
f.	United Way Payable		20.00	
	U.S. Savings Bonds Payable		10.00	
	Employee Benefit Payable (350 + 87.50 + 526.50)		964.00	
	Cash			994.00

Requirement 3

The total cost of the payroll includes gross salaries and wages plus all additional costs to the employer in the form of either fringe benefits or payroll related taxes paid by the employer. Summarized in entries (a) to (c) above, total December payroll for Green Stems, Inc. totaled $9,859.60 computed as follows:

Total December Payroll	
Gross wages:	$8,775.00
Payroll tax expense (entry b)	208.10
Employee benefits (entry c)	876.50
	9,859.60

Total cash spent by the business is also $9,859.60, as summarized by entries (d) through (f).

Demonstration Problem #2 Solved and Explained

Requirement 1

1.
12/1	Cash	15,000	
	Notes Payable		15,000

12/31	Interest Expense	112.50	
	Interest Payable		112.50

The company needs to accrue interest expense for December, calculated as follows:
$$\$15,000 \times .09 \times 1/12 = \$112.50$$

2. No entry required. However, the footnotes to the balance sheet should contain information about this lawsuit. This is an example of a contingent liability.

3.
12/31	Salary Expense	45,000	
	Salary Payable		45,000

4.
	Accounts Receivable	150,500	
	Sales		140,000
	Sales Tax Payable		10,500

12/31	Warranty Expense	945	
	Estimated Warranty Liability		945

The warranty expense is based on the cost to the company of repairing or replacing each unit. Therefore, the estimate is calculated as follows:

Unit sales × estimate × cost to repair/replace
$$700 \times .03 \times \$45 = \$945$$

Study Tip: Estimating warranty expense is another example of the matching principle.

Requirement 2 (Current liability section of balance sheet)

Notes Payable	$15,000.00
Interest Payable	112.50
Salaries Payable	45,000.00
Sales Tax Payable	10,500.00
Warranty Liability	945.00
Total Current Liabilities	$71,557.50

Chapter 12 - Partnerships

CHAPTER OVERVIEW

In Chapter 1 you were introduced to the three legal forms of business organizations: sole proprietorships, partnerships, and corporation. Since then, the focus has been on either sole proprietorships or corporations. We now turn our attention to the third type, partnerships. The differences in accounting for partnerships compared to sole proprietorships and corporations lies in the accounting for the creation of the business, how profits and losses are divided among the partners, and how the admission or withdrawal of partners is accounted for. Basically, all other business transactions are accounted for exactly the same as all other forms of business organizations. The learning objectives for this chapter are to

1. Identify the characteristics of a partnership.
2. Account for partner's investments in a partnership.
3. Allocate profits and losses to the partners.
4. Account for the admission of a new partner.
5. Account for the withdrawal of a partner from the firm.
6. Account for the liquidation of a partnership.
7. Prepare partnership financial statements.

CHAPTER REVIEW

Objective 1 - Identify the characteristics of a partnership.

A **partnership** is an association of two or more persons who are co-owners of a business for profit. Partners frequently draw up a **partnership agreement**, also called **articles of partnership**. This agreement is a written contract between the partners that sets forth the duties and rights of each partner.

The characteristics of a partnership are:

1. **Limited life**. The addition or withdrawal of a partner dissolves the partnership.
2. **Mutual agency**. Every partner has the authority to obligate the business to contracts within the scope of regular business operations.
3. **Unlimited liability**. If the partnership cannot pay its debts, the partners are personally responsible for payment.
4. **Co-ownership**. Assets of the business become the joint property of the partnership.
5. **No partnership income taxes**. The net income of a partnership is divided among the partners, who individually pay income taxes on their portions of the partnership's income.
6. **Partners' owner's equity accounts**. Separate owner's equity accounts will be set up for each partner, both a Capital account and Drawing account.

Exhibit 12-2 in your text summarizes the advantages and disadvantages of partnerships.

There are two basic types of partnerships:

- **General partnership.** Each partner is an owner of the business and shares 100% of the benefits and risks of ownership.
- **Limited partnership.** Two classes of partners exist: general partners and limited partners. The general partner(s) assumes the majority of the risk of ownership. There must be at least one general partner. The limited partners are so-called because their liability for partnership obligations is limited in some way—usually to the amount of their investment in the partnership. Because their risk is limited, so is their share of potential profits. Most of the large accounting firms are organized as **limited liability partnership (LLPs).** In an LLP, the individual partner's liability for the firm's debts is restricted in some way.

An **S Corporation** is treated similar to a partnership for tax purposes. This means that the partnership pays no income taxes on its income; rather, the individual shareholders pay taxes on the distributions they receive during the year. There are restrictions to forming S Corporations and their popularity fluctuates with changes in the legislation affecting them.

Objective 2 - Account for partner's investments in a partnership.

Partners may invest assets and liabilities in a business. The simplest investment to account for is cash:

Cash	XX	
Partner's Name, Capital		XX

Assets other than cash are recorded at their current market value. Suppose Woodard, an individual, invests land that he owns outright in a partnership. The land cost him $60,000 several years ago and now has a current market value of $95,000. The correct entry on the partnership's books is:

Land	95,000	
Woodard, Capital		95,000

Suppose Woodard still owed $10,000 on the land. The entry to record the initial capital investment by Woodard would be:

Land	95,000	
Note Payable		10,000
Woodard, Capital		85,000

Objective 3 - Allocate profits and losses to the partners.

If there is no partnership agreement, or the agreement does not specify how profits and losses are to be divided, then the partners share profits and losses equally. If the agreement specifies a method for sharing profits, but not losses, then losses are shared in the same manner as profits.

Several methods exist to allocate profits and losses. Partners may share profits and losses according to a stated fraction or percentage. If the partnership agreement allocates 2/3 of the profits and losses to Taylor, and 1/3 to Simpson, then the entry to record the allocation of $60,000 of income is:

			Taylor	Simpson	Total
Income Summary		60,000			
	Taylor, Capital (60,000 x 2/3)		40,000		
	Simpson, Capital (60,000 x 1/3)		20,000		

Suppose Taylor and Simpson have the capital balances listed below:

Taylor, Capital	240,000
Simpson, Capital	160,000
Total Capital balances	400,000

Sharing of profits and losses may also be allocated based on a combination of capital contributions and service to the business. The important point to remember is to follow the exact order of allocation specified by the partnership agreement. Assume that Taylor and Simpson's partnership agreement specifies that the first $20,000 will be divided according to each partner's capital contribution, the next $30,000 will be based on service with Taylor receiving $22,000 and Simpson receiving $8,000, and any remaining amount will be divided equally. The allocation of the $60,000 net income will be determined as follows:

		Taylor	Simpson	Total
Total net income				$60,000
Sharing of first $20,000 of net income based on capital contributions *:				
Taylor	(240,000 / 400,000) x 20,000	$12,000		
Simpson	(160,000 / 400,000) x 20,000		$8,000	20,000
Net income remaining for allocation				40,000
Sharing of next $30,000 based on service:				
Taylor		22,000		
Simpson			8,000	30,000
Net income remaining for allocation				10,000
Taylor		5,000		
Simpson			5,000	10,000
Net income remaining for allocation				$ 0
Net income allocated to the partners		$ 39,000	$ 21,000	$ 60,000

* To allocate income (loss) in proportion to the partner's capital contributions to the business, use this formula:

$$\text{Income allocated to a partner} = \frac{\text{Partner's capital}}{\text{Total capital}} \times \text{Net income (loss)}$$

Then, the entry to record the allocation of $60,000 of income is:

Income Summary		60,000	
	Taylor, Capital		39,000
	Simpson, Capital		21,000

When a loss occurs, the process does not change. Simply follow the terms of the agreement (or divide the loss equally in the absence of an agreement) in the order specified.

Partners generally make periodic withdrawals of cash from a partnership. If Simpson withdraws $5,000 from the partnership, the entry is:

Simpson, Drawing	5,000	
Cash		5,000

Just like in a sole proprietorship, the drawing accounts must be closed to the capital accounts at the end of the period. If Simpson's $5,000 withdrawal is the only withdrawal during the period, the closing entry is:

Simpson, Capital	5,000	
Simpson, Drawing		5,000

Objective 4 - Account for the admission of a new partner.

Remember that a partnership is dissolved when a new partner is added or an existing partner withdraws. Often a new partnership is immediately formed to replace the old partnership. CPA firms and law firms often admit new partners and have existing partners retire during the course of a year. All the current partners must approve the new partner in order for the new partner to participate in the business.

A new partner may be admitted into an existing partnership by either:
1. purchasing a present partner's interest, or
2. by investing in the partnership.

When **purchasing a partnership interest**, the new partner pays the old partner directly, according to the terms of the purchase agreement. Thus, the partnership receives no cash. The only entry the partnership will make is to close the old partner's capital account and open the new partner's capital account:

Old Partner, Capital	XX	
New Partner, Capital		XX

A person may also be admitted to a partnership by directly **investing in the partnership**. This investment can be a simple investment, and is recorded as:

Cash and Other assets	XX	
New Partner, Capital		XX

The new partner's interest in the business will equal:

$$\text{New partner's interest} = \frac{\text{New partner's capital}}{\text{Total capital}}$$

Note: The sharing of profits and losses is determined by the new partnership agreement, and not by the partnership interest allotted to the new partner.

Successful partnerships frequently require incoming partners to pay a **bonus** to existing partners. In this situation, the incoming partner will pay more for a portion of the partnership interest than the amount of capital he receives. The difference, which is a bonus to the existing partners, is computed by a three-step calculation:

1)   Total capital before new partner's investment
        + New partner's investment
        = Total capital after new partner's investment

2)   New partner's capital balance = Total capital after new partner's investment multiplied by the new partner's interest in the partnership

3)   Bonus to existing partners = New partner's investment - New partner's capital

The entry on the partnership books to record the transaction is:

Cash	XX	
New Partner, Capital		XX
Old Partner #1, Capital (Bonus)		XX
Old Partner #2, Capital (Bonus)		XX

Note: The bonus paid by the new partner is credited to the old partners' Capital accounts. The allocation of the bonus to existing partners is based on the partnership agreement of the existing partners profit-loss sharing ratio.

In some cases, a potential new partner may bring substantial future benefits to a partnership. In this situation, the existing partners may offer the newcomer a partnership share that includes a bonus. The calculation is similar to the calculation for a bonus to the existing partners:

1)   Total capital before new partner's investment
        + New partner's investment
        = Total capital after new partner's investment

2)   New partner's capital balance = Total capital after new partner's investment multiplied by the new partner's interest in the partnership

3)   Bonus to new partner = New partner's capital - New partner's investment

The entry on the partnership's books to record the transaction is:

Cash and Other Assets	XX	
Old Partner #1, Capital (Bonus)	XX	
Old Partner #2, Capital (Bonus)	XX	
New Partner, Capital		XX

Note: The bonus given to the new partner is debited to the old partners' Capital accounts. The allocation of the bonus to the existing partners is based on the partnership agreement of the existing partners profit-loss sharing ratio.

Objective 5 - Account for a partner's withdrawal from the firm.

Partners may **withdraw from a partnership** due to retirement, partnership disputes, or other reasons. The withdrawing partner may sell his or her interest or may receive the appropriate portion of the business directly from the partnership in the form of cash, other partnership assets, or notes.

The first step is to determine whether the partnership's assets are to be valued at book value or market value. If assets are to be valued at market value, an independent appraisal will be used to revalue the assets. Increases in asset values are debited to asset accounts and credited to the partners' capital accounts according to the profit-and-loss sharing ratio. Decreases in asset values are debited to the partners' capital accounts and credited to asset accounts according to the profit-and-loss sharing ratio. After recording the revaluation of the assets, the market value becomes the new book value of the assets.

A partner may withdraw from a partnership at book value, at less than book value, or at more than book value. (Remember that book value may or may not be equal to current market value, depending upon whether the assets have been revalued or not.) A partner willing to withdraw at less than book value may be eager to leave the partnership. A partner withdrawing at more than book value may be collecting a bonus from the remaining partners, who may be eager to have the partner withdraw.

Withdrawal at book value is recorded as:

Withdrawing Partner, Capital	XX	
Cash, Other Assets, or Note Payable		XX

Withdrawal at less than book value is recorded by:

Withdrawing Partner, Capital	XX	
Cash, Other Assets, or Note Payable		XX
Remaining Partners, Capital		XX

When a partner withdraws at less than book value, the difference between the withdrawing partner's capital and the payment to the withdrawing partner is allocated to the remaining partners based on the new profit-and-loss ratio.

Withdrawal at more than book value is recorded by:

Withdrawing Partner, Capital	XX	
Remaining Partners, Capital	XX	
Cash, Other Assets, or Note Payable		XX

When a partner withdraws at more than book value, the difference between the payment to the withdrawing partner and the withdrawing partner's capital is allocated to the remaining partners based on the new profit-and-loss ratio.

329

The death of a partner also dissolves the partnership. The books are closed to determine the deceased partner's capital balance on the date of death. Settlement with the partner's estate is made according to the partnership agreement.

Objective 6 - Account for the liquidation of a partnership.

Liquidation is the process of going out of business and involves three basic steps:

1. Selling the partnership's assets and allocating any gains or losses to the partners' capital accounts based on the profit-and-loss ratio.
2. Paying the partnership's liabilities.
3. Distributing the remaining cash to the partners based on their remaining capital balances.

When selling assets, gains result in credits (increases) to partners' capital accounts. Losses result in debits (decreases) to partners' capital accounts. Gains and losses are allocated between the partners according to their respective profit and loss sharing ratios.

The general worksheet for liquidation of a partnership is:

	Cash	+	Noncash Assets	=	Liabilities	+	Capital	
Balances before sale of assets	XX		XX		XX		XX	
Sale of assets and sharing of							XX	if gain, or
gains and (losses)	XX		(XX)				(XX)	if loss
Balances after sale of assets	XX		-0-				XX	
Payment of liabilities	(XX)				(XX)			
Balances after payment of								
liabilities	XX		-0-		-0-		XX	
Disbursement of cash to								
partners	(XX)						(XX)	
Ending balances	-0-		-0-		-0-		-0-	

Occasionally, allocation of losses on the sale of assets results in a capital deficiency for one or more partners. The deficient partner should contribute personal assets to eliminate the deficiency. If not, the deficiency must be allocated to the remaining partners.

Objective 7 - Prepare partnership financial statements.

Partnership financial statements are similar to the financial statements of a proprietorship. The exceptions are that a partnership income statement includes a section showing the division of net income to the partners, and the owners' equity section of the balance sheet includes accounts for each partner.

TEST YOURSELF

All the self-testing materials in this chapter focus on information and procedures that your instructor is likely to test in quizzes and examinations.

I. Matching   *Match each numbered term with its lettered definition.*

_____ 1. Articles of partnership
_____ 2. Capital deficiency
_____ 3. Unlimited personal liability
_____ 4. Dissolution
_____ 5. Liquidation
_____ 6. Mutual agency
_____ 7. Bonus
_____ 8. Limited partnership
_____ 9. General partnership
_____10. S Corporation

A. A debit balance in a partner's capital account that requires the additional investment of assets by the deficient partner or distribution to remaining partners.
B. Ending of a partnership
C. A business organization with shareholders that is treated as a partnership for tax purposes.
D. The ability of every partner to bind the business to a contract within the scope of the partnership's regular business operations
E. The process of going out of business
F. Type of partnership with at least one general partner who has unlimited liability and at least one limited partner whose liability is limited to their investment in the business.
G. When a partnership (or a proprietorship) cannot pay its debts with business assets, the partners (or the proprietor) must use personal assets to meet the debt
H. A contract among partners specifying such things as the name, location, and nature of the business; the name, capital investment, and the duties of each partner; and the method of sharing profits and losses by the partners
I. Results when assets contributed (or withdrawn) do not equal the amount credited (or debited) to a partner's capital account
J. Type of partnership in which each partner shares all the privileges and risks of ownership.

II. Multiple Choice   *Circle the best answer.*

1. If the partnership agreement does not stipulate how profits and losses will be divided, then by law, partners must share profits and losses:

   A. equally
   B. in the ratio of their capital balances.
   C. based on a ratio of time devoted to the business.
   D. in the same proportion as their initial investments.

2. Whitney invests cash of $20,000 and a building with a cost of $250,000 and accumulated depreciation to date of $95,000 in the Whitney and Becker Partnership. The building has a current market value of $345,000. A mortgage note payable of $105,000 is outstanding on the building and will be assumed by the partnership. Whitney's capital account would be credited for:

   A. $365,000.   C. $260,000.
   B. $175,000.   D. $165,000.

3. A partnership income statement includes:

   A. a listing of all of the partners' capital account   C. a section showing the division of net income
      balances.   to the partners.
   B. a listing of all of the partners' drawing   D. both a and b are correct.
      account balances.

4. All of the following are characteristics of a general partnership except:

   A. mutual agency.   C. limited life.
   B. limited liability.   D. co-ownership of property.

5. When a partner takes money out of the partnership, the partner's:

   A. drawing is credited.   C. capital is debited.
   B. drawing is debited.   D. capital is credited.

6. A new partner may be admitted to a partnership:

   A. only by investing in the partnership   C. by purchasing common stock of the partnership
   B. only by purchasing a partner's interest D. either by investing in the partnership or by
                                                purchasing a partner's interest

7. In a partnership liquidation, a gain from the sale of assets is allocated to the:

   A. payment of partnership liabilities.   C. partner with the lowest capital balance.
   B. partners based on their profit-and-loss ratio. D. partners based on their capital balances.

8. If a partner has a debit balance in his capital account and is personally insolvent, then the other partners:

   A. absorb the deficiency based on their   C. absorb the deficiency based on their profit-and-
      personal wealth.   loss ratio.
   B. absorb the deficiency based on their capital D. sue the insolvent partner's spouse.
      balances.

9. ABC partnership shares profits and losses in a 2:4:4 ratio respectively. This means:

   A. partner A receives 20% of the profits. C. partner B receives 60% of the profits.
   B. partner A receives 50% of the profits. D. partner C receives 20% of the profits.

10. In a general partnership, which of the following is true?

A. there must be more than one limited partner   C. all partners have unlimited liability
B. there must be at least one general partner   D. some partners have limited liability

III. Completion   *Complete each of the following statements.*

1. If the partnership agreement specifies how profits will be shared, but does not specify how losses will be shared, then the losses are allocated _____.
2. The five characteristics of a partnership are: 1) _____,
   2) _____, 3) _____,
   4) _____, and 5) _____.
3. The difference between a partnership and sole proprietorship is that a partnership has _____ _____ owners, while a sole proprietorship has _____ owner.
4. _____ refers to the ability of any partner to contract on behalf of the partnership.
5. A _____ occurs when a new partner is admitted or an existing partner leaves a partnership.
6. A partnership undergoes _____ when it ceases operations and settles all its affairs.
7. A debit balance in a partner's capital account is called _____.
8. The steps in liquidating a partnership are:
   a) _____
   b) _____
   c) _____
   d) _____
9. A partner with limited liability is called a _____.
10. When liquidating, cash is distributed to the partners according to the _____.

IV. Daily Exercises

1. Two sole proprietors, Wells Co. and Bank Co., decide to form a partnership called Wells Bank. Wells will contribute the following to the proprietorship:

	Book value	Market Value
Cash	8,000	8,000
Inventory	7,200	7,600
Equipment	11,700	9,000
Liabilities	6,100	6,100

Record the journal entry to reflect Wells' investment.

Date	Accounts and Explanation	PR	Debit	Credit

2. The X, Y & Z partnership reported $45,000 net income its first year of operations If the partners neglected to agree on the distribution of profits, how much should partners A, C, and E receive?

3. Refer to the information in Daily Exercise #2 above, but assume the partners agreed to a $12,000 per partner salary allowance, with any balance divided 3:2:1 among X, Y, and Z. Calculate the amount owed to each partner.

4. Review the information in Daily Exercises #3 above, but assume the first year resulted in net income of $6,000. Calculate the amount X, Y, and Z should receive.

5. Review the information in Daily Exercises #3 above, but assume the first year resulted in net loss of $10,000. Calculate the amount X, Y, and Z should receive.

6. Record the journal entry for Daily Exercise #4 above.

Date	Accounts and Explanation	PR	Debit	Credit

7. A partnership has decided to liquidate. After selling the assets and paying the debts, $9,000 in liabilities remains outstanding. To whom should the creditors look for payment?

8. Assume the same information in Daily Exercise #7, except the partnership is a limited partnership. How would your answer change?

V. Exercises

1. Frank Lord and Joseph Taylor formed a partnership. Lord contributed cash of $25,000 and land with a fair market value of $65,000 that cost $34,000. The partnership also assumed Lord's note payable on the land of $24,000. Taylor contributed $50,000 in cash, equipment with a fair market value of $62,000 and a book value of $26,000, and the partnership assumed his accounts receivable of $8,500.

Make journal entries to show each partner's contribution to the business.

Date	Accounts and Explanation	PR	Debit	Credit

2. Gapp and Kidd formed a partnership. Gapp invested $102,000 and Kidd invested $68,000. Gapp devotes most of his time on the road developing the business, while Kidd devotes some of his time to managing the home office and the rest of his time is spent at his second job. They have agreed to share profits as follows:

- The first $50,000 of profits is allocated based on the partner's capital contribution.
- The next $50,000 of profits is allocated $40,000 to Gapp and $10,000 to Kidd based on their service to the partnership.
- Any remaining amount is allocated 3:1.

A. If the partnership profits are $150,000, how much will be allocated to Kidd, and how much will be allocated to Gapp?
B. If the partnership has a loss of $80,000, how much will be allocated to Gapp, and how much will be allocated to Kidd?
C. If the partnership profits are $42,000, how much will be allocated to Gapp, and how much will be allocated to Kidd?

A.

	Gapp	Kidd	Total

B.

	Gapp	Kidd	Total

C.

	Gapp	Kidd	Total

3. Keith and Vince are partners in a landscaping business. Their capital balances are $24,000 and $16,000 respectively. They share profits and losses equally. They admit Amy to a one-fourth interest with a cash investment of $8,000. Make the journal entry to show the admission of Amy to the partnership.

Date	Accounts and Explanation	PR	Debit	Credit

4. Anne, Barbara, and Cathy are partners with capital balances of $15,000, $45,000, and $30,000 respectively. They share profits and losses equally. Barbara decides to retire.

A. Make the journal entry to show Barbara's retirement if she is allowed to withdraw $25,000 in cash.

Date	Accounts and Explanation	PR	Debit	Credit

B. Make the journal entry to show Barbara's retirement if she is allowed to withdraw $45,000 in cash.

Date	Accounts and Explanation	PR	Debit	Credit

C. Make the journal entry to show Barbara's retirement if she is allowed to withdraw $55,000 in cash.

Date	Accounts and Explanation	PR	Debit	Credit

5. The following balance sheet information is given for DJ's Tunes For Hire:

Cash	$ 16,000	Liabilities	$ 28,000
Noncash assets	56,000	Doug, Capital	6,000
		James, Capital	24,000
		Jerome, Capital	14,000
Total assets	$ 72,000	Total liabilities and capital	$ 72,000

Doug, James, and Jerome use a profit and loss ratio of 3:4:1, respectively. Assume that any partner with a deficit in his or her capital account is insolvent. Prepare the journal entries for liquidation assuming the noncash assets are sold for $20,000.

Date	Accounts and Explanation	PR	Debit	Credit

VI. Beyond the Numbers

Review the information in Exercises 5. Assume all information is the same except Doug is a limited partner. Prepare journal entries to record the liquidation.

Date	Accounts and Explanation	PR	Debit	Credit

VII. Demonstration Problems

Demonstration Problem #1

The partnership of Ben and Jerry is considering admitting Waldo as a partner on April 1, 20X6. The partnership general ledger includes the following balances on that date:

Cash	$ 40,000	Total liabilities	$ 50,000
Other assets	85,000	Ben, Capital	25,000
		Jerry, Capital	50,000
Total assets	$ 125,000	Total liabilities and capital	$ 125,000

Ben's share of profits and losses is 1/3 and Jerry's share is 2/3.

Required:

1. Assume that Waldo pays Jerry $75,000 to acquire Jerry's interest of the business, and that Ben has approved Waldo as a new partner.

    a. Prepare the journal entries for the transfer of partner's equity on the partnership books.
    b. Prepare the partnership balance sheet immediately after Waldo is admitted as a partner.

2. Suppose Waldo becomes a partner by investing $75,000 cash to acquire a one-fourth interest in the business.

    a. Prepare a schedule to compute Waldo's capital balance. Record Waldo's investment in the business.
    b. Prepare the partnership balance sheet immediately after Waldo is admitted as a partner.

3. Suppose Waldo becomes a partner by investing $20,000 cash to acquire a one-fourth interest in the business.

    a. Prepare a schedule to compute Waldo's capital balance. Record Waldo's investment in the business.

    b. Prepare the partnership balance sheet immediately after Waldo is admitted as a partner.

Requirement 1

a.

Date	Accounts and Explanation	PR	Debit	Credit

b.

Ben and Waldo

Balance Sheet

April 1, 20X6

Requirement 2

a. Computation of Waldo's capital balance:

Date	Accounts and Explanation	PR	Debit	Credit

b.

Ben, Jerry, and Waldo
Balance Sheet
April 1, 20X6

Requirement 3

a.   Computation of Waldo's capital balance:

Date	Accounts and Explanation	PR	Debit	Credit

b.

Ben, Jerry, and Waldo
Balance Sheet
April 1, 20X6

Demonstration Problem #2

The partnership of B, T, and U is liquidating. The partnership agreement allocated profits to the partners in the ratio of 3:2:1. In liquidation, the noncash assets were sold in a single transaction for $120,000 on August 31, 20X8. The partnership paid the liabilities the same day. The partnership accounts are presented at the top of the liquidation schedule that follows.

1. Complete the schedule summarizing the liquidation transactions. See the format on the next page. You may wish to refer to the partnership liquidation exhibits in the text. Assume that U invests cash of $4,000 in the partnership in partial settlement of any capital account deficiency. This cash is distributed to the other partners. The other partners must absorb the remainder of the capital deficiency.
2. Journalize the liquidation transactions.
3. Post the liquidation entries.

Requirement 1 (Summary of liquidation transactions)

	Cash	+	Noncash Assets	=	Liabilities	+	B (1/2)	+	Capital T (1/3)	+	U (1/6)
Balance before sale of assets	30,000		240,000		120,000		90,000		50,000		10,000
a) Sale of assets and sharing of loss											
Balances											
b) Payment of liabilities											
Balances											
c) U's investment of cash to share part of his deficiency											
Balances											
d) Sharing of deficiency by remaining partners in ratio of 3/5 to 2/5											
Balances											
e) Distribution of cash to partners											
Balances											

343

Requirement 2 (Journal entries to record the liquidation transactions)

a.

Date	Accounts and Explanation	PR	Debit	Credit

b.

Date	Accounts and Explanation	PR	Debit	Credit

c.

Date	Accounts and Explanation	PR	Debit	Credit

d.

Date	Accounts and Explanation	PR	Debit	Credit

e.

Date	Accounts and Explanation	PR	Debit	Credit

Requirement 3 (Post the liquidation transactions)

Cash		Noncash Assets		Liabilities	
30,000		240,000			120,000

B, Capital		T, Capital		U, Capital	
	90,000		50,000		10,000

345

SOLUTIONS

I. Matching

1. H	5. E	9. J
2. A	6. D	10. C
3. G	7. I	
4. B	8. F	

II. Multiple Choice

1. A   If the partnership agreement does not stipulate how profits and losses will be divided, then the partners must share profits and losses equally.

2. C   Partners in a new business will contribute assets and liabilities. Assets and liabilities are recorded at their fair market value. To determine a partner's capital account balance, add the fair market values of the assets contributed and subtract the fair market value of any liabilities. Whitney invests cash, $20,000; a building with a fair market value of $345,000, and a mortgage note payable of $105,000. Therefore, Whitney's capital balance is $20,000 + $345,000 - $105,000 = $260,000.

3. C   The only difference between a sole proprietorship income statement and a partnership income statement is that the partnership income statement includes a section that shows the allocation of net income among the partners.

4. B   Limited liability is a characteristic of a limited partnership. Partners in a general partnership, just like a sole proprietorship have unlimited liability for the debts of the business.

5. B   Withdrawing money from the partnership requires a credit to cash that is balanced with a debit to the partner's Drawing account. The balance of the partner's Drawing account will be closed to his Capital account at the end of the period.

6. D   Of the items listed, answer C "purchasing common stock of the partnership" is inappropriate since partnerships do not have stock; answers A and B are incorrect because of the use of the word "only" in the answers.

7. B   Gains and losses incurred in liquidation are allocated based on the partners' profit-loss sharing ratios specified in the partnership agreement.

8. C   The deficiency in a partner's capital account balance is allocated as if it were a loss based on the partners' profit-and-loss sharing ratios specified in the partnership agreement.

9. A   To determine a partner's fractional share, create a denominator by summing the integers (2 + 4 + 4 = 10) and use the partner's ratio as the numerator. Thus, A receives 2/10 or 20%; B receives 4/10 or 40%; and C receives 4/10 or 40%.

10. C   A general partnership has no limited partners. All partners in a general partnership have unlimited liability for the debts of the business.

III. Completion

1. in the same way as profits.
2. limited life, mutual agency, unlimited liability, co-ownership of property, no partnership income taxes
3. two or more, one
4. mutual agency
5. dissolution
6. liquidation
7. deficit
8. adjust and close the books, sell the assets, pay the debts, distribute any remaining cash to the partners (order is important)
9. limited partner
10. the balance in the capital accounts (*not* the profit/loss ratio)

IV. Daily Exercises

1.

Cash	8,000	
Inventory	7,600	
Equipment	9,000	
Liabilities		6,100
Wells, Capital		18,500

Assets contributed are recorded at their current market value. Well's net investment is $18,500, the difference between the fair market value of the assets ($8,000 + $7,600 + $9,000) less the liabilities.

2. Each partner receives an equal share, or $15,000. When the partnership agreement fails to specify how profits and losses will be shared among the partners, the distribution of profits (and losses) is always equal.

3.

	Partners			Amount	
	X	Y	Z	45,000	
Salary Allowance	12,000	12,000	12,000	(36,000)	
Balance				9,000	
3:2:1	4,500	3,000	1,500	(9,000)	
	16,500	15,000	13,500	0	

Proof: $16,500 + $15,000 + $13,500 = $45,000

Study Tip: After the calculating, always verify the individual amounts sum back to the original amount.

4.

		Partners		Amount
	X	Y	Z	6,000 —
Salary Allowance	12,000	12,000	12,000	(36,000)
Balance				(30,000)
3:2:1	(15,000)	(10,000)	(5,000)	(30,000)
	(3,000)	2,000	7,000	0

Proof: $-3,000 + $2,000 + $7,000 = $6,000 ◄─────────────

5.

		Partners		Amount
	X	Y	Z	(10,000) —
Salary Allowance	12,000	12,000	12,000	(36,000)
Balance				(46,000)
3:2:1	(23,000)	(15,333)	(7,667)	(46,000)
	(11,000)	(3,333)	4,333	0

Proof: $-11,000 + $-3,333 + $4,333 = $-10,000 ◄─────────────

6.

X, Capital	3,000	
Income Summary	6,000	
Y, Capital		2,000
Z, Capital		7,000

7. The partnership's creditors can look to any of the partners for payment. In a general partnership, each partner has unlimited personal liability for partnership's debts. Creditors would be wise to enforce their claims against the partner with the largest net worth.

8. In a limited partnership, two classes of partners exist—general and limited. The liability of a limited partner extends only to the amount invested. The fact that liabilities remain after all the assets have been sold and the cash proceeds distributed to creditors indicates the limited partners' obligations have been met. Therefore, the creditors can look only to the general partner(s) for payment.

V. Exercises

1.

GENERAL JOURNAL

Date	Accounts and Explanation	PR	Debit	Credit
	Cash		25,000	
	Land		65,000	
	Notes Payable			24,000
	Lord, Capital			66,000
	Cash		50,000	
	Equipment		62,000	
	Account Receivable		8,500	
	Taylor, Capital			120,500

2.

A.

	Gapp	Kidd	Total
Total net income			150,000
Sharing of first $50,000 of net income, based on capital contribution:			
Gapp (102,000/170,000 × 50,000)	30,000		
Kidd (68,000/170,000 × 50,000)		20,000	
Total			50,000
Net income remaining for allocation			60,000
Sharing of the next $50,000 based on service:			
Gapp	40,000		
Kidd		10,000	
Total			50,000
Net income remaining for allocation			10,000
Remainder shared equally:			
Gapp (3/4 × 10,000)	7,500		
Kidd (1/4 × 10,000)		2,500	
Total			10,000
Net income remaining for allocation			-0-
Net income allocated to the partners	77,500	32,500	110,000

B.

	Gapp	Kidd	Total
Total net income (loss)			(80,000)
Sharing of first $50,000 of net income (loss), based on capital contribution:			
Gapp (102,000/170,000 × 50,000)	30,000		
Kidd (68,000/170,000 × 50,000)		20,000	
Total			(50,000)
Net income (loss) remaining for allocation			(130,000)
Sharing of the remainder based on service:			
Gapp	40,000		
Kidd		10,000	
Total			(50,000)
Net income (loss) remaining for allocation			(180,000)
Remainder shared equally:			
Gapp (3/4 × 180,000)	(135,000)		
Kidd (1/4 × 180,000)		(45,000)	
Total			70,000
Net income (loss) remaining for allocation			-0-
Net income (loss) allocated to the partners	(65,000)	(15,000)	(80,000)

C.

	Gapp	Kidd	Total
Total net income			42,000
Sharing of first $50,000 of net income, based on capital contribution:			
Gapp (102,000/170,000 × 50,000)	30,000		
Kidd (68,000/170,000 × 50,000)		20,000	
Total			(50,000)
Net income remaining for allocation			(8,000)
Sharing of the remainder based on service:			
Gapp	40,000		
Kidd		10,000	
Total			(50,000)
Remainder shared equally:			(58,000)
Gapp (3/4 × 58,000)	(43,500)		
Kidd (1/4 × 58,000)		(14,500)	
Total			58,000
Net income remaining for allocation			-0-
Net income allocated to the partners	26,500	15,500	42,000

3. Total new partnerships equity is $48,000 ($24,000 + $16,000 + $8,000). One fourth of $48,000 is $12,000.

Date	Accounts and Explanation	PR	Debit	Credit
	Cash		8,000	
	Keith, Capital [1/2 × (12,000 - 8,000)]		2,000	
	Vince, Capital		2,000	
	Amy, Capital [1/4 × (24,000 + 16,000 + 8,000)]			12,000

4.

A.

Date	Accounts and Explanation	PR	Debit	Credit
	Barbara, Capital		45,000	
	Cash			25,000
	Anne, Capital			10,000
	Cathy, Capital			10,000

B.

Date	Accounts and Explanation	PR	Debit	Credit
	Barbara, Capital		45,000	
	Cash			45,000

C.

Date	Accounts and Explanation	PR	Debit	Credit
	Barbara, Capital		45,000	
	Anne, Capital		5,000	
	Cathy, Capital		5,000	
	Cash			55,000

5.

Date	Accounts and Explanation	PR	Debit	Credit
	Cash		20,000	
	Doug, Capital		13,500	
	James, Capital		18,000	
	Jerome, Capital		4,500	
	Noncash assets			56,000
	Sale of noncash assets at $36,000 loss			

Loss on sale = 36,000 (56,000 - 20,000). Therefore,

Doug = 36,000 × 3/8 = 13,500
James = 36,000 × 4/8 = 18,000
Jerome = 36,000 × 1/8 = 4,500

Date	Accounts and Explanation	PR	Debit	Credit
	Liabilities		28,000	
	Cash			28,000
	Paid liabilities			
	James, Capital		6,000	
	Jerome, Capital		1,500	
	Doug, Capital			7,500
	Allocated Doug's deficit to remaining partners			

Doug's deficit = 7,500 (6,000 - 13,500)
James   = 4/5 × 7,500 = 6,000
Jerome = 1/5 × 7,500 = 1,500

Date	Accounts and Explanation	PR	Debit	Credit
	Jerome, Capital		8,000	
	Cash			8,000
	Distributed remaining cash to Jerome based on remaining capital balance			
	James's balance = 0 (24,000 - 18,000 - 6,000 = 0)			

VI. Beyond the Numbers

Date	Accounts and Explanation	PR	Debit	Credit
	Cash		20,000	
	Doug, Capital		6,000	*
	James, Capital		24,000	**
	Jerome, Capital		6,000	
	Noncash Assets			56,000

* Because Doug is a limited partner, the amount of loss he must absorb is limited to the balance in his capital account.

** After debiting Doug's account for $6,000, the remaining loss is distributed between James and Jerome, as follows:

James   = 30,000 × 4/5 = 24,000
Jerome = 30,000 × 1/5 = 6,000

Date	Accounts and Explanation	PR	Debit	Credit
	Liabilities		28,000	
	Cash			28,000
	Jerome, Capital		8,000	
	Cash			8,000

VII. Demonstration Problems

Demonstration Problem #1 Solved and Explained

Requirement 1

a. Apr 1   Jerry, Capital   50,000   Debit closes Jerry's account
                 Waldo, Capital   50,000 Credit opens Waldo's account
            To transfer Jerry's equity in the partnership to Waldo.

Note that the book value of Jerry's capital account ($50,000) is transferred, not the price Waldo paid ($75,000) to buy into the business. Since the partnership received no cash from the transaction, the entry would be the same no matter what Waldo paid Jerry for the interest.

b.

Ben and Waldo
Balance Sheet
April 1, 20X6

Cash	40,000	Total liabilities	50,000
Other assets	85,000	Ben, Capital	25,000
		Waldo, Capital	50,000
Total assets	$125,000	Total liabilities and capital	$125,000

Requirement 2

a. Computation of Waldo's capital balance:
    Partnership capital before Waldo is admitted
        (25,000 + 50,000) $ 75,000
    Waldo's investment in the partnership   75,000
    Partnership capital after Waldo is admitted $150,000
    Waldo's capital in the partnership
        (150,000 1/4) $ 37,500

Date	Accounts and Explanation	PR	Debit	Credit
April 1	Cash		75,000	
	Waldo, Capital			37,500
	Ben, Capital (1/3 of $37,500)			12,500
	Jerry, Capital (2/3 of $37,500)			25,000
	To admit Waldo as a partner with a one-fourth interest in the business.			

Note that Ben's capital account increased by $12,500 and Jerry's capital account increased by $25,000. These amounts represent Ben and Jerry's proportionate share of the $37,500 amount by which Waldo's $75,000 payment exceeded his $37,500 capital account credit. When a partner is admitted by investment in the partnership, often the investment exceeds the new partner's capital account credit, and the original partners share proportionately in the difference.

b.

Ben, Jerry, and Waldo
Balance Sheet
April 1, 20X6

Cash (40,000 + 75,000)	$115,000	Total liabilities	$ 50,000
Other assets	85,000	Ben, Capital	37,500
		Jerry, Capital	75,000
		Waldo, Capital	37,500
Total assets	$200,000	Total liabilities and capital	$200,000

Requirement 3

a. Computation of Waldo's capital balance:

Partnership capital before Waldo is admitted	
(25,000 + 50,000)	$ 75,000
Waldo's investment in the partnership	20,000
Partnership capital after Waldo is admitted	$95,000
Waldo's capital in the partnership	
(95,000 × 1/4)	$ 23,750

Date	Accounts and Explanation	PR	Debit	Credit
April 1	Cash		20,000	
	Ben, Capital (1/3 of $3,750)		1,250	
	Jerry, Capital (2/3 of $3,750)		2,500	
	Waldo, Capital			23,750
	To admit Waldo as a partner with a one-fourth interest in the business.			

Note that Ben's capital account decreased by $1,250 and Jerry's capital account decreased by $2,500. These amounts represent Ben and Jerry's proportionate share of the $3,750 amount by which Waldo's capital account balance of $23,750 exceeded his $20,000 payment. When a partner is admitted by investment in the partnership, often the partnership interest received exceeds the new partner's cash investment, and the original partners share proportionately in the difference.

b.

Ben, Jerry, and Waldo
Balance Sheet
April 1, 20X6

Cash (40,000 + 20,000)	$60,000	Total liabilities	$ 50,000
Other assets	85,000	Ben, Capital	23,750
		Jerry, Capital	47,500
		Waldo, Capital	23,750
Total assets	$145,000	Total liabilities and capital	$145,000

Points to Remember

1. Partners may specify any profit or loss sharing method they desire. Common arrangements include:

   a. Sharing equally - unless the partners agree otherwise, profits and losses are required by law to be divided equally
   b. Sharing based on a stated fraction
   c. Sharing based on capital contributions
   d. Sharing based on salaries and interest
   e. Sharing based on a combination of the above and/or other factors

> **Study Tip:** Be alert to problems requiring an allocation of profits and losses when the capital account balances are given for each partner, but nothing is specified about the sharing method. When the sharing method is not specified, each partner receives an equal share.

2. New partners are often admitted to established partnerships. Technically, a new partnership is formed to carry on the former partnership's business, and the old partnership ceases to exist (it is dissolved). Although the old partnership dissolves, the business is not normally terminated, nor are the assets liquidated.

> **Study Tip:** Be sure you can distinguish between the admission of a partner by purchase of a partner's interest (Requirement 1) and admission by making a direct investment in the partnership (Requirements 2 & 3).

Demonstration Problem #2 Solved and Explained

Requirement 1 (Summary of liquidation transactions)

	Cash	+	Noncash Assets	=	Liabilities	+	B (1/2)	+	.T (1/3)	+	U (1/6)
							Capital				
Balance before sale of assets	30,000		240,000		120,000		90,000		50,000		10,000
a) Sale of assets and sharing of loss	120,000		(240,000)				(60,000)		(40,000)		(20,000)
Balances	150,000		-0-		120,000		30,000		10,000		(10,000)
b) Payment of liabilities	(120,000)				(120,000)						
Balances	30,000		-0-		-0-		30,000		10,000		(10,000)
c) U's investment of cash to share part of his deficiency	4,000										4,000
Balances	34,000		-0-		-0-		30,000		10,000		(6,000)
d) Sharing of deficiency by remaining partners in ratio of 3/5 to 2/5							(3,600)		(2,400)		6,000
Balances	34,000		-0-		-0-		26,400		7,600		-0-
e) Distribution of cash to partners	(34,000)						(26,400)		(7,600)		
Balances	-0-		-0-		-0-		-0-		-0-		-0-

Requirement 2 (Journal entries to record the liquidation transactions)

a.

Date	Accounts and Explanation	PR	Debit	Credit
	Cash		120,000	
	B, Capital [(240,000 – 120,000) × 3/6]		60,000	
	T, Capital [(240,000 – 120,000) × 2/6]		40,000	
	U, Capital [(200,000 – 120,000) × 1/6]		20,000	
	Noncash Assets			240,000
	To record the sale of noncash assets in liquidation, and to distribute loss to partners.			

b.

Date	Accounts and Explanation	PR	Debit	Credit
	Liabilities		120,000	
	Cash			120,000
	To pay liabilities in liquidation.			

c.

Date	Accounts and Explanation	PR	Debit	Credit
	Cash		4,000	
	U, Capital			4,000
	U's contribution to pay part of the capital deficiency in liquidation.			

After posting the entries above, U's capital account reveals a $6,000 deficiency, indicated by its debit balance:

U, Capital			
Loss on sale 20,000		Bal.	10,000
		Investment	4,000
Bal. 6,000			

d.

Date	Accounts and Explanation	PR	Debit	Credit
	B, Capital ($6,000 3/5)		3,600	
	T, Capital ($6,000 2/5)		2,400	
	U, Capital			6,000
	To allocate U's capital deficiency to the other partners in their profit and loss ratios.			

Prior to U's withdrawal from the partnership, the partners shared profits and losses as follows:

Ratio: B 3 = 1/2
        T 2 = 1/3
        U 1 = 1/6

The remaining partners are required to absorb the deficiency left by a partner who is unable to contribute sufficient capital to cover the deficiency. After a $4,000 contribution, U's deficiency was reduced to $6,000. Note that between B and T, profits and losses are shared in the ratio of 3 to 2 (or 60% and 40%). As a result, U's uncovered deficiency is allocated to B and T by reducing their capital accounts by $3,600 ($6,000 × 60%) and $2,400 ($6,000 × 40%), respectively.

e.

Date	Accounts and Explanation	PR	Debit	Credit
	B, Capital		26,400	
	T, Capital		7,600	
	Cash			34,000
	To distribute cash to partners on liquidation of partnership.			

Requirement 3 (Post the liquidation transactions)

Cash

Bal.	30,000	Payment of liabilities	120,000 (b)
(a) Sale of assets	120,000		
(c) U's contribution	4,000		
Bal.	34,000	Final distribution	34,000 (e)
Bal.	0		

Noncash Assets

Bal. 240,000	240,000 (a)	

Liabilities

(b) 120,000	Bal. 120,000	

B, Capital

(a) Loss on sale	60,000	Bal.	90,000
(d) Deficit from U	3,600		
(e) Final distribution	26,400	Bal.	26,400
		Bal.	0

T, Capital

(a) Loss on sale	40,000	Bal.	50,000
(d) Deficit from U	2,400		
(e) Final distribution	7,600	Bal.	7,600
		Bal.	0

U, Capital

(a) Loss on sale	20,000	Bal.	10,000
		Investment	4,000 (c)
Bal.	6,000	Allocate U's deficit	6,000 (d)
		Bal.	0

Chapter 13 – Corporations: Paid-In Capital and the Balance Sheet

CHAPTER OVERVIEW

In Chapter 12 you learned about the partnership form of organization. In this chapter, we begin an in-depth discussion of the corporate form of organization. Because the corporate form is more complex than either sole proprietorships or partnerships, our discussion of corporations continues in Chapter 14, 15, and 16. Therefore, an understanding of the topics in this chapter is important before continuing to the next chapter. The learning objectives for this chapter are to

1. Identify the characteristics of a corporation.
2. Record the issuance of stock.
3. Prepare the stockholders' equity section of a corporation balance sheet.
4. Account for cash dividends.
5. Use different stock values in decision making.
6. Evaluate return on assets and return on stockholders' equity.
7. Account for the income tax of a corporation.

CHAPTER REVIEW

Objective 1 - Identify the characteristics of a corporation.

1. A corporation is a **separate legal entity** chartered and regulated under the laws of a particular state. The owners' equity of a corporation is evidenced by shares of stock held by stockholders, and is referred to as stockholders' or shareholders' equity.
2. A corporation has **continuous life**. A change in ownership of the stock does not affect the life of the corporation.
3. **Mutual agency of owners is not present** in corporations. A stockholder cannot commit a corporation to a binding contract (unless that stockholder is also an officer of the corporation).
4. Stockholders have **limited liability**. That is, they have no personal obligation for the debts of the corporation. A stockholder's risk of loss is limited to the individual stockholder's investment in the corporation.
5. **Ownership and management are separated**. Every corporation is controlled by a board of directors who appoint officers to manage the day-to-day operations of the business. It is the stockholders who elect the board of directors. Thus, stockholders are not obligated to manage the business; ownership is separate from management.
6. **Corporate taxes** include state franchise taxes and federal and state income taxes. Corporations pay dividends to stockholders who then pay personal income taxes on the dividends they receive. This is considered double taxation of corporate earnings.

How do corporations compare to partnerships and sole proprietorships? Let's take a look:

	Corporation	Partnership	Sole Proprietorship
Separate legal entity	Yes	No	No
Continuous life	Yes	No	No
Ease of transferability of ownership	Yes	No	No
Mutual agency	No	Yes	Yes
Limited liability	Yes	No-General Yes-Limited	No
Separation of ownership and management	Yes	No	No
Taxable entity	Yes	No	No

Exhibit 13-1 in your text summarizes the advantages and disadvantages of a corporation.

Corporations come into existence when a **charter** is obtained from that state. The charter authorizes the corporations to issue (sell) a certain number of shares of stock. The **bylaws**, or the constitution governing the corporation, are then adopted. The stockholders elect a **board of directors**, who appoint the officers of the corporation. (Review Exhibit 13-2 in your text.)

Owners receive **stock certificates** when they invest in the business. The basic unit of investment is a **share**. A corporation's outstanding stock is the number of shares of its stock that are held by stockholders and represents 100% of the ownership of the corporation. Stockholders' equity is reported differently than owners' equity of a proprietorship or a partnership because corporations must report the sources of their capital.

Corporations have two primary sources of capital:

- **Paid-in capital or contributed capital** represents amounts received from the stockholders from the sale of stock. Generally, paid-in capital cannot be used for dividends.
- **Retained earnings**. Retained Earnings is the account that at any time is the sum of earnings (net income) accumulated since incorporation, minus any losses, and minus all dividends distributed to stockholders. Similar to partnerships and sole proprietorships, revenues and expenses are closed into Income Summary during the closing process. However, in a corporation Income Summary is closed to the Retained Earnings account, not the Capital account(s).

Stockholders have four basic rights, unless specifically withheld by contract:

1. Voting rights
2. Right to share in dividends
3. Right to receive proportionate share of any assets remaining upon liquidation of the corporation.
4. Preemptive right to maintain their proportionate ownership in the corporation.

There are different types of stock that a corporation can issue with rights that are specific to each type of stock. Stock may be **common** or **preferred.** Common stock is the basic form of capital stock. Every corporation must have common stock. A corporation may also issue preferred stock that provides its owners with certain "preferences" over common stock. Typically, preferred stock provides a fixed dividend that is paid to the preferred stockholders before any dividends are paid to the common stockholders.

Stock may also be issued with a **par value** or **no-par value**. Par value is an arbitrary value that a corporation assigns to a share of stock that is used to set the corporation's legal capital. If a corporation issues no-par stock, it may assign a **stated value** to establish the legal capital of the corporation. For accounting purposes, par value and stated value are accounted for in the same way.

A corporation may also issue different classes of common or preferred stock. Each class provides different rights to the respective owners. Each class of common or preferred stock is recorded in a separate general ledger account. Preferred stockholders receive their dividends before common stockholders and take priority over common stockholders in the receipt of assets if the corporation liquidates.

Objective 2 - Record the issuance of stock.

If a corporation issues common stock at a price that equals the par value, the entry to record the transaction is:

Cash (# of shares × issue price)	XX	
Common Stock (# of shares × par value)		XX

Par value is usually set low enough so that stock will not be sold below par. A corporation usually sells its common stock at an issue price above par value. The portion of the issue price that exceeds the par value is referred to as a premium. The amount of the premium also increases paid-in capital, but is recorded in a separate account called **Paid-In Capital in Excess of Par**. A premium is not a gain, income, or profit to the corporation. A corporation cannot earn a profit or incur a loss by buying or selling its own stock. The entry to record stock issued at a price in excess of par value is:

Cash (# of shares x issue price)	XX	
Common Stock (# of shares × par value)		XX
Paid-in Capital in Excess of Par - Common (# of shares × premium)		XX

- If no-par common stock is issued with no stated value, the entry is the same as when stock is issued where the issue price is equal to par value (above), except the credit to the common stock account is equal to the number of shares multiplied by the issue price (because no par value exists).
- Accounting for no-par common stock with a **stated value** is the same as the accounting for par-value stock, except the account that is used to capture the premium above the stated value is called **Paid-in Capital in Excess of Stated Value**.
- A corporation may issue stock and receive assets other than cash. When this occurs, the corporation records the assets at their current market value.

Accounting for preferred stock follows the same pattern as accounting for common stock. The difference is that instead of the word "Common," the word "Preferred" will appear in the titles of the general ledger accounts.

Objective 3 - Prepare the stockholders' equity section of a corporation balance sheet.

Preferred stock always appears before common stock in the stockholders' equity section of the balance sheet.

The format of the stockholders' equity section of the balance sheet is:

Stockholders' Equity

Paid-in Capital:	
Preferred Stock, $ par, number of shares authorized, number of shares issued	$ XX
Common Stock, $ par, number of shares authorized, number of shares issued	XX
Paid-in Capital in Excess of Par - Common	XX
Total Paid-in Capital	XX
Retained Earnings	XX
Total Stockholders' Equity	$ XX

Study Tip: Review the Decision Guidelines *Stockholders' Equity of a Corporation* in your text.

A **cash dividend** is a distribution of cash to the stockholders of a corporation. A corporation must have sufficient Retained Earnings in order to declare a dividend; meaning the declaration of the dividend cannot result in a negative balance in Retained Earnings. The company must also have sufficient cash to pay the dividend. (However, keep in mind that Retained Earnings and Cash are not the same.) Only the board of directors can declare a dividend. And, the board of directors must declare a dividend before the corporation can pay it. Once a dividend has been declared, it is a legal liability of the corporation.

There are three important dates related to dividends:
1. On the **date of declaration** the board announces its intent to pay a dividend to stockholders in the future; thus, a liability is created.
2. Stockholders owning shares of stock on the **date of record** will receive the dividend.
3. The **payment date** is the date the dividends are actually mailed.

Objective 4 - Account for cash dividends.

When a dividend is declared, the basic entry to record the transaction is:

Retained Earnings	XX	
Dividends Payable		XX

Dividends Payable is a current liability.

The date of record falls between the declaration date and the payment date and requires no journal entry. The dividend is usually paid several weeks after it is declared. When it is paid, this entry is recorded:

Dividends Payable	XX	
Cash		XX

When a corporation has issued both common and preferred stock, dividends must be split between the two types of stock. As we have mentioned, preferred stockholders have priority over common stockholders for receipt of dividends. In other words, common stockholders do not receive dividends unless the total dividend declared is large enough to pay the preferred stockholders first and then still have some amount left over to pay to the common stockholders.

The amount of the fixed dividend for preferred stock can be stated as a percentage of par or a dollar amount per share. Preferred stock may be "5% preferred" which means that each share of preferred stock will receive an annual dividend of 5% of the par value of the stock. Thus, if preferred stock is issued with a $50 par value per share, and is "5% preferred", stockholders will receive a $2.50 ($50 × 5%) annual dividend per share. Stockholders holding "$3 preferred" stock would receive a $3 annual cash dividend per share regardless of the par value of the stock. Once the dividend that will be paid to the preferred stockholders is determined, then, the dividend to common stockholders, if any, will be calculated as follows:

**Common dividend = Total dividend - Preferred dividend,
where total dividend > preferred dividend**

A dividend is passed when a corporation fails to pay an annual dividend to preferred stockholders. Whether a corporation has an obligation to make up a passed dividend depends on whether the preferred stock is issued as *cumulative or noncumulative*. When **cumulative preferred stock** is issued, any passed dividends are said to be in arrears. If multiple dividends are not paid, then cumulative preferred stock continues to accumulate annual dividends until the dividends are paid. *Therefore, a corporation must pay all dividends in arrears plus the current year's dividend to the preferred stockholders before it can pay dividends to the common stockholders.*

Dividends in arrears are not liabilities. Keep in mind that a dividend does not become a liability until a dividend is declared. Dividends in arrears have not been declared; therefore, they cannot be a liability to the corporation. However, dividends in arrears are disclosed in notes to the financial statements. Preferred stock is considered cumulative unless it is specifically labeled as noncumulative. Noncumulative preferred stock does not accumulate dividends in arrears.

The following table summarizes the effects of the stockholders' equity transactions discussed in this chapter:

Transactions:	Effects on Accounting Equation:				
			Stockholders' Equity		
	Assets	**Liabilities**	**Paid-in Capital**	**Retained Earnings**	**Total**
Issuance of stock	Increase	No effect	Increase	No effect	Increase
Declaration of a cash dividend	No effect	Increase	No effect	Decrease	Decrease
Payment of a cash dividend	Decrease	Decrease	No effect	No effect	No effect

Objective 5 - Use different stock values in decision making.

Market value (market price) is the price at which a person could buy or sell a share of stock. Daily newspapers report the market price of many publicly traded stocks. In addition, many Internet sites provide up-to-the-minute stock prices.

Book value is the amount of stockholders' equity per share of stock. If only common stock is outstanding:

$$\text{Book value} = \frac{\text{Total stockholders' equity}}{\text{Number of shares outstanding}}$$

If both preferred and common stock are outstanding, preferred stockholders' equity must be calculated first. Preferred equity is equal to the liquidation value of preferred stock plus any dividends in arrears. The book value per share of preferred stock is equal to its liquidation value plus any cumulative dividends in arrears divided by the number of preferred shares outstanding.

$$\text{Preferred book value} = \frac{\text{Liquidation value of preferred stock} + \text{Dividends in arrears}}{\text{Number of preferred shares outstanding}}$$

Once the book value of the preferred stock is calculated, to determine the book value of the common stock, subtract the preferred equity from the total equity and divide by the number of common shares outstanding.

$$\text{Common book value} = \frac{\text{Total equity} - (\text{Liquidation value of preferred stock} + \text{Dividends in arrears})}{\text{Number of common shares outstanding}}$$

Objective 6 - Evaluate return on assets and return on stockholders' equity.

1. **Rate of return on total assets** = $\dfrac{\text{Net income} + \text{Interest expense}}{\text{Average total assets}}$
   (return on assets)

The return on total assets measures how successfully the company used its (average) assets to generate income for those financing the business. The net income and interest expense in the numerator represent the return to the two groups that have financed the corporation: stockholders and creditors, respectively.

2. **Rate of return on common stockholders' equity** = $\dfrac{\text{Net income} - \text{Preferred dividends}}{\text{Average common stockholders' equity}}$
   (return on equity)

The denominator, average common stockholders' equity, is equal to total stockholders' equity minus preferred equity as you saw above in the calculation of common book value.

The rate of return on common stockholders' equity also measures the profitability of the company. The return on equity should always be higher than the return on assets. This is a sign of financial strength that shows that the corporation is generating a greater return with the money invested by stockholders than it is paying out in interest expense.

Objective 7 - Account for the income tax of a corporation.

Because corporations have a distinct legal identity (they have the right to contract, to sue, and be sued-- just as individuals have these rights), their income is subject to federal income tax. However, unlike individuals, the amount of tax actually paid will differ from the expense recognized for the period (for individuals, these amounts are generally the same). The difference results from the following:

- **Income tax expense** is calculated by multiplying the applicable tax rate by the amount of income before taxes from the income statement.
- **Income tax payable** is calculated by multiplying the applicable tax rate by the amount of taxable income reported on the corporate tax return filed with the Internal Revenue Service.

Because these results will differ, a third account, **Deferred Tax Liability**, is used to reconcile the entry, as follows:

Income Tax Expense	XX	
Income Tax Payable		XX
Deferred Tax Liability	XX	

The deferred tax liability account is a long-term liability account.

TEST YOURSELF

All the self-testing materials in this chapter focus on information and procedures that your instructor is likely to test in quizzes and examinations.

Matching *Match each numbered term with its lettered definition.*

_____ 1. Authorized stock
_____ 2. Book value
_____ 3. Convertible preferred stock
_____ 4. Cumulative stock
_____ 5. Legal capital
_____ 6. Market value
_____ 7. Outstanding stock
_____ 8. Stated value
_____ 9. Preferred stock
_____ 10. Stockholders' equity
_____ 11. Retained earnings
_____ 12. Deferred income tax

_____ 13. Board of directors
_____ 14. Bylaws
_____ 15. Common stock
_____ 16. Dividends
_____ 17. Paid-in capital
_____ 18. Par value
_____ 19. Preemptive right
_____ 20. Premium on stock
_____ 21. Contributed capital
_____ 22. Income tax expense
_____ 23. Income tax payable

A. An account which reconciles the difference between income tax expense and income tax payable
B. A corporation's capital that is earned through profitable operation of the business
C. A corporation's capital from investments by the stockholders
D. A group elected by the stockholders to set policy for a corporation and to appoint its officers
E. Another term for paid-in capital
F. A stockholder's right to maintain a proportionate ownership in a corporation
G. An arbitrary amount assigned to a share of stock
H. The portion of stockholders' equity that cannot be used for dividends
I. Distributions by a corporation to its stockholders
J. Owners' equity of a corporation
K. Similar to par value
L. Preferred stock that may be exchanged by the stockholders, if they choose, for another class of stock in the corporation
M. Preferred stock whose owners must receive all dividends in arrears before the corporation pays dividends to the common stockholders
N. Pre-tax accounting income multiplied by the tax rate
O. Shares of stock in the hands of stockholders
P. Stock that gives its owners certain advantages such as the priority to receive dividends and the priority to receive assets if the corporation liquidates
Q. The amount of owners' equity on the company's books for each share of its stock
R. Taxable income multiplied by the tax rate
S. The constitution for governing a corporation
T. The excess of the issue price of stock over its par value
U. The most basic form of capital stock
V. The price for which a person could buy or sell a share of stock
W. The maximum number of shares of stock a corporation may issue

II. Multiple Choice   *Circle the best answer.*

1. The board of directors for a corporation is:

    A. appointed by the state
    B. elected by management
    C. elected by the stockholders
    D. appointed by corporate officers

2. A stockholder has no personal obligation for corporation liabilities. This is called:

    A. mutual agency
    B. limited agency
    C. transferability of ownership
    D. limited liability

3. An owner's investment of cash in a corporation increases:

    A. assets and decreases liabilities
    B. one asset and decreases another asset
    C. liabilities and decreases stockholders' equity
    D. assets and increases stockholders' equity

4. A stock certificate shows all of the following except:

    A. additional paid-in capital
    B. stockholder name
    C. par value
    D. company name

5. The ownership of stock entitles common stockholders to all of the following rights except:

    A. right to receive guaranteed dividends
    B. voting right
    C. preemptive right
    D. right to receive a proportionate share of assets in a liquidation

6. When a corporation declares a cash dividend:

    A. liabilities increase, paid-in capital decreases
    B. liabilities increase, retained earnings decrease
    C. no effect on paid-in capital
    D. both B. and C.

7. When a corporation pays a cash dividend:

    A. liabilities decrease, assets increase
    B. assets decrease, retained earnings decreases
    C. liabilities decrease, assets decrease
    D. retained earnings decrease, liabilities increase

8. When a company issues stock in exchange for assets other than cash, the assets are recorded at:

   A. market value
   B. original cost

   C. book value
   D. replacement cost

9. Dividends Payable is a(n):

   A. expense
   B. current liability

   C. paid-in capital account
   D. stockholders' equity account

10. Dividends in arrears on preferred stock are reported:

   A. as a liability on the balance sheet
   B. as a reduction of retained earnings

   C. on the income statement as expense
   D. as a footnote to the financial statements

III. Completion   *Complete each of the following.*

1. Every corporation issues _____ stock.
2. The corporation's constitution is called the _____.
3. Preferred stockholders have preference over common stockholders in _____ and _____.
4. Dividends are declared by _____.
5. Taxable income multiplied by the applicable tax rate equals _____.
6. Stockholders' equity minus preferred equity equals _____.
7. The date of _____ determines who receives the dividend.
8. The date of _____ establishes the liability to pay a dividend.
9. The price at which a share of stock is bought or sold is called the _____ value.
10. Corporations come into existence when a _____ is approved by the _____ government.

IV. Daily Exercises

1. The following selected list of accounts with their normal balances was taken from the general ledger of Dayton Corporation as of December 31, 20X6:

Cash	173,500
Common stock, $1 par	190,000
Retained earnings	131,500
Preferred stock, $100 par	500,000
Paid-in capital in excess of par-common	380,000

a. Prepare the stockholders' equity section of the balance sheet at December 31, 20X6.

b. How many shares of common stock have been issued? _____

c. How many shares of preferred stock have been issued? _____

2. Einstein Corporation has 20,000 shares of noncumulative, 5%, $100 par, preferred stock outstanding as well as 100,000 shares of $3 par common stock. The board of directors has passed dividends for the past three years, not counting the current year. The board of directors wants to give the common stockholders a $1.25 dividend per share. The total dividends to be declared must be:

3. A company issues 40,000 shares of common stock for $30 per share. Record this transaction (omit explanation) assuming each independent situation below:

   a. the stock had a par value of $1 per share
   b. the stock had no par value, but a stated value of $1 per share
   c. the stock had no par or stated value

Date	Accounts and Explanation	PR	Debit	Credit

4. On September 10, the board of directors declares an annual dividend of $30,000 payable on October 30 to stockholders of record on September 30. Make the journal entries that would be recorded on the following dates:

   a. the declaration date
   b. the date of record
   c. the payment date.

Date	Accounts and Explanation	PR	Debit	Credit

5. Refer to the information in Daily Exercise #4 and assume the company has 4,000 shares of $50 par, 4% preferred stock issued and 10,000 shares of $1 par common stock. The preferred stock is non-cumulative and the corporation has no dividends in arrears. Make the journal entries that would be recorded on the following dates:

   a. the declaration date
   b. the date of record
   c. the payment date.

Date	Accounts and Explanation	PR	Debit	Credit

6. Refer to the information in Daily Exercise #5, but assume the preferred stock is cumulative and the company has two years of dividends in arrears. Calculate the amount due each class of shareholder.

V. Exercises

1. The charter of Berger Corporation authorizes the issuance of 25,000 shares of preferred stock and 300,000 shares of common stock. During the first year of operation, Berger Corporation completed the following transactions:

March 1   Issued 40,000 shares of $1 par common stock for cash of $15 per share.

March 10   Issued 5,000 shares of 6%, no-par preferred stock with stated value of $50 per share. The issue price was $50 per share.

March 28   Received inventory valued at $25,000 and equipment with a market value of $60,000 in exchange for 2,000 shares of $1 par common stock.

Prepare the journal entries for each transaction.

Date	Accounts and Explanation	PR	Debit	Credit

2. Review the information in Exercise #1 and assume retained earnings has a balance of $95,000. Prepare the stockholders' equity section of the Berger Corporation's balance sheet at the end of the first year.

3. The Hot Springs Corporation has 3,000 shares of $100 par, cumulative, 8% preferred stock outstanding. There were no dividends in arrears at the end of 20X3, and no dividends have been paid for 20X4, 20X5 & 20X6. Hot Springs has 20,000 shares of $2.50 par common stock outstanding.

   a. How much will each class of stockholders receive if Hot Springs declares an $80,000 dividend at the end of 20X6?

   b. How much will each class of stockholders receive if Hot Springs declares a $50,000 dividend at the end of 20X6?

4. Natural Fibers Corporation reported income before taxes of $242,000 on their income statement and $186,000 taxable income on their tax return. Assuming a corporate tax rate of 45%, present the journal entry to record Natural Fibers taxes for the year.

Date	Accounts and Explanation	PR	Debit	Credit

VI. Beyond the Numbers

Using the information in Daily Exercises #5 and #6, analyze the effect (increase, decrease, no effect) of the dividend payment, as of 12/31 on the return on assets and return on stockholders' equity.

VII. Demonstration Problems

Demonstration Problem #1

On January 1, 20X5, the state of Vermont approved Video Productions, Inc. corporate charter which authorized the corporation to issue 100,000 shares of 6%, $25 par preferred stock and 1,000,000 shares of common stock with a $1 par value. During January, the corporation completed the following transactions:

Jan 10 Sold 50,000 shares of common stock at $15 per share.
    11 Issued 6,000 shares of preferred stock for cash at $25 per share.
    17 Issued 20,000 shares of common stock in exchange for land valued at $420,000.
    27 Sold 2,000 shares of preferred stock at $25 a share.
    31 Earned a small profit for January and closed the $3,800 credit balance of Income Summary into the Retained Earnings account.

Required

1. Record the transactions in the general journal.
2. Post the journal entries into the equity accounts provided.
3. Prepare the stockholders' equity section of Video Productions, Inc. balance sheet at Jan. 31, 20X5.

Requirement 1 (journal entries)

Date	Accounts and Explanation	PR	Debit	Credit

Requirement 2 (postings)

Common Stock	Paid-in Capital in Excess of Par-Common

Preferred Stock	Retained Earnings

Requirements 3 (Stockholders' equity section)

Video Productions, Inc.
Balance Sheet - Stockholders' Equity Section
January 31, 20X5

Demonstration Problem #2

Wilcox Corporation has the following capital structure: 5,000 shares of $25 par, 4% preferred stock authorized and outstanding, and 100,000 authorized shares of $2 par common stock, 20,000 shares issued. During years X1 through X6, the corporation declared the following dividends:

X1	$0
X2	2,000
X3	40,000
X4	120,000
X5	0
X6	20,000

A. Assume the preferred stock is noncumulative; calculate the amount of dividends per share for each year.

Year	Dividend Amount	Preferred	Common

B. Assume the preferred stock is cumulative; calculate the amount of dividends per share each year.

Year	Dividend Amount	Preferred	Common

SOLUTIONS

I. Matching

1. W	5. H	9. P	13. D	17. C	21. E
2. Q	6. V	10. J	14. S	18. G	22. N
3. L	7. O	11. B	15. U	19. F	23. R
4. M	8. K	12. A	16. I	20. T	

II. Multiple Choice

1. C The common stockholders of the corporation elect the board of directors. Each share of common stock usually gives the stockholder one vote.

2. D Recall that mutual agency is a characteristic of partnerships not present in corporations. Transferability of ownership is a characteristic that the corporate form of organization simplifies as compared with partnerships. Limited agency has no meaning.

3. D When cash is invested in a corporation, assets increase and stockholders' equity, specifically, paid-in capital increases.

4. A Additional paid-in capital is the excess of the price paid to the corporation over the par value of the stock. It is an amount that is calculated to account for the sale of stock, but not shown on the stock certificate.

5. A Dividends represent the distribution of the earnings of the corporation and are not guaranteed.

6. D The declaration of a dividend reduces retained earnings and increases the liability account, Dividends Payable, and has no effect on paid-in capital.

7. C The payment of a cash dividend results in cash being paid to stockholders to settle the liability created by the declaration of the dividend.

8. A When capital stock is issued in exchange for non-cash assets, the assets should be recorded at fair market value. Any excess amount over the par value will be recorded in the Paid-in Capital in Excess of Par account.

9. B The declaration of a dividend by the board of directors creates a current liability.

10. D Dividends in arrears are not a liability since a dividend must be declared to create a liability. However, dividends in arrears do impair the amount of capital available to common stockholders. Dividends in arrears are usually disclosed by a footnote.

III. Completion

1. common (Corporations may also issue preferred stock, but that is optional.)
2. bylaws
3. receiving dividends and in event of a liquidation
4. the board of directors
5. Income Tax Payable
6. common stockholders' equity
7. record
8. declaration
9. market
10. charter; state

IV. Daily Exercises

1.   a. Prepare the stockholders' equity section of the balance sheet for December 31, 20X6.

Dayton Corporation
Balance Sheet (partial)
December 31, 20X6

Paid-in Capital:	
Preferred Stock, $100 par	500,000
Common Stock, $1 par	$190,000
Paid-in capital in excess of par-common	380,000
Total paid-in capital	1,070,000
Retained earnings	131,500
Total Stockholders' Equity	$1,201,500

b. How many shares of common stock have been issued? $190,000/$1 par = 190,000 shares

c. How many shares of preferred stock have been issued? $500,000/$100 par = 5,000 shares

2.   Step 1: Calculate the fixed dividend due the preferred stockholders:
5% x $100 par = $5.00 dividend per share of preferred stock
$5.00 x 20,000 shares = $100,000 dividend to preferred stockholders.

Step 2: Calculate the amount of dividend desired for the common stockholders:
100,000 shares x $1.25 dividend per share = $125,000 dividend to common stockholders

Step 3: Calculate the total dividend that needs to be declared to meet the goal of the board of directors:

Preferred dividend	$100,000
Common dividend	125,000
Total dividend required	$225,000

3.

a.	Cash (40,000 shares x $30 per share)	1,200,000	
	Common Stock (40,000 shares x $1 par)		40,000
	Paid-in Capital in Excess of Par - Common		1,160,000
b.	Cash (40,000 shares x $30 per share)	1,200,000	
	Common Stock (40,000 shares x $1 stated value)		40,000
	Paid-in Capital in Excess of Stated Value - Common		1,160,000
c.	Cash (40,000 shares x $30 per share)	1,200,000	
	Common Stock (40,000 shares x $30 per share)		1,200,000

4.

9/10	Retained Earnings		30,000	
	Dividends Payable			30,000
9/30	No entry			
10/30	Dividends Payable		30,000	
	Cash			30,000

Study Tip: Remember no entry is required on the record date. This simply determines who will receive the dividend when paid.

5.

9/10	Retained Earnings		30,000	
	Dividends Payable-Preferred*			8,000
	Dividends Payable-Common**			22,000
9/30	No entry			
10/30	Dividends Payable-Preferred		8,000	
	Dividends Payable-Common		22,000	
	Cash			30,000

*Preferred: $50 × 4% = $2 per share × 4,000 shares = $8,000.
**Common: $30,000 - $8,000 = $22,000, or $2.20 per share ($22,000/10,000 shares).

Since the preferred stock is noncumulative, the preferred shareholders are only entitled to the current year's dividend ($8,000). The balance is distributed to the common stock.

6.

Preferred dividends in arrears: $8,000 per year (see above) × 2 years	$16,000
Preferred current year dividend:	8,000
Total dividend to the preferred stockholders:	$24,000
Total dividend to the common stockholders ($30,000 - $24,000)	$6,000

Since the preferred stock is cumulative, the preferred shareholders are entitled to the two years of dividends in arrears and the current year's dividend. The balance, if any, is distributed to the common stockholders.

V. Exercises

1.

3/1	Cash (40,000 shares x $15 per share)	600,000	
	Common Stock (40,000 shares x $1 par)		40,000
	Paid-in Capital in Excess of Par - Common		560,000
3/10	Cash (5,000 shares x $50 per share)	250,000	
	Preferred Stock (5,000 x $50 par)		250,000
3/28	Inventory	25,000	
	Equipment	60,000	
	Common Stock (2,000 x $1 par)		2,000
	Paid-in Capital in Excess of Par - Common		83,000

2.

Stockholders' Equity

Paid-in capital:

Preferred stock, 6%, no-par, $50 stated value, 25,000 shares authorized, 5,000 shares issued	$ 250,000
Common stock, $1 par, 300,000 shares authorized, 42,000 shares issued	42,000
Paid-in capital in excess of par – common stock	643,000
Total paid-in capital	935,000
Retained earnings	95,000
Total stockholders' equity	$ 1,030,000

3.

A. Preferred: $100 par $\times$ 8% $\times$ 3,000 shares $\times$ 3 years $= $72,000$
    Common: $80,000 - $72,000 = $8,000

B. Preferred: $50,000

   Since $50,000 is less than the $72,000 preferred stockholders must receive before common stockholders receive anything, all $50,000 goes to the preferred stockholders. And the common stockholders receive nothing!

4.

Income Tax Expense	108,900	
Income Tax Payable		83,700
Deferred Tax Liability		25,200

Income Tax Expense = $242,000 $\times$ 45% = $108,900
Income Tax Payable = $186,000 $\times$ 45% = $83,700
Deferred Tax Liability = $108,900 - $83,700 = $25,200

VI. Beyond the Numbers

Here's the solution—see below for the explanation. This is more difficult than you might have thought.

Situation	Return on Assets	Return on Stockholders' Equity
a. preferred stock is non-cumulative	increase	decrease
b. preferred stock is cumulative	increase	decrease

The formulas are:

Rate of return on total assets $\quad = \quad \dfrac{\text{Net income + Interest expense}}{\text{Average total assets}}$

Rate of return on common stockholders' equity $\quad = \quad \dfrac{\text{Net income - Preferred dividends}}{\text{Average common stockholders' equity}}$

For the return on assets, neither net income nor interest expense change because dividends of $30,000 were paid (regardless of who got how much.) However, average total assets will decrease because of the $30,000 reduction in cash. Therefore, return on assets will increase in both situations.

For return on stockholders' equity, the numerator (net income less preferred dividends) is smaller because of the dividend payment. The denominator (average stockholders' equity) is also decreasing because the total dividends are debited to Retained Earnings. In Exercise #5, the numerator is decreasing by $8,000 while the denominator is decreasing by $30,000. In Exercise #6, the numerator is decreasing by $24,000 while the denominator is decreasing by $30,000.

VII. Demonstration Problems

Demonstration Problem #1 Solved and Explained

Requirement 1

1/10	Cash	750,000		
	Common Stock (50,000 × $1 par)		50,000	
	Paid-in Capital in Excess of Par - Common (50,000 × $14)		700,000	
	Sold common stock at $14 per share.			

The payment of cash is recorded by debiting Cash and crediting Common Stock for the number of shares times the par value of the stock (50,000 × $1). The balance is recorded in the premium account, Paid-in Capital in Excess of Par - Common Stock.

1/11	Cash (6,000 × $25)	150,000	
	Preferred Stock (6,000 × $25 par)		150,000
	Issued preferred stock at par.		

Preferred Stock is credited for the number of shares multiplied by the par value (6,000 × $25).

1/17	Land	420,000	
	Common Stock (20,000 × $1 par)		20,000
	Paid-in Capital in Excess of Par - Common ($420,000 - $20,000)		400,000
	To issue common stock at a premium price.		

When a corporation issues stock in exchange for an asset other than cash, it debits the asset received (in this case, land) for its fair market value and credits the capital accounts, the same as it would if cash were the asset received.

1/27	Cash	50,000	
	Preferred Stock (2,000 × $25 par)		50,000

Preferred Stock is credited for the number of shares multiplied by the par value (2,000 × $25).

1/31	Income Summary	3,800	
	Retained Earnings		3,800

To close Income Summary by transferring net income into Retained Earnings.

At the end of each month or year, the balance of the Income Summary account is transferred to Retained Earnings. Video Productions, Inc. earned a small profit in January. The closing entry will debit Income Summary (to reduce it to zero) and credit Retained Earnings (increasing stockholders' equity to reflect profitable operations for the month).

Requirement 2

Preferred Stock		Common Stock	
	1/11 150,000		1/10 50,000
	1/27 50,000		1/17 20,000
	Bal. 200,000		Bal. 70,000

		Paid-in Capital in Excess of Par – Common	
Retained Earnings			1/10 700,000
	1/31 3,800		1/17 400,000
	Bal. 3,800		Bal. 1,100,000

Requirements 3

Video Productions, Inc.
Balance Sheet - Stockholders' Equity Section
January 31, 20X5

Stockholders' equity:	
Preferred stock, 6%, $25 par, 100,000 shares authorized, 8,000 shares issued	$ 200,000
Common stock, $1 par, 1,000,000 shares authorized, 70,000 shares issued	70,000
Paid-in capital in excess of par - Common	1,100,000
Total paid-in capital	1,370,000
Retained earnings	3,800
Total stockholders' equity	$1,373,800

Demonstration Problem #2 Solved and Explained

A. Preferred stock is noncumulative.

Year	Dividend Amount	Preferred	Common
X1	$0	$0	$0
X2	$2,000	$0.40 per share ($2,000 dividend ÷ 5,000 shares)	$0
X3	$40,000	$1.00 per share 5,000 shares × $25 par × 4% = $5,000 $5,000 ÷ 5,000 shares = $1.00	$1.75 per share $40,000- $5,000 = $35,000 $35,000 ÷ 20,000 shares = $1.75
X4	$120,000	$1.00 per share 5,000 shares × $25 par × 4% = $5,000 $5,000 ÷ 5,000 shares = $1.00	$5.75 per share $120,000 - $5,000 = $115,000 $115,000 ÷ 20,000 shares = $5.75
X5	$0	$0	$0
X6	$20,000	$1.00 5,000 shares × $25 par × 4% = $5,000 $5,000 ÷ 5,000 shares = $1.00	$.75 per share $20,000 - $5,000 = $15,000 $15,000 ÷ 20,000 shares = $0.75

The preferred stock is noncumulative so the shareholders are only entitled to the current year's dividend, which is $1/share for a total of $5,000. Any (and all) excess goes to the common shareholders.

B. The preferred stock is cumulative.

Year	Dividend Amount	Preferred	Common
X1	$0	$0	$0

There are now $5,000 of preferred dividends in arrears.

Year	Dividend Amount	Preferred	Common
X2	$2,000	$0.40 per share ($2,000 ÷ 5,000 shares)	$0

There is now $8,000 of preferred dividends in arrears.

Year	Dividend Amount	Preferred	Common
X3	$40,000	$2.60 per share $8,000 in arrears + $5,000 current = $13,000 $13,000 ÷ 5,000 shares = $2.60	$1.35 per share $40,000-$13,000 = $27,000 $27,000 ÷ 20,000 shares = $1.35
X4	$120,000	$1.00 per share 5,000 shares × $25 par × 4% = $5,000 $5,000 ÷ 5,000 shares = $1.00	$5.75 $120,000 - $50,000 = $115,000 $115,000 ÷ 20,000 shares = $5.75

Preferred has no arrearage so they receive $1.00 per share with the remainder going to common.

Year	Dividend Amount	Preferred	Common
X5	$0	$0	$0

There is now $5,000 of preferred dividends in arrears.

Year	Dividend Amount	Preferred	Common
X6	$20,000	$ 2.00 per share $5,000 in arrears + $5,000 current = $10,000 $10,000 ÷ 5,000 shares = $2.00	$ .50 per share $20,000-$10,000 = $10,000 $10,000 ÷ 20,000 shares = $0.50

> **Study Tip:** Most preferred stock is cumulative. The term has no meaning when applied to common stock.